KABIR JAFFE • RITAMA DAVIDSON
MARGARETHA BESSEL • CHRISTIANE BECHT

Your ENERGY in ACTION!

»Energy Balancing« for daily living

Illustrated by Antonia Baginski

ENERGY BALANCING INSTITUTE

Copyright © 2013 by Energy Balancing Institute

All rights reserved. This book or any portion thereof may not be reproduced or used in any manner whatsoever without the express written permission of the publisher except for the use of brief quotations in a book review.

Printed in the United States of America
First Printing, 2013

ISBN 978-1-940458-01-4

Energy Balancing Institute
610 SW 34th St
Suite 21-0184,
Fort Lauderdale, FL 33315

Table of Content

Introduction 7

Section One: The World of Energy and You 16

1	The Energy World	17
2	Your Sensitivity to Energy	29
3	Clearing your Energy Field	39
4	Centering Yourself	66
5	The Four Directions of Energy Flow	89

Section Two: The Horizontal - The Plane of Action - IN and OUT
Part I: IN 102

6	Taking Energies IN	103
7	Not taking Energies IN	119
8	Energy Leaks and the Ring-Pass-Not	137
9	The Healthy and the Unhealthy IN	146

Section Two: The Horizontal – The Plane of Action - IN and OUT
Part II: OUT 158

10	Creatorship - Your Power to Create	159

11	The Art of Impacting	170
12	Energy Violations	186
13	The Art of Bringing Your Essence Out	196

Section Three: The Vertical – The Plane of Consciousness – UP, BEYOND and DOWN

Part I: UP and BEYOND 208

| 14 | UP - The Shift in Consciousness | 209 |
| 15 | Beyond - Meeting the Magic of the Higher | 230 |

Section Three: The Vertical – The Plane of Consciousness – UP, BEYOND and DOWN

Part II: DOWN 244

| 16 | Bring the Higher Down - Make it Real | 245 |
| 17 | Energy and Consciousness – Your Higher Calling | 258 |

Section Four: Orchestrating your Energy 266

18	Our fundamental Energy Balancing Exercise and its Variations: FEBE, QEBE and EEBE	267
19	Issue Quick Reference List	278
20	All 18 Energy Principles at one Glance	287
21	Glossary of the most important Energy Terms	290
22	Overview of all Energy Balancing Exercises	297
23	The Energy Balancing Institute	301
24	Coming soon	303
25	Indigo Adults	303
26	The Inner Work School	304

Introduction

How it started

In 1975, I, Kabir, had an energy explosion. I had attended a workshop on Tai Chi/Chi Gung that focused on the energy of Chi, the life force. Something awakened. For the next three weeks I didn't sleep. I was living in the mountains, it was winter with snow on the ground, and I was walking around in a tee shirt. My energy was burning and overflowing. After three weeks the intensity of this experience diminished but life has never since been the same. A whole new dimension of life had opened to me with many resultant changes.

I had become aware of the world of energy. Within and around me were powerful forces of energy I previously had no knowledge of. Not only were these forces affecting me, but for better and worse they were shaping my life in countless ways.

'Energy Balancing'

Almost 40 years later energy is even more profoundly the center point of my life through 'Energy Balancing'. Energy Balancing is an understanding of how energy flows within the human energy field and between ourselves and the world around. It has its roots in the Energy Sciences – Energy Healing and Medicine, Energy Psychology, and Energy Spirituality as taught in Yoga and the Indian Chakra system.

What is new in Energy Balancing is the application of energy to daily living. It teaches energy skills for keeping our selves in balance and center, for better relating, greater effectiveness and higher consciousness. Its focus is on creating energy awareness in everything we do, and to develop the energy skills to make our lives work better.

Energy Balancing puts powerful tools directly in our hands that we can use in everyday situations. It takes the richness of the Energy Sciences and makes them immanently practical and accessible.

The Goal of this Book

Our primary goal is immanently practical – to give you the energy skills to make your life better. The book focuses on day-to-day situations and the energy forces you are dealing with in them.

We explore three aspects of Energy:

- Your own energy - what you are doing with your energy and how you can bring yourself in balance and center
- Energy in action - dynamic energy skills to better create life situations
- Energy in relating - skills for interacting with others

Our secondary goal is to help you "get energy" - to look at life with an energy understanding. This book is an introduction into the incredible world of energy and how it is playing itself out in your life. This is a profound insight into the powerful forces that are shaping you and it sheds light on to many aspects about who you are, why you act, feel and think the ways you do, and why certain things happen in your environment.

We hope to start a journey into energy that will take you to some incredible places. Becoming 'energy aware' opens a path of self-development that leads to a whole new way of living and Being that is incredible, wondrous, magical and potent.

The Larger Perspective

Energy Balancing is the reflection of an immense phenomenon happening on an unprecedented scale. There is emerging in millions of people a new faculty of perception - the ability to perceive the previously hidden world of energy.

In the past, energy, though always present, went mostly unnoticed. At best it was perceived as a gut feeling, an intuition, or an instinctive reaction. A few advanced souls - medicine men and women, mystics and healers perceived more, but for the major of people this sense remained mostly dormant.

In the last 100 years a radical change is taking place globally. Millions are suddenly exploring energy, and entire new energy-based branches of existing bodies of knowledge have burst upon the scene - Energy Medicine, Energy Psychology and Energy Spirituality. The deeper purpose of this book is to help people understand their new perceptions and consciously use energy.

Energy in Action – The Experiential Dimension

This book is an invitation to get more involved in evolving our planet through using energy to further mature yourself and lift consciousness. We have found energy immensely powerful in the process of awakening consciousness and bettering our lives, and we passionately believe in this work.

You can simply read this book and it will open your eyes to another dimension of life that you will find fascinating and of great value. However, we can't encourage you enough to jump into the energy world and to take your experience to a whole other level by directly experimenting with the included exercises.

Sensitivity to energy and the skills of using energy is something that grows. In the beginning you may feel nothing or only faint sensations. But gradually it becomes so clear that you will be amazed that you hadn't noticed these things before.

Online and Live Trainings

We also have support resources online to help the material and the many "close to real life" exercises of this book to go deeper:

- There are videos of many of the exercises as well as talks and illustrations.
- For those of you who would like a more in-depth experience, we will have an online Energy Balancing course that will help you more deeply understand and get this material.
- In addition, you get live trainings in our school and in workshops, where you can experientially immerse yourself in the world of energy.

Check out our website at www.energybalancing.me

About the Writing of this Book

This book was a team effort. We chose to write as a team for four reasons. First, each of us brings our own unique experience of energy to the book. Second, working together created a 'group field' that was bigger than any one of us, and this brings more potency to the book. Third, the Energy Balancing Institute is a team endeavor and we wanted to represent the whole team. And lastly, it was simply more fun. There is something so enjoyable in working together when a team really syncs. We amplify each other's strengths, and come to some incredibly highs of group consciousness.

The subject of energy is vast. Our greatest challenge in writing this book was to exclude. Our tendency was to put everything into one book – an experience that would have overwhelmed the reader. We worked hard to delete and simplify the material to make the book accessible. For this reason we decided to focus on 'Fieldwork', the work with the Human Energy Field. The other main area of energy, 'Centerwork', the work with the energy centers or chakras, will be covered in a later book.

We have tried to visually depict energy as accurate as possible; and we know our illustrations are semi-accurate at best! We say semi-accurate because the images are a simplistic representation of a tremendously complex and three-dimensional world we find almost impossible to illustrate accurately.

About Us

Kabir Jaffe
Founder of Essence Training, Energy Balancing Institute and the Science of Human Potential

Kabir Jaffe is a pioneer in the new energy-based psychology and spirituality. He is a psychologist, astrologer, energy therapist, author, and the Founder of Essence Training, the Energy Balancing Institute and the Science of Human Potential Institute.

Kabir started his journey of inner work more than 40 years ago. With an extensive professional background as a clinical psychologist and 18 years' experience living an ashram in India, Kabir describes himself as a "man with two wings—scientist on one side and mystic on the other".

In 1995, he and his partner Ritama founded Essence Training, an Inner Work School helping people learn how to use energy to awaken consciousness and bring positive change to the world. Fascinated by the evolution of consciousness, Kabir has developed a new branch of psychology: the Science of Human Potential. His models of the psyche map the interrelationship of energy, consciousness, evolution and spirituality with the aim of helping others better understand the profound evolutionary step humanity is currently undergoing at this time in history.

Now, after decades of training holistic professionals, Kabir has launched the 'Energy Balancing Institute' and a think-tank called the 'Science of Human Potential Institute'. His book collaborations include *Indigo Adults: Forerunners of the New Civilization* and *Your Energy in Action: Energy Balancing for Daily Living*.

Ritama Davidson
Co-founder of Essence Training, Energy Balancing Institute and the Science of Human Potential

Ritama Davidson is a gifted energy reader, author and co-founder of Essence Training, the Energy Balancing Institute and the Science of Human Potential.

Since she was a child, Ritama has always looked for truth about life beyond the material world. Even in her work as a professional dancer and choreographer, she would create dances about the energy matrix of life. While living in New York, Ritama worked as a shiatsu and massage therapist.

But then, at age 32, she had a car accident that triggered her ability to see and hear the full spectra of the soul itself. Now even more highly sentient to the world of energy than before, Ritama decided to move away from practicing physical therapies and acquire training in energy work. When she met her lifelong and professional partner Kabir Jaffe in 1994, she saw the immense potential of combining their unique perspectives on energy.

Her book collaborations include *Indigo Adults: Forerunners of the New Civilization* and *Your Energy in Action! Energy Balancing for Daily Living*. Ritama believes that energy work can help us develop a profound understanding, compassion and love for ourselves and others, and can be a doorway to relieving suffering on this planet.

Margaretha Bessel
Dean of Essence Training
Director of the Energy Balancing Institute

Margaretha Bessel is an energy therapist, writer, professional singer and vocal coach. She is also Director of the Energy Balancing Institute and its Certification Programs as well as Dean of Essence Training.

Originally from Germany and half Dutch, Margaretha grew up as a minister's daughter. As a child, whenever she heard music, something magical resonated in her body, making her feel deeply connected to a power beyond herself. In 1995 when she came in touch with Essence Training, she learned how to come into even higher states of resonance using energy work.

Margaretha is one of four co-authors of *Your Energy in Action! Energy Balancing for Daily Living.* She brings a groundedness, clarity and down-to-earth understanding of spirituality to this work. Also, her experience as a concert singer and voice therapist, which gives her a highly-attuned sensitivity to the energy of sound, brings a unique depth to her energy work.

Based on a combination of energy tools with Bel Canto techniques, she has developed a new method of training singers called *Free your Voice & Sing your Song*. Margaretha's passion is to help ignite energy awareness in others and contribute to the spiritual awakening throughout the world.
www.MargarethaBessel.de and *www.FreeYourVoice.de*

Christiane Becht
Teacher within Essence Training
Director of Marketing of the Energy Balancing Institute

Christiane Becht is a writer, teacher for Essence Training, international seminar leader and the Director of Marketing for the Energy Balancing Institute.

A native of Germany, she was a first league field hockey player and comes from a background in corporate marketing for Fortune 500 companies like Kraft and Proctor & Gamble. When she was a CEO of her own marketing research company, Christiane first started to notice how the energy of rooms affected people. This observation drove her to embark on the study of Feng Shui, energy healing practices involving chakras and auras, spirituality, mediumship and psychology.

In 2005, she became acquainted with Essence Training and Energy Balancing. Passionate about these unique methods, Christiane went on to develop Energy Balancing workshops and courses. After seeing the rapid, positive impact this work had on her clients, she and three of her colleagues went on to co-author the book *Your Energy in Action! Energy Balancing for Daily Living*.

In this work, Christiane brings her extensive practical experience in applying Energy Balancing to "real life" situations, along with her knowledge of how people quickly learn this simple and highly effective method, as a "fast track" catalyst to higher levels of living and personal transformation.

Essence Training Inner Work School and the Energy Balancing Institute

For the past 17 years Energy Balancing has been exhaustively put through its paces with many thousands of people in the Essence Training Inner Work School. Essence Training is a 5-year study in Energy and Inner Work and is one of the most intensive self-development training programs available today (*www.essencetraining.com*). The Energy Balancing Institute within the school offers a spectrum of courses in Energy Balancing, from introductory programs up to advanced therapist certification *(www.energybalancing.me)*.

Section One

The Energy World and You

1 The Energy World

The Ordinary is Extra-Ordinary

Kabir's story:

I am sitting in dread at the family dinner table. The food is not yet served but already I'm in knots. As my mother enters the room with the main dish my anxiety doubles; I know there isn't going to be enough salt. She never uses enough salt.

It isn't really the salt that's the issue; it's the asking for it. The salt lives at the other end of the table. I have to speak up; everybody is going to look at me.

My 'problem' is that I am painfully shy. I just get all tongue-tied around people. My insides feel like they've twisted into a pretzel, and it seems someone is strangling me with their hands around my neck. I can't breathe, and when I speak it feels like I am inside this big hollow drum, everything booming and echoey. The longer I go without asking, the worse I feel. I start beating myself up me; "What's wrong with me? Why can't I speak up? Everyone's thinking that I'm such a jerk. I'm so screwed up."

Looking back at that young boy I marvel at the miracle that I've been standing in front of groups for the last 40 years as a seminar leader and public speaker. I am again and again grateful that I came across Energy and Inner Work.

There were several ways my transformation came about.

Shyness as a Form of Protection

First, I came to understand. I realized that what I experienced then as shyness was actually a form of protection from the people I was surrounded by.

> *"What I experienced as shyness was actually a form of protection against the people I was surrounded by"*

Now that sounds strange, given, that I came from a "good" family. There were no major problems such as alcoholism or violence. My parents were educated, well-mannered, cultured and gentle people. The family atmosphere was generally supportive and positive.

So why had I become protective?

An ordinary family dinner...

We live in a world that is for the most part familiar. But even the most ordinary of situations is anything but when seen through the eyes of energy.

Because asking for the salt was never the simple request it sounds to be. It was the undercurrents. Inevitably, my brother would make a snide comment like, "Oh, he never has enough salt." Or my father, who was nearest the salt and speaking to his neighbor, would cast me a dirty look for disturbing him.

Now these don't appear to be big things, yet I seemed to be making them into a big deal. Why was I so disturbed by them?

> *Subtle ridicules and irritations were not just subtle things; they were powerful energy streams that went right into me.*

**...is an extra-ordinary occurrence
when seen through the eyes of energy**

What's really going on in even the simplest of situations is mind-blowing.
Energies of all sorts are moving within and between people.

Living without Skin

It was because these subtle ridicules and irritations went right in to me. I felt like I didn't have any skin. A look felt like hot burning barbs streaming from someone's eyes skewering me. An interaction felt like I had brushed up against a cactus with spiky barbs that penetrated me with judgment and condemnation, and would be still painful hours later. Dealing with people was often awful.

I couldn't have verbalized it then, but in looking back with more understanding eyes I realize that I lived in fear. Everyone seemed dangerous; they were full of anger, judgment, resentment or bitterness. It seemed they were wrapped in clouds of emotions; pain, depression, excitement or disappointment.

Even when someone was nice, it didn't feel nice. My mother would say, *"Why don't you have some more of these vegetables. I made them especially for you. They're so healthy and you'll grow big and strong."* Though I felt her care, I more strongly felt something undefined that I reacted to.

> *I was living in fear. Everyone seemed dangerous; they were full of anger, judgment, resentment or bitterness. It seemed they were wrapped in clouds of emotions; pain, depression, excitement or disappointment.*

Later in my life, as I traveled the paths of inner work to track back to the source of my struggles, I realized that behind her care were her own fears. Growing up shortly after the Great Depression her childhood had been one of lack punctuated by illness due to malnutrition. Her childhood traumas still lived on in her. Though we now lived comfortably middle class, her fears permeated her mothering; she was always worried, anxious there wouldn't be enough. When she offered food, her underlying anxiety toxically wove through her words, and her panicked energy held and ensnared me.

My mother's care sent powerful control and attachment cords into my body.

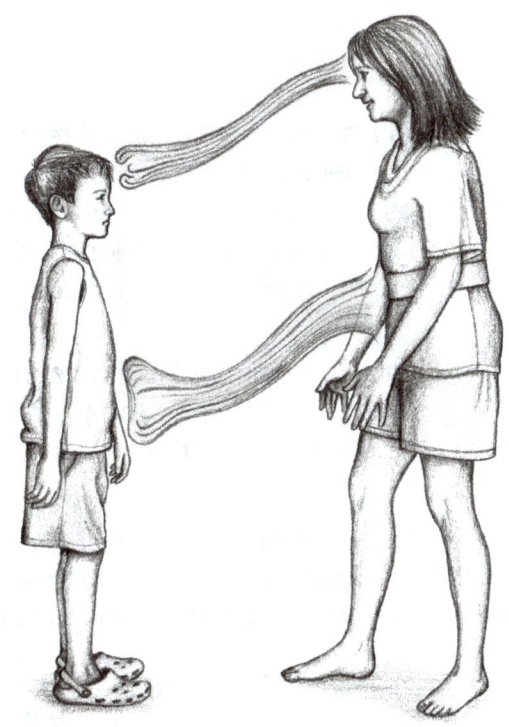

A Mother's Care

I came to understand that my shyness was a protection mechanism I had learnt to survive. If they can't see me, they can't get me. Drawing attention was dangerous.

My flight reaction had kicked in at a young age. My way of flight was to withdraw into a tight, cramped ball within myself. The moment I had to speak my defense system would start sounding the alarm, screaming loudly through the only ways it knew; knots, tensions, feelings of strangulations, self-criticism and projected judgments.

This really puzzled me. Why was I so affected by these undercurrents in human nature? Why did I feel them so painfully, and become so threatened, by nuances that for most people passed right by them? Why had I developed this extreme protection mechanism?

The Root Problem – Sensitivity

As I learnt about energy I recognized my real 'problem' wasn't shyness, it was sensitivity. I felt everything. I didn't have strong boundaries, with the result that I felt trespassed, violated, used and abused in so many interactions. Rarely did someone feel clean to me. The moments I felt safe with another person could be counted on one hand.

I initially wondered if I had some paranoid tendency to see darkness when there wasn't any, or to take a minor nuance and twist it out of proportion, making the proverbial mountain out of the molehill.

> *My real problem was sensitivity. I felt everything. I realized that everyone was sensitive, in pain and floundering to survive. Things others did that caused me pain were due to their protection mechanisms.*

The 'Ah Ha' moment came when I looked around me and I realized that most people were also sensitive and feeling the same pain I was. It was just that they had developed different coping mechanisms. Where I would retreat, another person would become aggressive, a second loud, a third retreated into their mind and disconnected from their body. It seemed that almost everyone was in pain and floundering to survive. I came to see that even the things that others did that caused me pain were mostly due to their protection mechanisms that they had adopted so they could survive.

Everyone is wrapped in Clouds of "Stuff"

It was unbelievable what I was beginning to see; that everyone was in protection, wrapped in clouds of "stuff" that befogged and distorted them, and that all this "energy" was flying back and forth between us like darts, daggers, vacuum cleaner suckers and toxic clouds. This was really weird!

Some Common Energy Survival Mechanisms

Everyone is sensitive to energy and is struggling to survive. Here are a few of the mechanisms we use to do so.

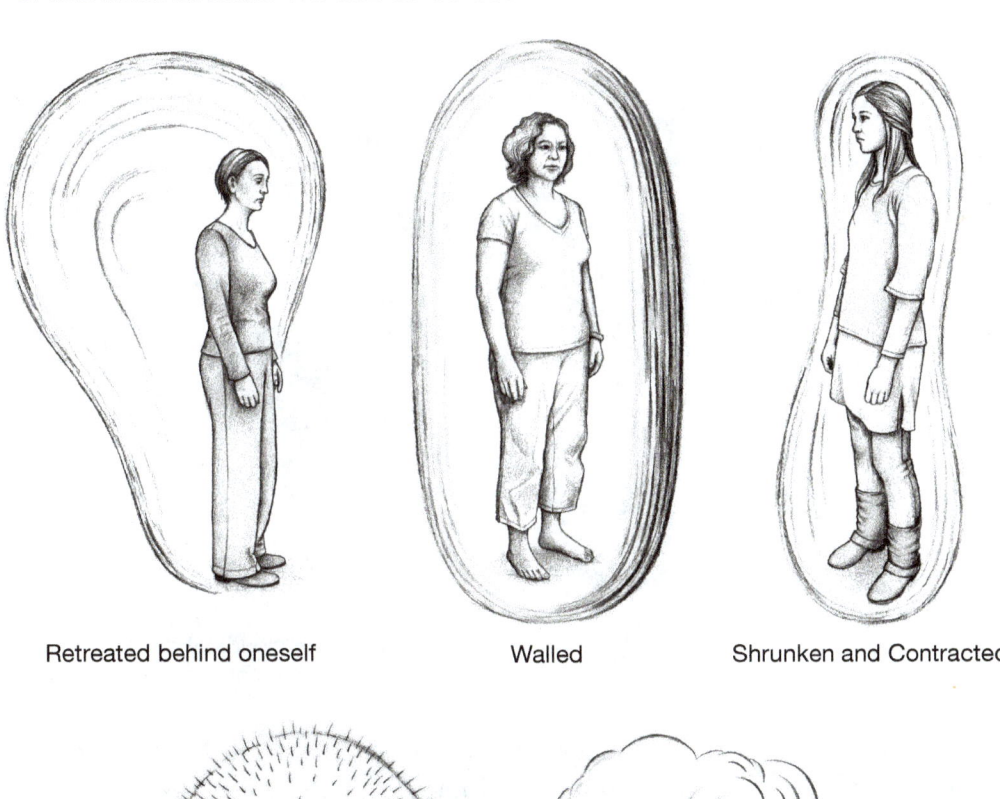

Retreated behind oneself   Walled   Shrunken and Contracted

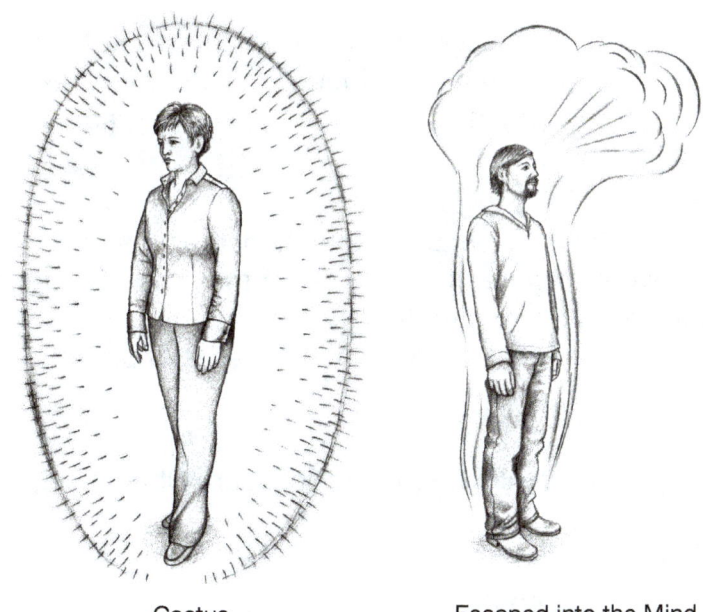

Cactus   Escaped into the Mind

Everyone is wrapped in clouds of "Stuff"

Everyone is wrapped in clouds of dense energies that befog and distort them

And to make it even weirder, it was as if no one noticed it. No one spoke about it. When I would mention it, I got looked at like I was crazy. Maybe I was crazy. This was like living in some sort of bizarre B grade science fiction movie that only I could see.

Luckily I came to realize that I wasn't the only one who saw it. I came to meet others who were experiencing the same thing I was. Together, we would be in a situation where something would happen and we'd turn to each other and say, "Did you see that?" - and yes, the other had experienced exactly what I had.

This was incredible. It was real! I wasn't making it up. Oh my god, what had I stumbled across?

That question became the central point of my life.

What is going on?

What are these energies that everyone carries but no one notices? Why don't we see them? Why do they affect us so powerfully? And the million-dollar question, what can I do about them?

I had awoken to the energy world.

Energy

As I explored, read and discussed with others I realized that what I now saw was not a new discovery, but had been written about in every culture and age. Spiritual, mystical and healing lore everywhere addressed it. It was the focus of shaman and mystics, monks, meditators and healers.

When I stripped away the different cultural packaging, the common thread pointed to a powerful world of energies that existed within each human being and also in the world around us. Though invisible to the eye and hidden from the normal waking mind, it none-the-less powerfully affects us. When explored and studied, we could become alert to it and work with it to profoundly alter our lives. I came to understand that what we refer to as mystic experiences, altered states of consciousness and spiritual awakening, were all openings to the capacity for a human being to perceive this subtle dimension and through various methods to let ourselves be transformed by it.

> *We are energy beings living in a world of energy.*

This was great stuff. Mystics and medicine men. Wow. I was in good company. But there was just one problem. I didn't want to become a mystic or a medicine man. I just wanted to feel good around people, be at ease in myself and be able to have a decent conversation without knots inside. I needed all this great spiritual stuff to be down to earth in the most immediate of ways here in the 21st century. I needed to be able to survive the meeting at work and my next conversation.

Energy Awareness - The Magic Key

So began the most incredible adventure. Initially it was learning to survive situations I was in. But the journey became so much more. It was not just about surviving but thriving in the wondrous world of energy. This tiny thread I had grasped began to unravel a very big ball of yarn. What I have inside me, what we all have inside of us, is amazing.

Not only had I stumbled on the energy world, I came to recognize that we all are magical beings of energy living in a magical energy world. And what a spectrum of energies there are! Though it had started with me struggling with more difficult energies, I begin to recognize the incredibly bright and uplifted energies we all have. Becoming energy aware provides a key to unlocking the immense potential of joy, abundance, creativity and love that is in each of us.

How does energy provide such a magic key to unlock such joy and abundance?

Understanding energy
A new view of the world

First, the understanding of energy is in itself mind blowing. By simply understanding and learning to "think" in terms of energy, you realize the vast world of forces that is tossing your little boat this way and that in a turbulent energy sea.

Perceiving energy
Seeing what's really going on

Secondly, you start paying more attention to energy and your energy perception grows. You notice nuances you might have missed before, and your energy perception gets clearer. Imagine having x-ray eyes and seeing clearly to the heart of every situation you are in!

Energy skills
Using energy to make life work

Third, "getting" energy will give you a whole new skill set for handling life in more healthy ways. It will create greater fulfillment in relationships and will help you keep balanced, centered and "on track" in all areas of your life.

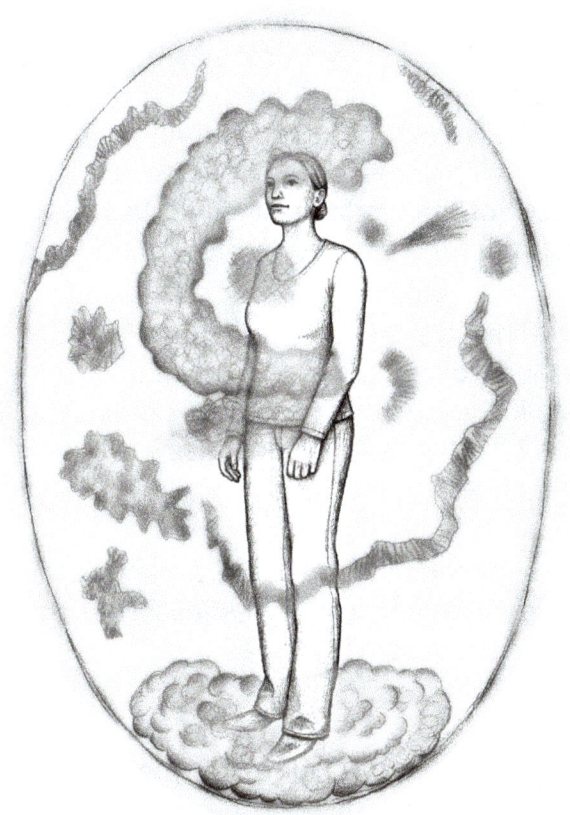

Stuff clouding the Field

Energy is a magic key that once discovered has the potential to revolutionize every area of your life.

I saw that within the clouds of density that wrap us…

… we are golden beings of light in our center.

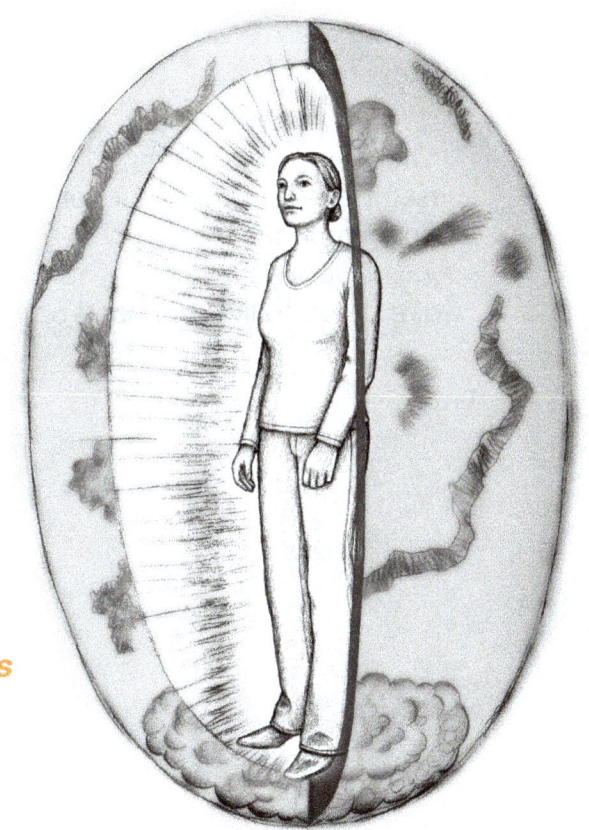

Golden Being

> **Finding center**
> Life works better when you are balanced and aligned

Fourth, through learning to use energy you discover "center". Center is when your energy is balanced and aligned. It's invaluable when life is coming at you fast and you are dealing with stressed out people, difficult situations, and the "normal madness" of the world we live in. And when you're in center, it becomes the platform for a whole new state of living.

> **You are an energy being**
> Accessing the awesome energies we contain within our self

Your thinking is clearer, you have more energy and your actions are more direct and dynamic. You realize just how potent you are and the tremendous energies that are at your disposal.

> **Realizing your potential**
> Becoming the person you know you can be

We are immense beings. The potentials we have for creativity, consciousness, love and power are awesome.

Ultimately, getting energy initiates a momentous self-development process. It opens a path of inner development that uses everyday life as the training grounds for personal unfoldment. It will help you become the person you've always known you can be, and help all of us create a world that we're proud to live in, based on healthy and mature human beings.

2 Your Sensitivity to Energy

Becoming Energy Aware

The goal of this book is to help you unfold the wondrous being that you are. The first step towards that is to help you "get energy".

We focus on three ways to help that happen. The first is to understand energy. The second is developing your sensitivity to energy. The third is learning to consciously use energy.

One of the most important insights is that you are ALREADY sensitive to energy; just most of us don't know it. You are feeling a myriad of energies – it's just that most of what you are feeling is happening beneath the threshold of conscious awareness.

Now, you may wonder, "How is this possible? If something so momentous is going on, how come I don't notice it?"

Well, ask yourself this: how much is going on in your body that you don't notice? Millions, billions of processes are at work yet you hardly notice them at all unless they reach a critical level (usually pain) that gets your attention.

What we normally see
Our mind is used to perceiving in a certain known bandwidth, as if we are wearing glasses that allow only a certain range of perception.

Or think about this; you live on an immense ball of matter called the Earth. Nearby is the moon, waxing and waning, creating vast tidal movements in the oceans of the earth. And not so far away is this huge ball of nuclear fire, the sun, burping magnetic storms, billions of tons of cosmic matter in your direction. All of this is affecting you. These huge forces affect your moods, your thinking, your body clocks, and your energy levels; and yet most of the time you hardly notice them.

What that tells us is that our awareness is very partial; we are perceiving with our conscious mind only a small percentage of what is going on. It registers only a small area of the spectrum of energy; the rest of which we don't consciously get but none-the-less is there and affecting us.

What's really going on
When we become alert and take our glasses off, a whole other world of perception opens up, and we perceive the energy dimension that's within and around us

So can you become more consciously aware of energy? The answer to that is absolutely yes. That's because it's not about becoming more sensitive, it's about become alert to the sensitivity that is already there.

Image you are an art student and you begin to pay attention to color. Within the visible bandwidth of light that the eye sees are tremendous ranges of colors. Great nuances are there. As you study art you begin to notice that there are a thousand shades of white; that the blue of the sky covers a great spectrum of different blues, and that the light of the sun is so very very different at sunrise or noon or sunset.

As an art student you don't develop a new sensitivity to light, you become conscious of the sensitivity that you already have but hadn't noticed before.

ENERGY PRINCIPLE 1:
The human energy field is an antenna

The human energy field is like an antenna of the finest sensitivity.

You are immensely perceptive to Energy

This is exactly how it works with energy. You already are immensely perceptive to energy. The human energy field is an antenna of the finest sensitivity, picking up a tremendous range of vibratory frequencies. You're just not paying attention to it. Only when it reaches a certain threshold of "loudness", perhaps pain or joy, does it get your attention.

But because you don't notice it, doesn't mean that energy doesn't notice you! It is affecting you in a myriad of ways. As mentioned in the previous chapter, in many ways it is the primary force that is shaping your feelings, thoughts, actions and interactions.

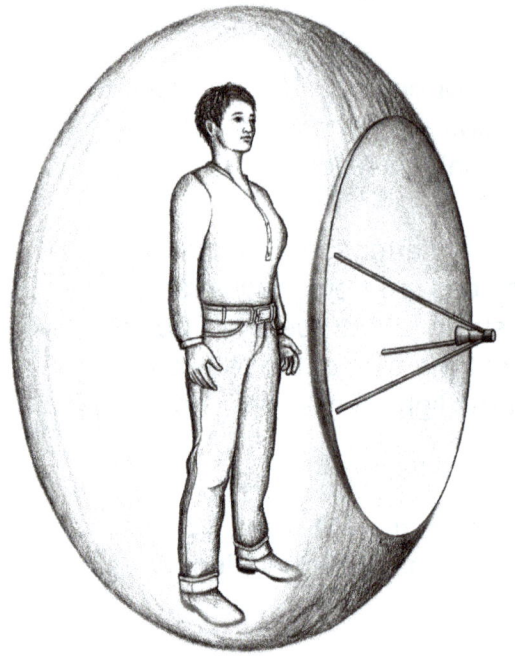

The human energy field is an antenna of immense sensitivity
The human energy field can be metaphorically likened to a tremendously sensitive satellite dish, receiving an immense array of energies.

So how can you become more energy aware?

Every section of this book is really about becoming aware of a certain aspect of energy. Though we focus on energy in action and how you can use energy to make life work better for you, at the root of this is a growing energy perception coupled with a mental understanding of the energy principles at work.

The moment you understand energy you start to identify its presence. Before you would feel something or be in a situation where something was happening but you didn't really notice the energy phenomenon that was going on there. Now you begin to notice things in a whole new way.

You start paying attention to subtleties of feeling and sensation. You notice when your gut gets a knot, or when something opens or closes between you and another. And on a mental level you suddenly understand. You suddenly say to your self, "Ah ha, such and such energy phenomena just happened. That's why I'm feeling this. That's why that just happened". Understanding brings energy to your attention. Together, understanding supports a deepening perception, and your growing sensitivity to energy widens your understanding.

There are many ways to train energy awareness. All the many exercises in this book, though they focus on using energy, have becoming aware of energy at their root. That said, there are a few key principles that we'd like to offer you here in the beginning of the book that will be threads woven through all the subsequent chapters.

Key Principles of Energy Awareness:

1. Feel your Feelings

You are feeling energy all the time. You are just not aware that you are feeling it. So the first energy awareness key is to pay attention to your sensations. You can try this right now in the following simple awareness exercise.

Exercise 2.1

Bring your awareness to your self. What are you feeling? Are you relaxed or tense, hard or soft, low energy or high, receptive or out going? These descriptive words are just a few examples to help you to tune in. Add your own. For now, don't worry about whether it's physical, emotional or energetic. They are all connected anyway. Simply pay attention.

2. Feelings have Location

Exercise 2.2

Next, notice where in the body you are feeling your feelings. Sometimes it's all over. Often it's in a particular location. You might feel warmth in your heart area, or an opening sensation in your solar plexus. You might notice yourself tightening in your shoulders or perhaps feeling blobby in your belly. It's amazing just how many different kinds of sensations we can have at different locations in our body/energy field.

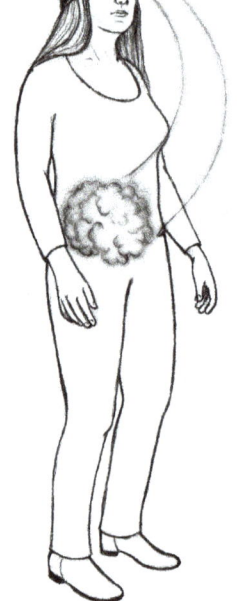

Turning your awareness inwards to look at what you're experiencing

3. Watch your Hands and your Body

Have you ever watched a person who gesticulates with their hands when they are speaking? Their hands are tracing their energy state. You can make a small experiment right now to see this.

Exercise 2.3

Think of something that has emotional content for you. Doesn't matter if it's happy or sad, good or bad. Just something that gets your emotions moving. Now, become an Italian! That's right – Italians' are known for their "eloquent" use of their hands when speaking. So for a moment, imagine you are an Italian and speak out loud for a moment about this emotional subject, and as you do, let your hands express what you are feeling.

Now continue doing this but in slow motion. Say the same words and make the same hand movements but now pay extra attention to what your hands are doing. Your hands are sculpting the energy that's at play.

It's the same with the rest of your body, though not always as obvious as the hands. Simply pay attention to your posture, to how you are sitting or standing, to what your body is reflecting. Your body reflects the energy state.

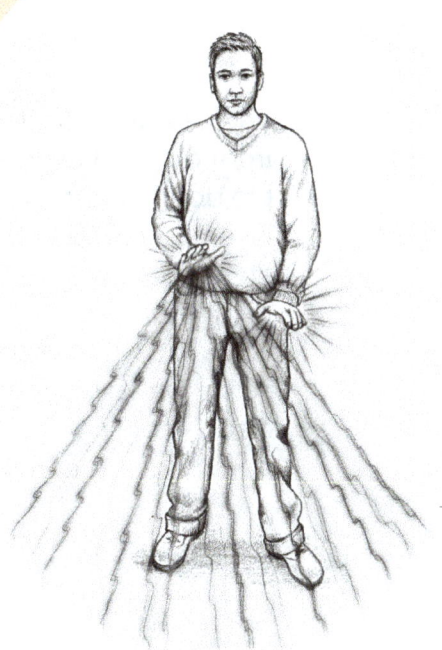

Our hands speak the language of energy
When we gesticulate while speaking our hands are tracing the energies at play

4. **Think Energy – ask yourself, "What's going on with the energy here"?**

Exercise 2.4

Ask yourself the question, "What is happening with the energy here?" In every moment energy is at work. You can ask yourself any time, and particularly in moments that are stronger emotionally or socially, "What is going on"? You might be surprised at just how much you know but didn't know you knew. We find in our trainings that we'll have a total beginner and when we ask them specific questions they so clearly describe the energy state.

Each exercise in this book highlights a certain facet of energy. We know from our own experience of reading "exercise" type books that most people don't do the exercises and we debated whether to include many exercises or not. But we felt these exercises to be different. Once you understand that such and such energy phenomena happens and what you can do about it, you will forever after be alert to those dynamics at play in your life. When they happen, you will almost automatically apply the energy skills you've read about to work with them. So whether you do each exercise or not, we'd encourage you to at least read them - they are becoming part of your repertoire of living skills.

The Gift and the Challenge of Sensitivity to Energy

As your sensitivity to energy grows you will become aware of a great spectrum of energies. They range from some wonderfully light, uplifting and inspiring energies to others that are darker and more difficult.

Energy Balancing explores the full spectrum of life energies with the emphasis on unfolding the higher frequency energies that bring joy and wellbeing. It's amazing just how incredibly uplifting some of the energies we contain are. One of the greatest of all joys is to access and live these higher vibrational energies. We refer to this as becoming "filled with light", because these energies, when seen with the inner eye, are bright.

To reach this light we will have to work with energies that are not so bright. Many of the energies you are dealing with in your day-to-day life are denser and more difficult. We wish we could tell you, "Just open your sensitivity to energy and you'll feel wonderful." But the truth is you are dealing with some difficult and dense energies that are affecting you adversely. These energies come from challenging situations with people, machines and electronics, as well as from within your own self. Learning to recognize these energies and handle them in appropriate ways is a critical energy skill. We're going to start our work with one of the most basic of all these skills. We call it "energetic dusting".

Energetic "Stuff"
Stuff cluttering the energy field, coming from external sources

3 Clearing your Energy Field

Energetic "Stuff"

Unless you've been sitting for the past week in some gorgeous place in nature, your energy field is cluttered with "stuff". By stuff we mean energetic debris; the residue of your own and others emotions and thoughts, and discordant energies from machines, cell phones, computers and the like.

To better imagine stuff, envision a beautiful piece of wood furniture sitting in an empty room gradually accumulating a layer of dust. This is exactly like the human energy field; it accumulates energetic "dust" that clogs it.

We live at and run a retreat center in the Caribbean. The environment here is very pure and peaceful. You hear only the sounds of the breeze and the waves rolling in. The nature is pristine and untouched.

A guest from New York arrived here. He looked very uncomfortable. He said, *"The environment is so quiet and peaceful. It's a bit unsettling. I'm feeling myself so noisy inside, so stuffy and clogged."*

He was really disturbed. In this quiet environment without all the usual distractions he became aware of his state. He then commented, *"I need to get into the ocean. I need to do something, to clear myself. I feel I've got to wash myself clean."*

His experience is a good example of the effect of stuff. He wasn't busy with any particular emotions or concerns, just a general feeling of being clogged, sluggish, chaotic and cloudy.

His experience was typical. Many guests upon arriving here initially feel uncomfortable. They often need to distract themselves by driving here and there, booking trips, anything to avoid how they are feeling. After a few days the power of nature and the sea begins to clear out the stuff people are carrying as well as relaxing their tensions. They start spending more time at the beach, just hanging out, doing nothing in particular. They start winding down, letting go and recharging. You can actually see them getting clearer, lighter and brighter.

But even if they come from a small town, or live out in the country and have a more quiet and simpler life style, they are still carrying stuff. It comes from everywhere in our environment, as well as from within our selves. Every interaction with others, every machine we deal with, even every thought and emotion that moves through us – all of this leaves a residue of stuff in our fields.

Try it out

Frequently throughout this book we're going to ask you to think of something, or to direct your awareness inwards to how you're feeling or thinking. We would highly suggest that you stop reading for a moment and try what's being suggested. This "simple" exercise of directed awareness is a magic key that will open the world of energy to you. It will bring you a living experience versus a mental concept. It's the difference between listening to a recording of a guitar or actually playing the guitar.

An experiment you can make to experience "stuff"

Exercise 3.1: Experience "Stuff"

1. Tune to a Situation with unhealthy and "stuffy" Energies

To give you a real experience of stuff, think back to the last place you've been in the past hours where you would say the energy is not clean, clear, flowing and uplifting. Perhaps where you're sitting right now? Or that conversation you just had, or that store/car/building you were recently in?

Environment with "unhealthy" energies

2. Tune to the underlying Energies

In your minds eye, see if you can imagine the quality of the energy there. Perhaps it's charged with tensions and underlying emotions. Or maybe there are many different people, things, happenings going on; a cacophony of discordant non-harmonic energies. As you tune to this, take note of the feeling in your body. It's not just a mental picture you want to access; tune to your body's sensations that come along with this mental image.

3. Tune to a Situation with healthy and clean Energies

To help you experience this, we're going to put it into contrast: bring to mind now a beautiful clean place in nature; fresh pure air, living plants, the elements in their purity. There is something serene and peaceful, yet invigorating. Again, note the sensations in your body. This natural place creates distinct feelings in you.

Environment with healthy and clean energies

4. Go back and forth and note the Difference

Now that we have these two pictures, go back and forth between them. Put yourself in the first picture for a moment, then the second. Repeat both images a couple of times. Each time as you go back and forth, note your body's sensations. It might take a moment to get in touch with the feelings as they can be subtle, but they will come. How does the first picture of the more stuff-filled environment make you feel? And how does the beautiful place in nature make you feel?

What you're experiencing is the effect of energetic debris on your energy field. This stuff clogs you. Seen energetically your field becomes muddy, your energy flow is disturbed, your brightness dims, your vibration drops and blockage ensues. Stuff is not good for you!

A Definition of Energy

In a moment we're going to begin to use Energy Balancing to clear the stuff. But before we do, we'd like to speak for a moment about what stuff really is. Through understanding, it becomes easier to clear it.

We've been using the term "energy" from the beginning of this book. Let's state clearly exactly what energy is.

Imagine a fish in the ocean. Water everywhere. Not only is water outside of the fish, but it's inside the fish too. Water moves in and out of its gills as it breathes. It courses through its veins as blood. Its very cells are composed of water and minerals that are part of the ocean. The fish and the ocean are integral with each other.

This example of the ocean has many parallels to what we refer to as energy. There is a fabric that underlies everything. It is the "sea" that all things swim within, the underlying "ocean of being" that everything is composed of. We call this "energy". Energy is everywhere, in everything. There is only "energy".

ENERGY PRINCIPLE 2:

Energy – the subtle fabric that underlies everything

The term Energy as we use it refers to a subtle world of forces that exist within ourselves, flows between us and other people, and is everywhere and in everything.

When we use energy in this book, we are referring to this fabric. We are also referring to particular aspects of it – areas that affect us as human beings. For not only does energy refer to those energies commonly described in physics – electromagnetic forces, atoms, sub-atomic particles, etc. -; it's composed of something else as well – the energies of Life. Every living thing is part of the fabric. Life energy (the animating force in you, us, animals and plants) is also part of the fabric of Existence.

ENERGY PRINCIPLE 3:
Energy is substance

Our thoughts, our feelings and our very life energy are a substance.

There is one more important understanding here: that the fabric of Life is a substance. Just as the water in the ocean is a substance, so too is this underlying fabric a substance. This has tremendous implications. It means our thoughts are a substance. Our emotions are a substance. Our love is a substance. Our highest moments of aspiration are a substance. Our very life force is a substance.

Take a look at this image – a very common visual representation of a person having a thought. We all recognize this image for a reason – because this visual representation is communicating a deeper truth about energy; that this thought is actually a substance. The person has created a substance vibrating in the frequencies we call "thought".

Thoughts are Substance
Every thought is a substance sitting in the field vibrating at the frequencies we call "thought"

High vibration
High vibrations can make us happy and manifest as love, creativity, inspiration, etc.

Low and dense vibration
All energy is vibration. Low-vibrational energies make us dense and can be harmful.

What mystics have come to understand is that the substance of Life, our Life Energy, is much larger than our body.

Commonly called the aura, it extends about three feet out from the body in all directions, with a larger area around the upper body, and a bit smaller area around the lower part of the body, making the field look roughly like an upside down egg.

Energy Principle 4:
Everything is vibration

Not only physical matter, but life energy, thoughts and feelings are all composed of frequencies of vibration in the substance of energy.

Within the aura energies are flowing at many rates of vibration. Some energies vibrate in the frequency we call emotion, some at the frequency we call thought. Some vibrate at very high frequencies we call inspiration, genius or enlightenment. Others vibrate at frequencies we call sad or anger. Some thoughts and emotions are so-called negative because their vibrations are destructive and harmful to us. Others are deemed positive because their vibrations are life supportive and uplifting. All are substance at various levels of vibration.

The Method of Clearing

Let's apply this understanding of vibration to what happened with our guest arriving here in the Caribbean. He was carrying a lot of stuff from the city, energetic substance vibrating at particular frequencies.

What can he do about this?

He can take this substance out of him self.

If it can be put in, it can be taken out. We call this clearing. Clearing is the process of removing unwanted energies from our energy field.

DEFINITION: **Clearing**

Clearing is the process of removing unwanted energies from our energy field.

Before we actually do this we'd like to comment that just the realization that we carry stuff and that this stuff is not us, is already gold. So many things we feel are not our feelings!

Realizing you carry stuff is already gold

Earlier in my life I, Kabir, would be around people and feel all weirded out, and think there was something wrong with me. I was taking on all kind of things from others but not knowing it, and then that stuff was vibrating me in creating further disturbance that I then personalized thinking I was weird. What a valuable insight to realize that so many of my "problems" were the result of stuff that I was carrying. There's was nothing wrong with me!

This realization put my mind at peace. It helped me to feel better about myself. I could then become pro-active because I could do something about it. And because I could do something about it, I felt a new confidence.

Most people, because they don't know they are carrying stuff and don't have the tools to remove it, deal with it in unconscious ways that lessen the discomfort but don't solve the problem. Because stuff is uncomfortable, we do things to distract ourselves from it. We watch TV, eat, browse the net, listen to music, go somewhere, drink or do drugs - anything to put our attention elsewhere so we don't have to feel what we are feeling.

Though this to some degree alleviates the discomfort, it doesn't get to the root of the issue. The stuff still stays in us, building up layer upon layer, creating more and more dis-ease. In fact, distracting our selves from the stuff versus doing something about it leads to even greater problems.

You have another option: if you don't feel good and you're carrying stuff – get it out!

So let's begin our journey into Energy Balancing with learning to remove the stuff. There are many ways to do this. We'll start with the most basic now to introduce certain principles of energy. Later we'll add more advanced methods.

Sensing and Intention

The work begins by sensing and then directing energy. In the beginning we use our imagination to visualize energy. We call it using "intention". You are "intending" that energy move in a certain way. What you'll discover is that once you set an intention for energy to move, you will begin to have a physical sensation of it doing just that. This is not imaginary. The sensation comes because you have begun to move energy.

ENERGY PRINCIPLE 5:
Energy follows awareness

Energy flows where your attention goes

One of the fundamental laws of energy work is "Energy follows thought" – what you think of moves energy. Said differently: "Energy flows where your attention goes".

Exercise 3.2: **Experience Energy following Awareness**

There's a simple experiment you can make to verify this:

1. Place both your hands in front of you, palms facing up. They can be resting on your lap or the arms of the chair, or simply extended in front of you in a way that you're relaxed.

2. Now focus your attention on the palm of one hand only, doesn't matter which one. Just rest your awareness there. Don't try to do or change anything; simply put your attention there. Do this for one minute.

3. Now take note, does the hand you were resting your awareness on feel different than the other hand? For almost everyone who does this, you will notice a significant difference. Energy flowed where attention goes.

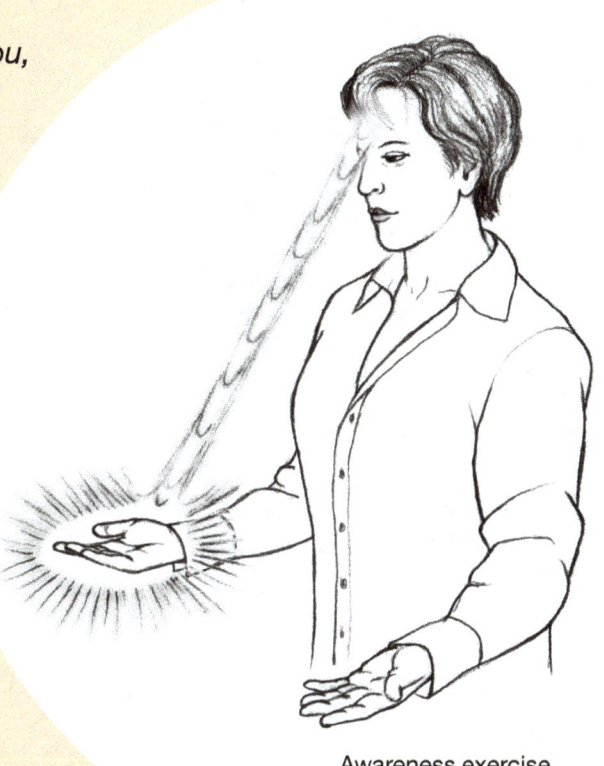

Awareness exercise with hands, part 1: Energy follows thought

Awareness exercise with hands, part 2: Energy building through hands opposite each other

One more simple exercise:

1. Put your hands in front of you, palms facing each other, about 1 foot apart. Take note of the sensation in your palms.

2. Now move them slowly towards each other. Come as close as one inch but don't let the palms touch.

3. Now move them slowly away, ending with the hands about two feet apart.

4. Now move them in again, then out, playing with the distance, taking note of the sensations as you do this.

You are experiencing energy. The sensation between your hands is the flow of energy that the hands radiate. For some people it can be very subtle, barely noticeable. For others it can be highly tangible. You may even notice your palms getting hot or cold, start sweating or becoming blotchy. These are all effects of the energy flow becoming more active.

Clearing the Energy Field

Let's now begin our work of clearing the energy field. We want to remind you to listen to and trust your intuition. If your hands want to work in one area a little longer, stay there. If some debris needs stronger movements, use stronger movements. For some areas you might feel the need to move more quickly. Generally however, we recommend slow hand movements so you can breathe with them and keep your attention fully focused. Throughout the whole exercise be sure you take deep breaths to support the clearing and releasing. Especially emphasize the exhalation.

Exercise 3.3: Dusting the Energy Field

1. Charge and sensitize your Hands with Energy

Rub your palms together quickly, like you were cleaning them with soap. Then hold them a few inches apart. Notice the energy flowing between them. Do this three times.

2. Set your Intention

Set the intention that the energy flowing through your hands will clear and cleanse your energy field. You may also say (internally or loudly) the affirmation "Powerful cleansing energy is flowing through my hands. It releases energetic debris".

Charging and Sensitizing the Hands

3. Dust the Field in the Front

Using your imagination, "see" the dirt that's clogging your energy field. With your palms facing outwards, slowly move your hands through your field away from your body and exhale. See yourself sweeping out the dust and energetic debris.

4. Clearing your Head and Shoulders

Now that you've cleared the front of your body, bring your hands to the sides and top of your head. Imagine clearing away mental stuff from your mind; a cloud of unnecessary thoughts that are hanging there.

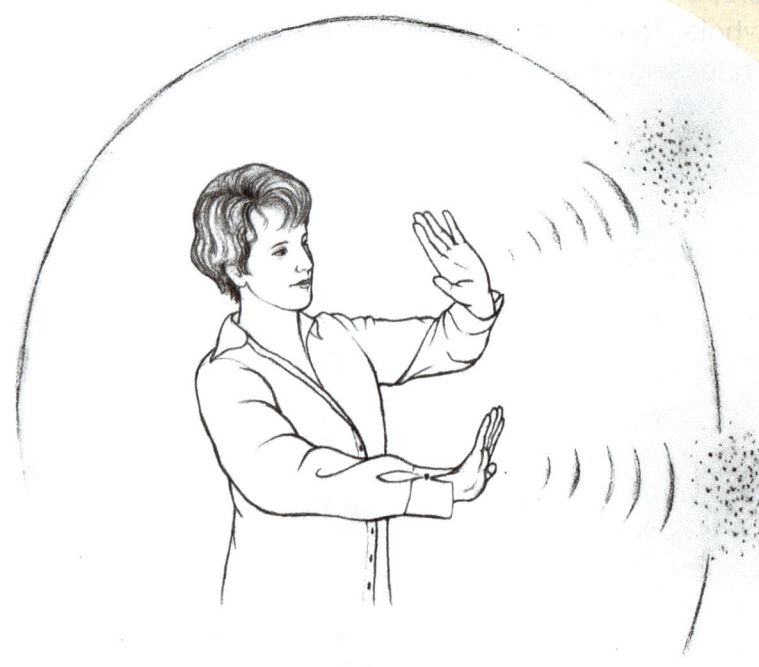

Dusting the Field

5. Clearing the Sides and Back

From your head slowly move downwards. Clear the sides of your body, and then behind you. Where your arms can't reach (e.g. behind the middle of your back), just visualize the energy extending from your hands doing the job.

6. Clearing the Legs and Feet

Now use your hands to clear your legs and feet. Energetic stuff tends to get caught here and thicken. You can also shake your legs and feet to help release.

7. Shake out your Hands

Energetic stuff can stick to your hands. From time to time shake out your hands to release this. Do it with arms stretched out, away from your body. Don't throw this stuff on anyone else! Trust that the earth will naturally transform this stuff. You can also shake stuff off into salt or salt water, as it's a good absorber of negative energies.

8. Completion: Breathe and take Note

To complete, stand with your arms relaxed and your feet shoulder width apart. Take some last deep breaths to relase any last debris. Feel your body and the area around your body. You might notice feeling lighter or brighter. Perhaps you can breathe more easily, or you feel more relaxed or more vital. You may notice your mind is clearer and your perception sharper.

Shaking out the Hands

Quick Reference Points:

1. *Charge and sensitize your Hands with Energy*
2. *Set your Intention*
3. *Dust the Field in the Front*

4. Clearing your Head and Shoulders
5. Clearing the Sides and Back
6. Clearing the Legs and Feet
7. Shake out your Hands
8. Completion: Breathe and take Note

You've just used energy flowing through your hands to dust your field, removing energetic debris that's been cluttering you. It's amazing how many things change when we remove the stuff. And if you don't notice anything, don't worry. It's not that you did the dusting wrong, or that it doesn't work. It just takes a little time to become sensitive to energy as well as being alert to the nuances of your own thoughts and feelings. Give it a little practice; you'll be amazed at the results.

* * * * *

Through Dusting you've removed what we could call the first layer of stuff, a layer that is constantly accumulating every day, every conversation, and that needs to be cleaned daily or even many times throughout the day.

The question might arise in your mind: "As I'm only learning now how to clear this dust, and since I hadn't been clearing it before, has it built up layer upon layer, like an old house that's been closed up for twenty years?"

The answer to that is yes and no. Yes, that there is stuff sitting there for a very long time, and in a way we are almost always covered, very rarely being clear and clean. No, in that there are things we do in our day to day life that do help remove some of this stuff, so that it doesn't build up to intolerable levels.

For example, taking a shower not only cleans your body, but it helps to clean your energy field as well. Being out in nature – the fresh air and sunlight, remove some of the stuff. Going to the gym and having a good workout helps flush some of the stuff. Many normal activities contribute to keeping our fields cleaner. So we are clearing stuff, even whilst we are accumulating.

These daily activities are great, and we would encourage you to find those that work for you. And we can't say enough; use your hands to dust the field. There is a power and effectiveness in deliberately clearing, that daily activities alone can't manage. Deliberately clearing stuff is tremendously powerful.

But even with all of this, not all of the stuff gets cleared.

Goop - the thicker stuff

There is another kind of stuff that builds up in us that also needs to be removed.

This stuff is more powerful. It has greater substance and it impacts you more strongly. This stuff lodges into the substance of your field in more powerful ways. This is the stuff of powerful emotions, thoughts and energetic discharges from others.

Returning back to our metaphor of a piece of furniture accumulating dust, imagine someone eating on a beautiful wooden table and spilling their food. A large mass of goop is now sitting on the table that needs to be cleaned up. This goop is different than dust. While dust is a general, diffuse film that is everywhere on the table, goop is thick, substantial and sits in a particular spot. Goop also has greater impact than dust. Where dust just accumulates and generally clouds things, goop can stain the table, going deeper and creating more lasting damage. Goop can be seriously destructive.

I (Kabir) ran into a friend, Antonio, and we stopped to talk for a few minutes. I could see he was upset. When I asked him what was going on he hesitated, then blurted out that he'd just had a big blow-up with his partner, Sandi.

Antonio is Italian and for him having family and kids is really important. But Sandi isn't so sure if she's ready for kids, at least not yet. The relationship is relatively new and she's going through a lot of personal changes. She wants time to feel herself, get on her feet and find her new direction. She's not saying no to a child but she wants to make the decision in her own time.

Antonio feels an urgency. Sandi just turned forty, and it makes him frightened that they'll miss this opportunity. As we spoke I could see that this urgency was acting like a lens, making him misinterpret Sandi's responses. He was taking her reticence to have a child as a rejection and feeling hurt, projecting that she doesn't really love him and that she's not committed to the relationship.

During our short conversation Antonio's many bottled up feelings of anger, blame, fear, hurt and pain spewed forth.

I could empathize with Antonio's pain. My own heart hurt in resonance with his. But I also felt something else. I felt

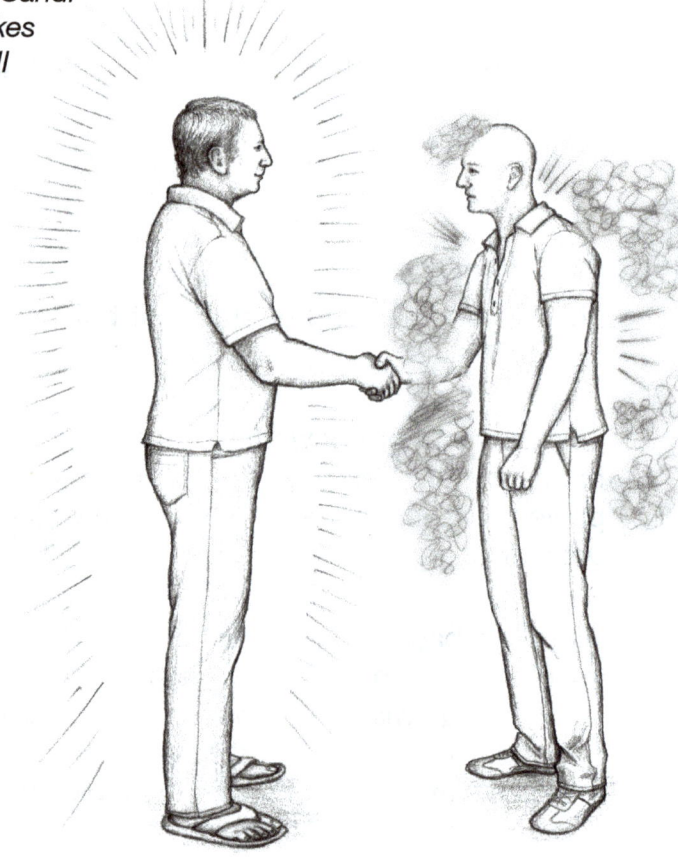

Kabir and Antonio meet. Antonio carries upset.
Kabir is relaxed

awful! Speaking bluntly, I felt like I had just been vomited on. His frustration and pain and anger vibrated in my body. I knew these feelings weren't mine. I hadn't been feeling this a moment before meeting him, nor had it "pushed my buttons"; children and committed relationships weren't my issue. I was carrying a load of stuff that had just been spewed into me.

Antonio shares his upset and dumps into Kabir

Kabir now carries Antonio's dumped energy. Antonio feels better.

ENERGY PRINCIPLE 6:
Energy Transference

Energy can be transferred between people, places and things.

The transference of energy from one person to another is very real. If a person is carrying a positive and uplifted energy it can transfer to you, lifting your spirit and vitalizing your field. Think of a person who loves and respects you. You may not have thought of it this way, but their positive attitude is more than just a belief or feeling they are carrying towards you; they are also sending positive energy your way; it is this energy that brings such a nice feeling to both your body and your mind.

But when the energy coming towards you is disturbed, it can disturb to you. Not only is it unpleasant, it can actually be toxic. Imagine throwing a handful of dirt into the oil in your car's engine. It's the same for your energy system. Disturbed and negative energies are like dirt thrown into your inner workings; they throw you off balance, aggravate your emotions, clog your system and befuddle your mind.

Antonio was carrying many disturbed emotions. Unknowingly in his sharing with me he released those emotions – directly into my energy field!

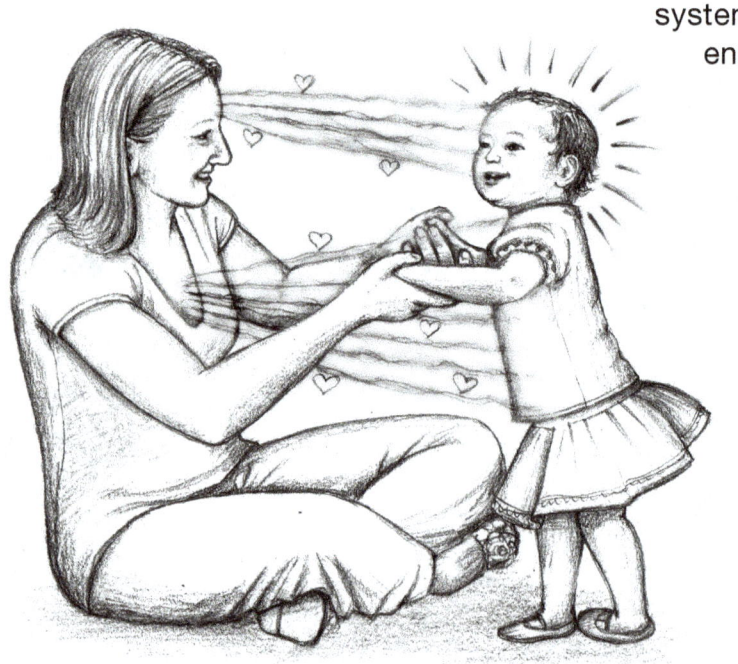

Person sending love or a positive energy substance

He actually felt better afterwards; he was no longer carrying such a large load of stuff. But I felt terrible. I needed to get it out.

This is a bit different method of clearing the field from dusting. We'll call this 'scooping the goop'.

Exercise 3.4: Scooping the Goop

1. Set the Intention

Charge your hands and set the intention to clear and release thicker energetic stuff, the "goop", out of your field.

2. Tune into Goop

Tune to your energy system and try to sense the area in which that energetic debris sits.

3. Scoop the Goop

Put your hands into this area, hold them together like a bowl and start 'scooping': Slowly move your hands from inside out, taking external energies back out, and empty that goop out once your hands are further away from your body (or whenever your hands feels full).

4. Use your Imagination

You can imagine the energies there like porridge that you scoop back out of your energy system.

Scooping the Goop

5. Shake it out

From time to time shake out your hands and breathe deeply out to release this thicker energetic stuff. Again trust that the earth will naturally transform it.

6. Completion

Stand with your arms relaxed and your feet shoulder width apart. Take a few deep breaths and take especially note of the area that you just cleared.

> **Quick Reference Points:**
> 1. Set the Intention
> 2. Tune into Goop
> 3. Scoop the Goop
> 4. Use your Imagination
> 5. Shake it out
> 6. Completion

The Onion

Now that we have learnt to dust and scoop the field, there is one more level of stuff that we'd like to address here.

ENERGY PRINCIPLE 7:

The Energy Field has layers

A human being is like an onion, composed of many layers

Your energy field has different layers. It can be likened to an onion. The outer layers hold more superficial and surface feelings and thoughts. The deeper layers hold more powerful and significant feelings and thoughts.

The stuff that accumulates every day and from interactions like with Antonio is more on the surface layers. These layers can be cleaned relatively easily. The energy tools of dusting and scooping work well here.

The deeper layers are more complex and need more understanding and skill to clear them. When you were younger you experienced many powerful emotions and events. These things made powerful impacts on you. Many became woven into your system. They've now been integrated into your very fabric. Over time, new things happened. These earlier energies became buried beneath later layers, in many cases forgotten but not gone.

The Energy Field has Layers like an Onion
"Stuff" accumulates in the different layers of the field

It's very much like archaeology. A culture comes into being, builds its buildings, artwork, tools, etc. Then that culture is superseded by a later culture that builds on top of it. Again and again this happens. The original culture's remains are now deeply buried beneath layers of archaeological ages.

We are mentioning these deeper layers because some of you are experiencing them and you are ready to begin to work with them. We cannot provide methods to work with those deeper layers here, as this is too involved for this book. If you are interested in doing this deeper work, check our website for the trainings we offer.

* * * * *

You are like an archaeologist, gradually clearing layer by layer until you get to your very roots. This Energy Balancing work we have just begun starts a process of clearing, opening and discovery. We would highly encourage you to practice clearing your field every day. Not only will it make you feel better and keep you functioning at a more optimal level; your energy skills will strengthen, your vitality will be greater, and your life will work better on all levels. Ultimately, this holds the promise of revealing the greatest archaeological treasure of all: your Essence, the Golden Being at your core.

The Golden Being
In our Essence, each one of us is incredibly bright

Exercise 3.5: Clearing Energy in Public

It's great if you can take the time to clear your field. But realistically, you can't always get a private moment to do this. So here are some ways you can inconspicuously clear yourself when you're with others.

1. The Forward Stretch

Put your hands in front of your chest at roughly the heart level. Turn the palms facing outwards. Then push outwards as if you are stretching. When the hands have reached full extension towards the front, then sweep them out towards the sides. You can do this a few time in a row and no one will notice.

2. Your powerful Mind

Though your hands are powerful in guiding energy, just your thinking alone can accomplish the same. Remember, Energy follows awareness; by visualizing energy moving, energy moves. Imagine your hands clearing your field. Just as if you were using them, do it just in your imagination.

3. Breathing moves Energy

In India they developed breathing into a powerful science called Pranayama. One of the simplest of breathing techniques is one you do naturally; take a deep breath. As you do, let your awareness focus on the life force (Chi or Prana) that comes in through the air. See this filling you from the inside and expanding outwards to push out the stuff that's clouding you. Then, let your exhale be a bit stronger than normal, kind of a sharp, strong, fast exhale. As you do this, see the stuff being blown away from your field.

Exercise 3.6: Some other Tools for Clearing in Daily Life Situations

In addition to these core tools of using the hands to clear the field, there are a number of quick-fix energy-based tools that you are probably already using and that you can now use more deliberately and skillfully. Each of these things is a "normal" daily activity that moves energy.

Clearing using the body: Move your Energy

If you are a runner, run. If you like dancing, dance. If you go to a gym, work out. Whatever movement you like to do, do it now. Getting your energy moving flushes your system and shakes off stuff.

Clearing using the breath: Deep Breathing

One of the simplest, most powerful and easily available tools that you can use anywhere is breathing. When you are full of stuff and your system is clogged, you unconsciously breathe shallow. To move your energy start by taking a number of deep breaths; open your jaw, move your shoulders and hips as you breathe.

Clearing using energy and the body: Pumping

At the bottom of the spine is a great reservoir of energy. Most of us know it as sexuality, but it has a deeper significant. In India they call it Kundalini, or the "reservoir of life energy". It can be activated through a pumping motion.

Clearing using emotions: Scream it out

Emotions are energy. Sometimes they just need to be released. There's nothing like a good scream or a Lion's roar to move them. Scream your

emotions out in a pillow or into the windshield of your car, or the waves or the forest. You can also try the method of gibberish; "talking" in non-sense sounds.

Clearing using the mind: Use a Positive Mental Image

Direct your attention towards a positive idea or image. As energy follows awareness, this image will positively enliven your energy field. A mental image can be strengthened through verbal repetition. You can use the expression we've written below or create your own:

"I am a golden being of light. This is just stuff that is clogging my system and I release it."

4 Centering Yourself

Ritama's Spiritual Path begins

Ritama:

"My spiritual path started at my dance academy. I remember the exact moment that birthed the new me. When I arrived at the academy I was eager and full of talent. Dance was a joy and I loved performing. I had confidence in myself - I knew I was good at this. I was even a bit cocky! You can imagine my shock when I received a D in a course. 'Why? How is this possible? Me? I'm one of the best dancers in the school. There must be something wrong with this instructor. I really need to talk to her.'

Upset, I went to her. She said: 'Ritama, you don't have a connection to your center'" I had no idea what she was talking about. My immediately response was, 'And you give me a D for this? Can't you change it? I have A's in all my other classes'"

She said, "No. I am doing this because I need to get your attention. Being centered is one of the most important things for becoming an excellent dancer."

I could feel that she meant well, and I intuitively felt she was right, but mentally I had no idea what she was talking about. I did not understand the concept. Where is my center? What center? How do I get the contact? If I wasn't in my center, where was I?

That moment started a quest for me to discover my center. However, center eluded me for a long time. What I did find early on however was an important step on the way – and that was how I was off center.

How do you know that you are off-center?

We all know the feeling of being off-center; we have spent a lot of our life there!
- You have certainly experienced being insecure or tense.
- Perhaps you weren't fully present or were preoccupied.
- Maybe your actions were not as powerful or effective as you would have liked them to be.
- Or your emotions were turbulent and clouded the situation.
- If you were doing something physical, perhaps you were clumsy.

All these exemplify ways we are off center.

Being off-centered is well embodied in language:

"I'm all over the place."
"I'm not together."
"I'm spaced out."
"I feel besides myself."

These expressions are more than metaphorical descriptions of how we are feeling; they accurately describe what is happening in our energy body!

The Main Directions to which we go Off-Center

The following images show the energetics of some of the ways we go off center and the text gives hints on how to recognize that off-center state. As you look at the pictures, you may notice each evokes particular sensations in your body. This is your energy body reshaping itself, just by looking at the picture. You'll probably recognize all of them, but which ones do you tend to resonate with the most?

There are many other ways we go off center that we haven't listed here, such as going off-center to the side or to the diagonal. Add your own off-center direction.

Your energies are in front of yourself

Caught in doing and pushing
to achieve your goals

Overdoing things to care for
and please others

In Front of Yourself:
- *Hooked into doing or action*
- *Spun-up or scattered*
- *Aggressive*
- *Bossy or pushy*
- *Proving yourself*
- *Juggling too many balls*

In Front of Yourself:
- *Pleasing others*
- *Caretaking another*
- *Emotionally over-invested*
- *Trying to get attention*

Your energies are contracted

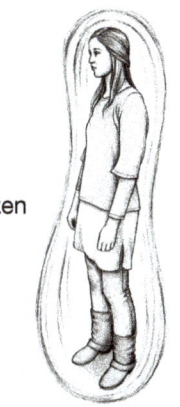
Tight and frozen

Your energies are behind yourself

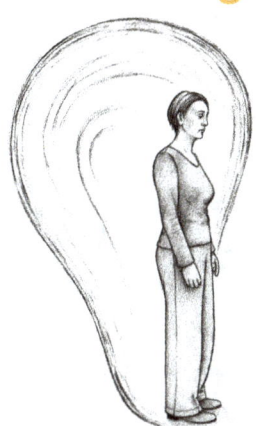

Contracted or Behind Yourself:
- *Tight or frozen*
- *Oversensitive*
- *Protective*
- *Feeling like a victim*
- *Hiding, escaping*

Knotted and behind yourself

Your energies are above yourself

Above Yourself:
- *Disconnected from your body*
- *Ungrounded*
- *Spaced out, daydreaming*
- *Too much in the mind*
- *Too "spiritual", not realistic*

Overly mental and disconnected from body/feelings

Spaced-out, dreamy

Your energies are down

Low energy, dragging yourself

Down:
- *Tired, flat, low energy*
- *Lazy, "couch potato"*
- *Lost your drive*
- *Addictions – food, drink, drugs, sex*
- *Hopeless, sad, depressed*

"Blobby" and sluggish

Ritama:

As I became more aware of my energy field my first insight was that I was in front of myself. This had many implications. On a technical level while dancing I had problems with my balance. On a performance level I received the feedback after a dance presentation that I was giving too much. And in my personal life I would often be overpowering and bossy, and others would get overwhelmed by me.

The awareness that I was in front of my self led to my next step - how to come back in. A whole new department in the school that before was of no interest to me suddenly drew me strongly. The quest of finding center became such a fire that I decided to change to the Faculty of Modern Dance. There the classes were based on breath and yoga and I began training in Tai Chi. Through all these new methods I came to understand what it meant to bring myself back and drop in.

Bringing your Field back to Center

Here's an exercise you can experiment with to bring your field back to center. In the following steps you will be directed to use your hands to guide your energy from the off-center state back to a state of center. When you move your hands, generally speaking, move them slowly. But trust your intuition to move more strongly or gently as needed. As you move your hands visualize the energies coming back to a healthier flow.

Exercise 4.1: Bring your Energy Field Back to Center

A: Preparation

1. Choose your Off-Center State

Choose one image from the previous pictures that reflects your most common way of going off center.

2. Enter that Off-Center State

Take a moment to enter that state and feel the physical sensation.

B: Core exercise

3. Choose (according to your off-center state) one of the following centering movements and bring your energies back to center:

"In Front of Yourself"

Feel where your energies are extended and simply use your hands to pull them closer to your body. Gather your energy and breathe it back in.

"Behind Yourself"

Let your hands be a bit behind you, one on each side, palms facing to the front. Slowly move the hands towards the front, bringing your energies back to center.

"Contracted In"

Use your hands to expand the retreated or contracted energies. Open your energy up and breathe it out to the front. Visualize the energy streaming out and forwards.

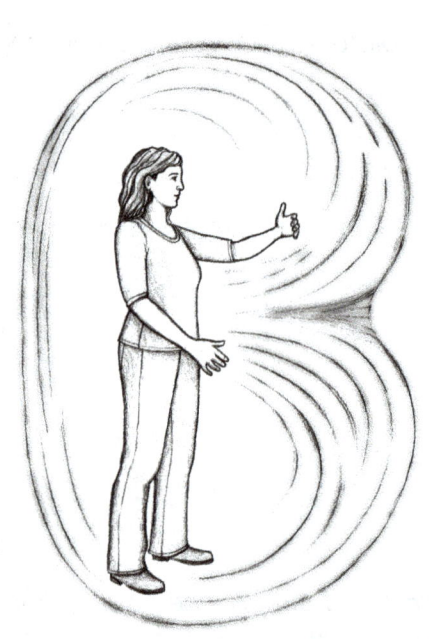

In Front of Yourself
Bringing energy back in

Behind Yourself or Contracted
Opening contracted energies out

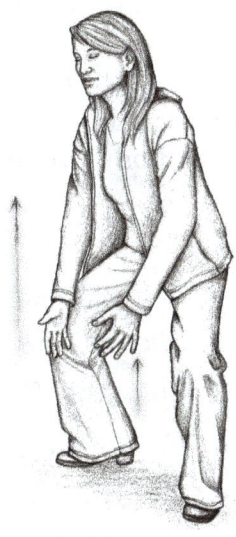

Above Yourself
Bringing spaced out energies down

Down
Lifting energies up

"Above Yourself"

Bring your energy, thoughts and ideas down to earth. With your hands pull and sweep the energies down, into your body and to the lower part of your spine.

"Down"

Lift your blobbing energies back up, using your hands to collect the energies around your lower body. Breathe in and sweep it up to the top of your head.

4. Use your Breath to center

Gather your energies with an in-breath and expand your energies with an out-breath.

> **C: Completion**
>
> **5. Tune to your new Balance**
>
> Take a moment to be with the feeling of this balanced state and how it affects your body, emotions and mind.
>
> > **Quick Reference Points:**
> >
> > 1. Choose your Off-Center State
> > 2. Enter that Off-Center State
> > 3. Choose your Centering Movement and balance Yourself
> > 4. Use your Breath to center
> > 5. Tune to your new Balance

What it means to be in Center

Ritama:

> *I realized something about center that had to do with my very core, the physical and energetic center of myself.*
>
> *My Tai Chi teacher told me to feel my spinal column and then to imagine a channel of energy in front it, right in the middle of my body. I was focused so much on the outside that it was difficult to pull my attention into my body. I had to turn my awareness 180°, from looking outwards to looking in.*
>
> *It was an overwhelming experience to slowly come into my body and be in the middle of it. I could feel the resistance and discomfort. But it was also new and exciting. When I would touch center it brought an incredible feeling of joy and peace. And then I'd lose it again! It was like a*

flicker of light, there and then gone. I knew in this moment I had to make this my mission. This was the most incredible feeling that I had ever felt. So no matter how often I would lose it, I was determined to find it - and keep it!

And slowly this magical feeling of being in my center grew into a bigger flame. I had found a space inside where I felt I had come home, like I was resting in my most delicious self.

Can you remember a moment when you just felt wonderful because you were at your optimum; where you were in a state of balance, clarity, and "in the flow"?

There are many ways this might have occurred. You might have been working and were highly productive. Perhaps you were with a loved one and things were just flowing between you. Or you were doing something active - sport, driving your car, walking in nature, and there was a state of balance, clarity, and being in the flow that made you feel just wonderful.

In all of these moments you were centered. Something was balanced within you. For a moment you were integrated – the many parts of you were working harmoniously together.

Being centered feels great! There's nothing like it. You feel so essentially you, your optimum self, the one you always knew was there.

> **Being centered is a sense of:**
> - Coming home to yourself
> - Resting in yourself
> - Your energies are aligned and working together harmoniously
> - You feel in the NOW and in the FLOW

The Core Channel

ENERGY PRINCIPLE 8:

Center – an energetic location

Center is an energetic location in the middle of your body. It is a vertical channel of energy running from the base of the spine to the top of the head

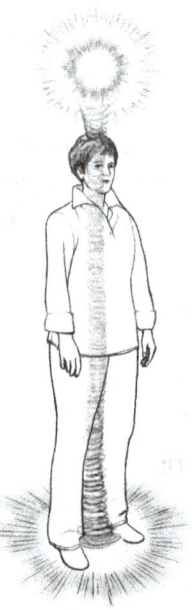

There's a reason the experience of center is called "center". That's because you are literally connected to the center of your self. This is a real location, a real physical place within your energy field.

Center and the Core Channel

DEFINITION: **The Core Channel**
In the very center of your energy body there is a vertical channel of energy that runs from the base of the spine to the top of the head. It parallels the spinal column but sits in front of it, in the middle of your torso.

Experience your Core

Through becoming aware of your core channel you can deliberately cultivate the connection to center. The best way to do that is to experience it.

Exercise 4.2: **Experience Your Core Channel**

We'd suggest you do this standing up. Second best is sitting in a chair with your back straight. Third option is lying down, again, with your back straight.

1. Close your eyes and bring your awareness inside.

2. Feel your spine. Imagine there is a column of energy right in front of your spine. It rises from the bottom of your spine to the top of your head. We call this the core channel.

3. Visualize your core channel. Maybe you see it as a channel of bright light. For some it feels more like a night sky, dark but full of sparkling stars. Find an image that works best for you.

4. Spend a few minutes there. This is a beautiful place to rest. It's like coming home to your self.

5. Take slow deep breaths. With each breath let yourself drop deeper into your core. Rest more and more within.

The core channel is going to become your center point, the place you come to rest.

Dynamic Center:
The Joy of Flow within Center

Ritama:

I thought I had found it – this wonderful feeling of resting in my center. Little did I know that there was more to come. My teacher began to guide me to a new and dynamic place of center where I could feel a flow of energy running through my core. It was so dynamic and alive. There was a feeling of movement inside. It brought so much energy that I felt my consciousness exploding. It was like a jolt of lightening opening at the bottom of my spine and running all the way up my body to burst forth like a shining sun at the top of my head. It was an incredible experience. It was the best high I had ever had – better than sex, better than drugs, even better than dance!

DEFINITION: Dynamic Center
The experience of a flow of energy that runs through your core, from the bottom of your spine to the top of your head.

Center is not static, that once you reach it you're there. It's dynamic and evolving; layers upon layers, depths upon depths gradually unfold. Throughout this book we'll add new understandings and tools to help you deepen your connection to center.

ENERGY PRINCIPLE 9:
Center - an energetic state

Being centered is an energetic state where your energy is rooted within the core channel, creating alignment and integration throughout your entire energy system.

This deep state of center and the life force flowing within it have been known in many cultures and mystery schools. In India the entire science of Yoga, and not just the Hatha Yoga that most people are familiar with (the stretching and strengthening exercises done at many fitness studios), focuses upon the core channel and the awakening and movement of energy within it.

Branches of Yoga, focused around the core channel:

1. Raja Yoga: the yoga of meditation
2. Kriya Yoga : the yoga of moving energy up the spine
3. Laya Yoga: activation of the energy centers (chakras)
4. Kundalini Yoga : awakening energy at the base of the spine and moving it upwards
5. Tantra Yoga: awakening sexual energy and moving it up the spine

The Tree

There is a metaphor dating back into antiquity that helps one to open the deeper core. Though this uses a pictorial metaphor it is much more than that – it is describing a real energetic state.

The image is of a tree. The tree has its roots deep into the earth where it is grounded and draws from the earth's nutrients. The trunk rises above the

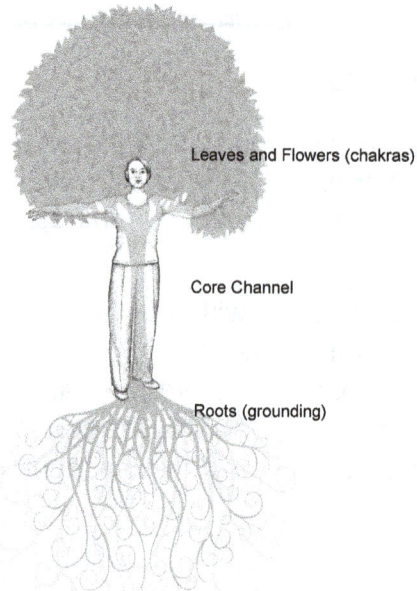

ground vertically and high into the sky. At the top of the tree is a broad canopy of foliage and flowers that opens the tree to the infinite sky above, and through which it absorbs the life-giving rays of the Sun.

We can't say enough about the energy truths hidden behind this image, and the value you will derive through working with it. Ideally, if you can do this exercise once a day for ten minutes, it will transform your life. Even done on an irregular basis, the 'tree exercise' is powerful beyond measure.

The Tree
The human energy system is like a tree with roots, a trunk and branches

Exercise 4.3:   Ground and Expand like a Tree

You can do this exercise standing or sitting. The important thing is that your spine is erect and not slouched.

A: Preparation: Grounding

1. Tune to Your Base

At the very bottom of the spine, where the coccyx is, is an energy center called the base. Take a few deep breaths into the base. Now visualize your core channel extending downwards through the base and into the earth, like a tree growing deep roots. (If you are standing, have the energy go down the legs, through the feet and into the earth.)

2. Grow Your Roots

Put one hand in front of your base and one behind, palms facing down, and gently move them downwards. Imagine that your hands are helping to open the energies of the base downwards. Connect to the earth. See your "root" anchored deeply within it. Feel the grounding and solidity this gives you.

B. Core Exercise

3. Charge Your Base

Keeping this root solidly in the earth, now inhale the energies from the earth up into the base. Each inhale is like sucking liquid up a straw, pulling the earth energies upwards. As you do this, use your hands, palms facing upwards, to sweep the energies of the earth upwards into the base. Do this for a few minutes.

4. Bring energy UP to the Crown

Now, inhaling strongly, suck the energy all the way up the core channel to the top of the head. We call this place the crown. Now use your hands, sweeping them fully up the core and to the top of the head. Do this four times.

5. Expand your Crown

Breathe into your crown. Imagine it as the flowers at the top of your tree. As you do this, use your hands all around your head in an upwards-sweeping movement to help the energies open here.

6. Breathe the Energies DOWN

Now as you exhale, breathe the energies from the top of the head down the core to the base. Support this with your hands if you like. Bring these high frequency energies down into the body. Do this four times, each time on the exhale.

> **C. Completion**
>
> **7. Rest within**
>
> *Feel the entire tree. Your roots are deep in the earth. Your crown is open and connected to the heavens above. Feel your core and rest within.*
>
> > **Quick Reference Points:**
> >
> > 1. *Tune to your Base*
> > 2. *Grow your Roots*
> > 3. *Charge your Base*
> > 4. *Bring Energy up to the Crown*
> > 5. *Expand your Crown*
> > 6. *Breathe the Energies down*
> > 7. *Rest within*

After you finish this exercise, look around you. For many people it's as if their eyes are a little clearer. Things seem different – more fresh and alive.

Putting Centering into Practice in Daily Life

Being centered opens up vast possibilities for living and consciousness. In the more advanced stages it unfolds what could be called, for lack of better words, higher consciousness.

But center is also immanently practical. It's for how we walk, talk and go about our daily business.

Ritama:

Struggling to hold center in daily life, I asked my Tai Chi teacher for advice. He said to me, "Even while I'm talking to you, one part of me is focused in my own center. Even when I'm doing other things, it's as if one eye is turned inwards and resting in my center, whilst the other eye is turned out."

We've covered several tools now to connect to center. These tools have brought you to the experience of your core channel and to the flow of life energy that moves here. But it might feel a bit strange to do the Bringing Your Field Back to Center Exercise or the Tree Exercise in the middle of a business meeting. You probably won't feel so comfortable saying, "Could we stop the meeting for a moment, I want to balance my energies by waving my hands around here in front of myself." Right!

So here are some ways you can center in the midst of normal life activities.

Exercise 4.4: A Ten-Seconds Centering

1. Take a full inhale. Now exhale deeply. Focus the exhale on the base, the bottom of the spine. Imagine tensions flowing out there. Get the feeling of grounding.

2. Inhale into the base and bring the energy up into the core channel, all the way to the top of the head and expand.

3. Now exhale the energy down your core to the base again.

Go back to what you were doing. As much as possible, keep one eye inwards and continue breathing into center whilst you go about your business.

Exercise 4.5: A Two-Seconds Centering

And if you can't even take the 10 seconds to do the above, then simply take one deep breath from your base up your core to the top of your head, and exhale down your core channel back to the base.

Now continue what you were doing.

Centering Quickly

Life comes at us fast! So we need to find center fast as well. It's great when you can take the time to really center, but what to do when you're in the thick of things and energies are flying. That's when you need center the most, and that's also probably the moment when it's least possible to take the time to do so.

Here's a form of "fast center". Though it may not be as effective as taking the time to fully center, you'll be amazed at just how useful it is.

Being Centered in Action

Now that you're familiar with the basics of centering, let's bring this to some of our daily action situations.

> **Exercise 4.6:** **Center while Walking**
>
> *1. First, come to center using any of the methods we've previously discussed.*
>
> *2. Now simply start walking around. As you walk, it's as if one eye is focused outwards on your environment, and the other eye is focused inwards on your center.*
>
> *3. Imagine you are walking "in balance". Maintain the connection to your core; stay grounded and open to the crown, all whilst you are in motion.*

It's amazing how quick the attention will drift and we'll lose connection to ourself. As a result we're quickly out of balance. So if that happened, just re-center yourself again. You will have to do this many times before you can regularly hold center.

Being centered in Action

Exercise 4.7:   Center while in Activity

1. For example, go wash your hands, or butter a piece of toast, or do laundry. Find something simple that takes eye/hand coordination.

2. Again, one eye is focused outwards on your environment, and the other eye is focused inwards on your center. Maintain the connection to your core all whilst you are in motion.

Good. When you're ready, let's jump into deep waters:

Exercise 4.8:   Center while Relating

Go and interact with someone whilst remaining in center.

This is not easy! Relating to another is one of the most powerful things that can pull us out of center. People can be the most challenging of all with regards to holding center. So if you find yourself off-balance when with others, don't be hard on yourself. This happens for everyone. It might take a while before you can hold center with people. With each chapter we deepen the process of holding center and coming back to yourself.

"Steh-auf-Männchen"

You probably remember these toys from when you were a kid. They were like a doll or a punching bag, with sand or water in the bottom. When you would knock them over they would simply come back up. In Germany they call them "Steh-auf-Männchen" (Stand up Man).

These dolls are a model for who you will become. You are going to get knocked over 1001 times. And you are going to learn to quickly come back up to center. Though in the beginning it will take more time to find center, you'll get it faster and faster. As center deepens you won't fall over as far or as often. And after a while, you will begin to find that you are living in center the majority of your time with only a little wobble here and there.

Being Centered – the foundation for higher things

Being centered is tremendously fulfilling. It's an incredible state to live in, and a joy within itself. You are here; present, dynamic, vital and potent. Your energies are aligned and in balance, and your actions carry that. Being centered in it self is a worthy goal of having.

Yet this is just the beginning, for being centered becomes the foundation for something more to happen. Everything else you do in life gains the benefit. Now your energy is available. The potency of your creativity, your higher intelligence, your soul and spirit have a balanced and integrated energy system through which they can work. When you are in center the way you relate is more loving, your communication more clear and your actions more effective. Center becomes the basis for all the many aspects of your Being to flower. Center benefits everything.

The Four Directions of Energy Flow

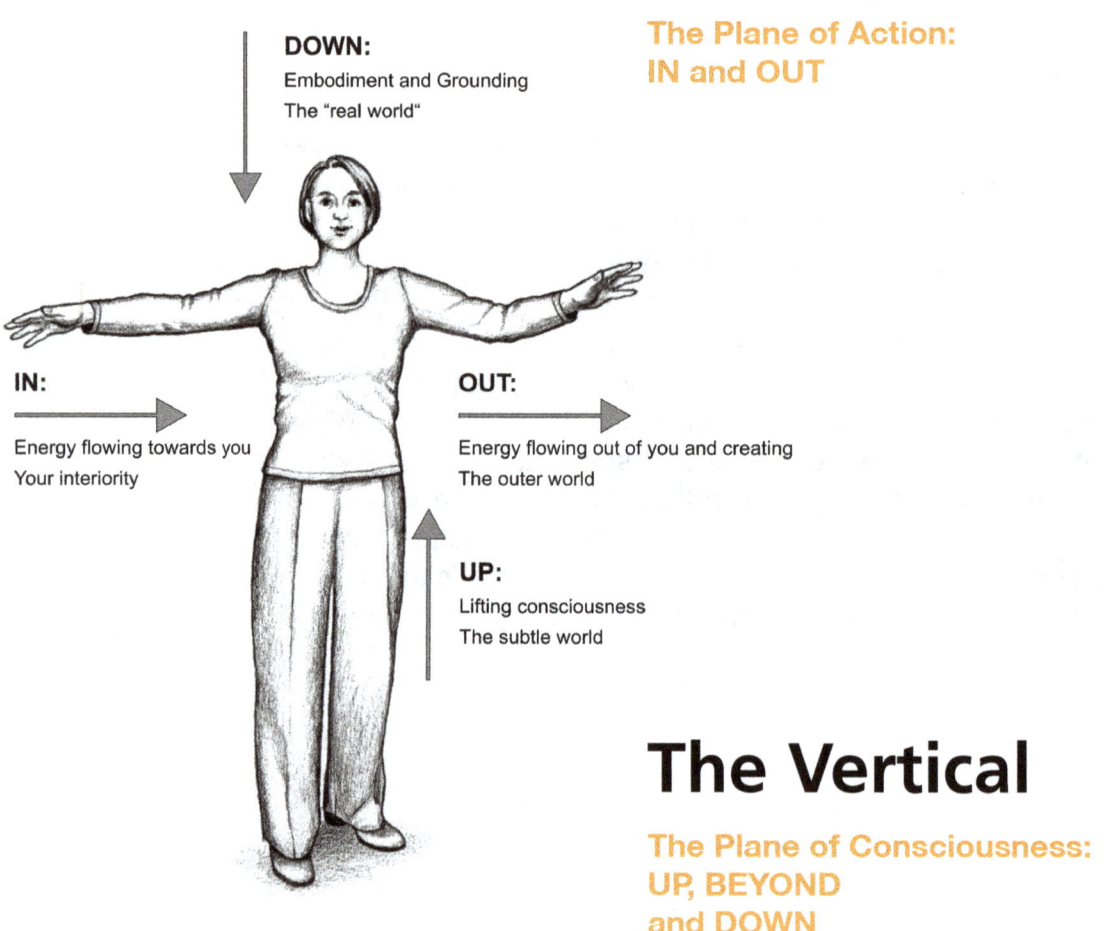

DOWN:
Embodiment and Grounding
The "real world"

IN:
Energy flowing towards you
Your interiority

OUT:
Energy flowing out of you and creating
The outer world

UP:
Lifting consciousness
The subtle world

The Horizontal

The Plane of Action:
IN and OUT

The Vertical

The Plane of Consciousness:
UP, BEYOND
and DOWN

5 The Four Directions of Energy Flow

The Four Directions of Energy Balancing

We are a meeting point of energies, an energy vortex, a center point around which energies flow. At every moment a remarkable array of energies are flowing into and out from our energy field.

We are also a powerful transformer of energy. Within us energy is moving and circulating, continually changing state and form as its vibration is altered in the service of various purposes.

The Two Planes of Energy Flow

There are many planes and directions of energy flow. We are going to focus on two of them – the horizontal and the vertical.

The horizontal has to do with action and relating. Energy flows OUT from us to the world around and energies flow IN towards us from others and the environment.

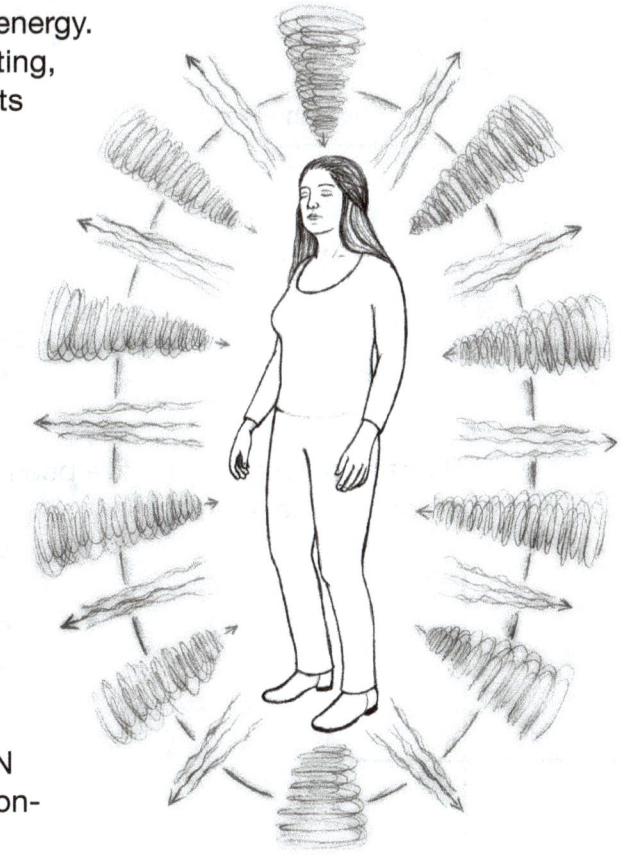

We are a meeting point of energies, an energy vortex

89

When you speak you are expressing horizontally. When you connect to others you are connecting horizontally. When you are in relationship to another, whether it's love flowing back and forth between you or even anger, it's a horizontal flow of energy.

The horizontal is the plane of action and relating

The vertical is the plane of consciousness

The vertical is the plane of consciousness. It is an internal dimension, having to do with energy flowing within our core channel and with how we feel and think. The way the energy flows here changes the quality of our thoughts and feelings.

Though we describe the vertical as internal it also has an external aspect to it; it connects and grounds us to the Earth below and opens us to the wonders of consciousness above.

These two dimensions have been represented in a symbol dating back to antiquity – the cross.

The cross has been used as a spiritual symbol in many cultures and religious traditions. The esoteric meaning behind the cross is the meeting of spirit and matter. The vertical arm of the cross represents the descending force of spirit (consciousness). The horizontal arm represents the plane of matter (form). The cross is said to be the symbol of Man in who spirit and matter, consciousness and form meet.

ENERGY PRINCIPLE 10:

The four directions of energy flow

Energy flows in four primary directions relative to a human being

The Four Directions in which Energy flows

When these two planes intersect we get four components of the cross – left horizontal, right horizontal, above and below. Each arm represents a direction that energy flows – IN and OUT, and UP and DOWN. Each direction represents a particular aspect of life and consciousness.

A master key to using energy effectively comes through understanding these four directions and gaining skills in each. Each direction has a profound effect upon an area of your life where it creates specific types of feelings, thoughts and behavior.

Each direction represents a pathway for the flow of energy.

Horizontal
- IN represents energy flowing in to you, energy you take in to your system
- OUT represents energy flowing out of you and what that creates in the world around of you

Vertical
- UP represents energy raising in consciousness and vibration
- DOWN represents energy concretizing and grounding

Each direction also represents an area of life.

- IN represents your inner life – the rich world of thoughts, feelings and sensations within.
- OUT represents the world outside of you – people, things and places
- UP represents a dimension of higher consciousness that is available to everyone – commonly referred to by names such as higher intelligence, soul, or spirit.
- DOWN represents you being in the body, in this moment, in the here and now.

We will cover these four directions in some detail in the coming chapters. Here we'd like to give you an overview, the 'bigger picture' of how they all fit together.

IN - OUT - UP - DOWN

A brief overview

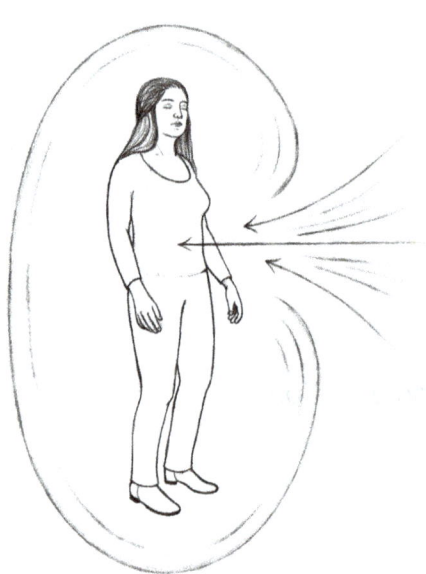

IN

IN as a direction represents energies that flow in towards you. For example, someone says, "I love you". It's not only their words that reach you, there's a warm and caring energy of love as well that flows towards you and enters your energy field.

A host of energies from the world around are constantly entering your field. An important aspect of keeping your energy in balance is to

IN
Direction of energy flow: IN – energies flowing in to you
Location: Your interiority

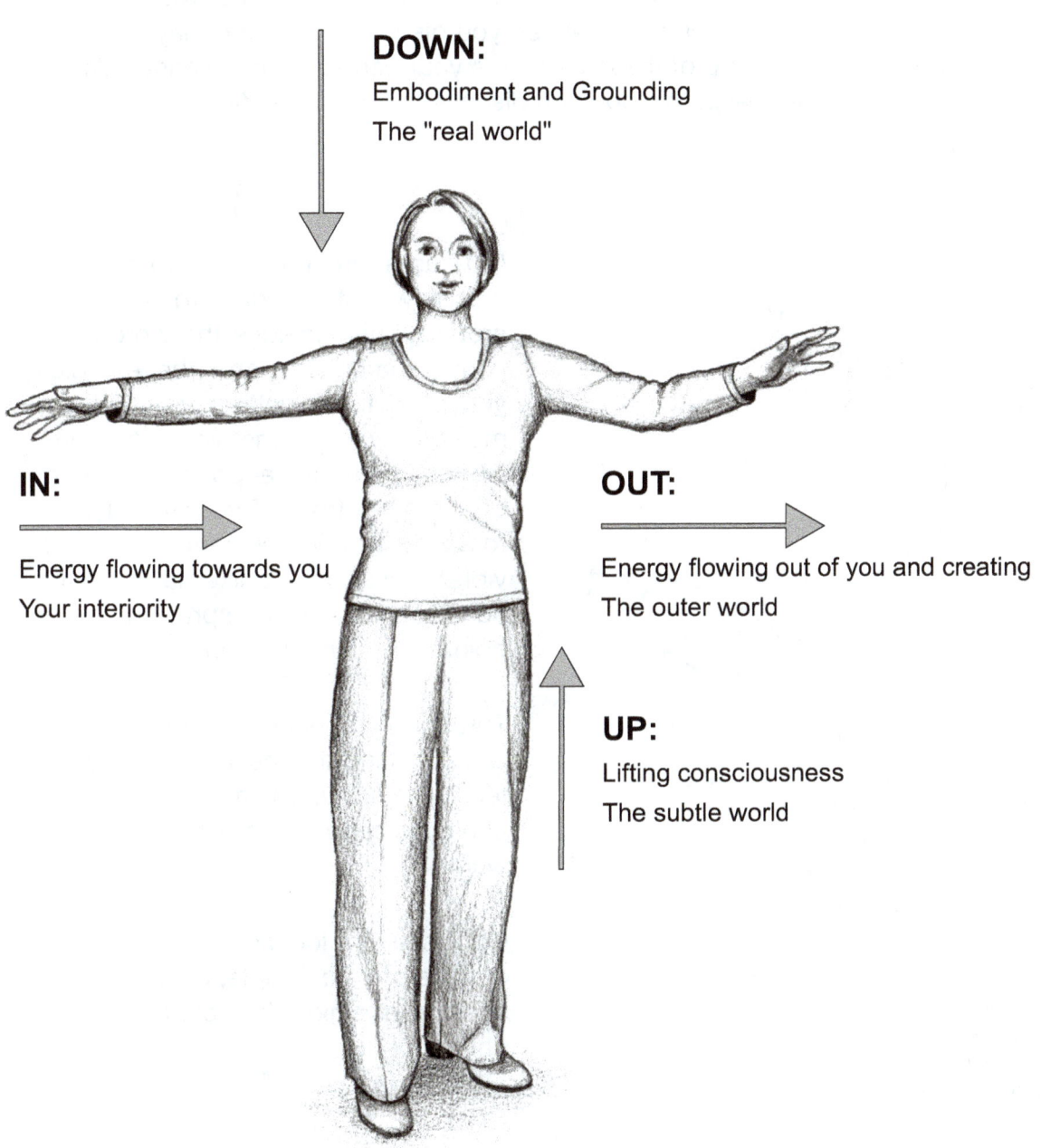

understand how these energies affect you, deliberately taking in those that are good for you, and not taking in those that aren't.

IN as a location also refers to your interiority, your rich inner world of feelings, thoughts and energies. When you discover layer upon layer of who you are. At the core of these depths is your center, your Essence. We will focus a great deal in this book on discovering and living from Essence.

Out

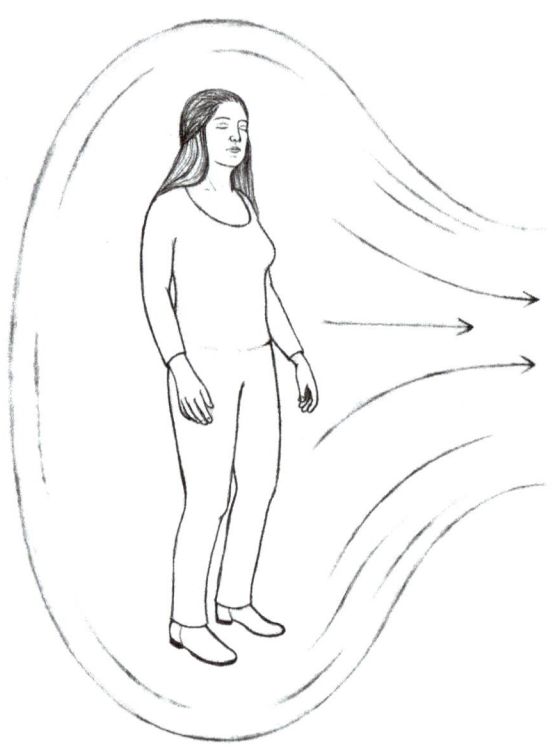

OUT
Direction of energy flow: energies flowing OUT from you
Location: The Outer world outside of you

OUT as a direction refers to energies that flow out of you into the world around. This includes the words that you communicate and the energies you send forth. Let's say you determinedly want something. Your will vibrates forth as a powerful stream of energy in front of you. If you were to speak to another person with this vibration strong, it's like having a fire hose of powerfully spraying water pointed in their direction.

Through OUT energy you impact the world around and have a powerful effect upon it. Learning to handle OUT energy is central to creating what you want.

OUT is also a location – that which is outside of you: people, places, things and the energies they contain are all part of OUT.

Up

UP refers to the process of moving energies from lower in the body upwards. Every feeling and thought has a location somewhere in your energy body. The denser or slower vibrational feelings and thoughts sit lower in the body, and as you move upwards you have feelings and thoughts that become progressively lighter and faster in their vibration.

For example, anger sits in the area of the solar plexus. You might be angry with a person and then come to understand that their behavior came from a tragedy that had just befallen them; suddenly your anger turns into compassion. The energy moved from your solar plexus upwards to your heart.

Not only did the energy move upwards, but it changed its vibrational state as well. "Up" also refers to this process of movement from energies of a denser vibration (such as anger) to energies of a more refined vibration (such as compassion).

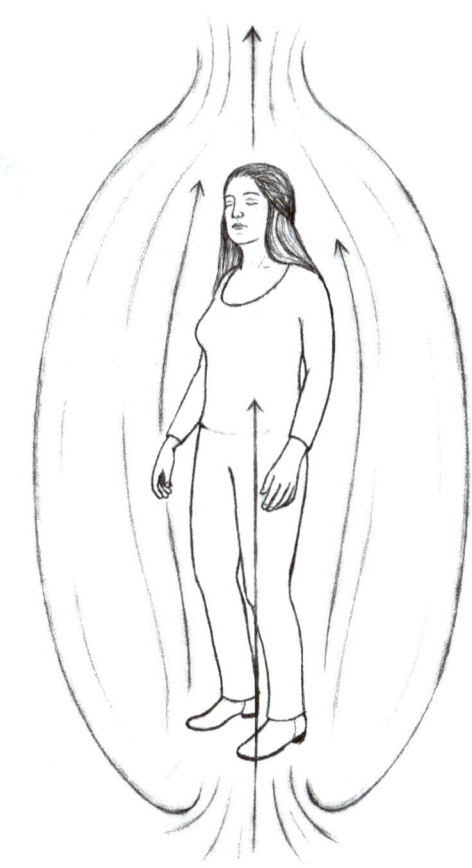

UP
Direction of energy flow:
Energies flowing within you from lower UP to higher places
Location: UP – at the top of your head and above it

When self-development is looked at through the eyes of energy, the entire process can be seen as an upward movement of energy, where we open to more refined and subtle states of consciousness and energy.

UP also refers to the location at the top of your body – the top of your head and above it. There are powerful energies of a high frequency that sit here. They contain your highest thoughts, feelings and aspiration. To live connected to UP is an Uplifted Experience.

Beyond

Though we speak of In, UP, Down and Out as your primary four directions, there is a fifth place that plays a central role in Energy Balancing. We call it "Beyond". This is an experience that opens at the top of the head. It's here that you touch a dimension of consciousness and energy that can, for lack of better words, be called "Enlightened", Higher Consciousness, your Soul or your Spirit. We refer to this dimension as "Beyond" because it's so much beyond normal awareness. This place is so immense and so illuminating, that once touched your life is never the same.

Down

The following example refers to the process of moving energies Down: bringing higher aspects of your self – love, compassion, vision and inspiration - into your mind, body and personality.

> *I, Kabir, was working on a book at an isolated resort in Thailand. I would sit in meditation with a laptop computer on my lap. A flash of insight would suddenly illuminate my mind. I would immediately type it out. If I got a tenth of what I saw, that was a lot. It was so frustrating! There was a place of higher intelligence in me that was showering me with insight, but I wasn't able to hold those insights and bring them down through my mind and into words.*

Another, more down to earth example of "Down" is one that most of you know. We have many ideals. Let's say you imagine yourself trim and healthy. You set the intention to go on a diet and put in place an exercise plan. This is your higher mind at work. But now you have to apply your ideal to eating and working out. Your higher is trying to guide your lower. You are attempting to "Bring Down" a higher understanding into your body.

"Down" as a direction is about bringing down your ideals, higher frequency energy, and the more enlightened self that you know you can be, into your mind, feelings, energy field, body and personality.

Down is also a location – the lower part of your body and the earth beneath you; it's "down here" in your body. You're grounded, solid, here and now.

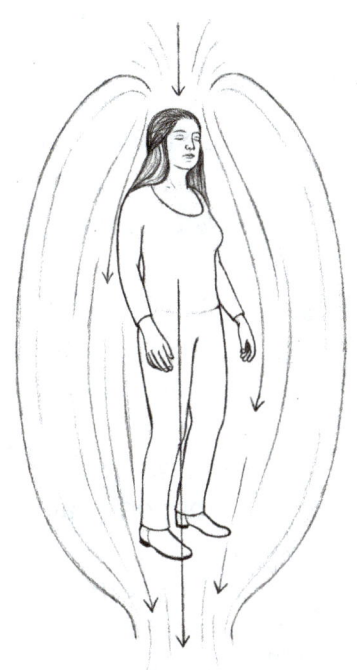

Down
Direction of energy flow:
Down from above your head into your body to your feet and the earth
Location: Down, both the lower part of your body and the earth beneath you

* * * * *

The Circular Flow of IN – UP - DOWN and OUT

Though we've structured this book in two sections - the horizontal plane of action, the energies we send IN and OUT, and the vertical plane of consciousness, UP and DOWN - there is a different organization that we use in the deeper teachings of energy balancing: the circular flow of IN - UP - DOWN and OUT and its corresponding steps:

Step One

IN refers to the turning inwards of your awareness. It begins a process of self-knowledge and exploration.

Step Two

As you turn in, you begin to work on yourself. Things begin to change. Your energies start moving UP – they increase in vibration, and they literally move upwards in your energy system to higher energy centers or chakras.

At some point you touch BEYOND, the higher states of consciousness that open at the top of your head, the crown chakra.

This is the first half of the journey – to attain consciousness. But it's only the first half. There's still more to go. The second half is the return back -bringing your consciousness here.

Step Three

DOWN represents the process of bringing the higher energies, thoughts and feelings down into your body and psyche. Your vibration shifts. You literally "hold more light". Your emotions and thinking undergo significant shifts as they become clearer and more potent.

Step Four

But even this isn't the end point. Ultimately, you're here to "live your light". To express in this world the consciousness you've attained, the love you carry, the insights that have emerged. You are here to contribute, to make the world a little better. You are here to create the outer as a reflection of the inner. OUT means to bring the richness of your consciousness out into the world around.

We refer to this entire process in the specific sequence as IN UP DOWN OUT. This is the full circle of Energy Balancing.

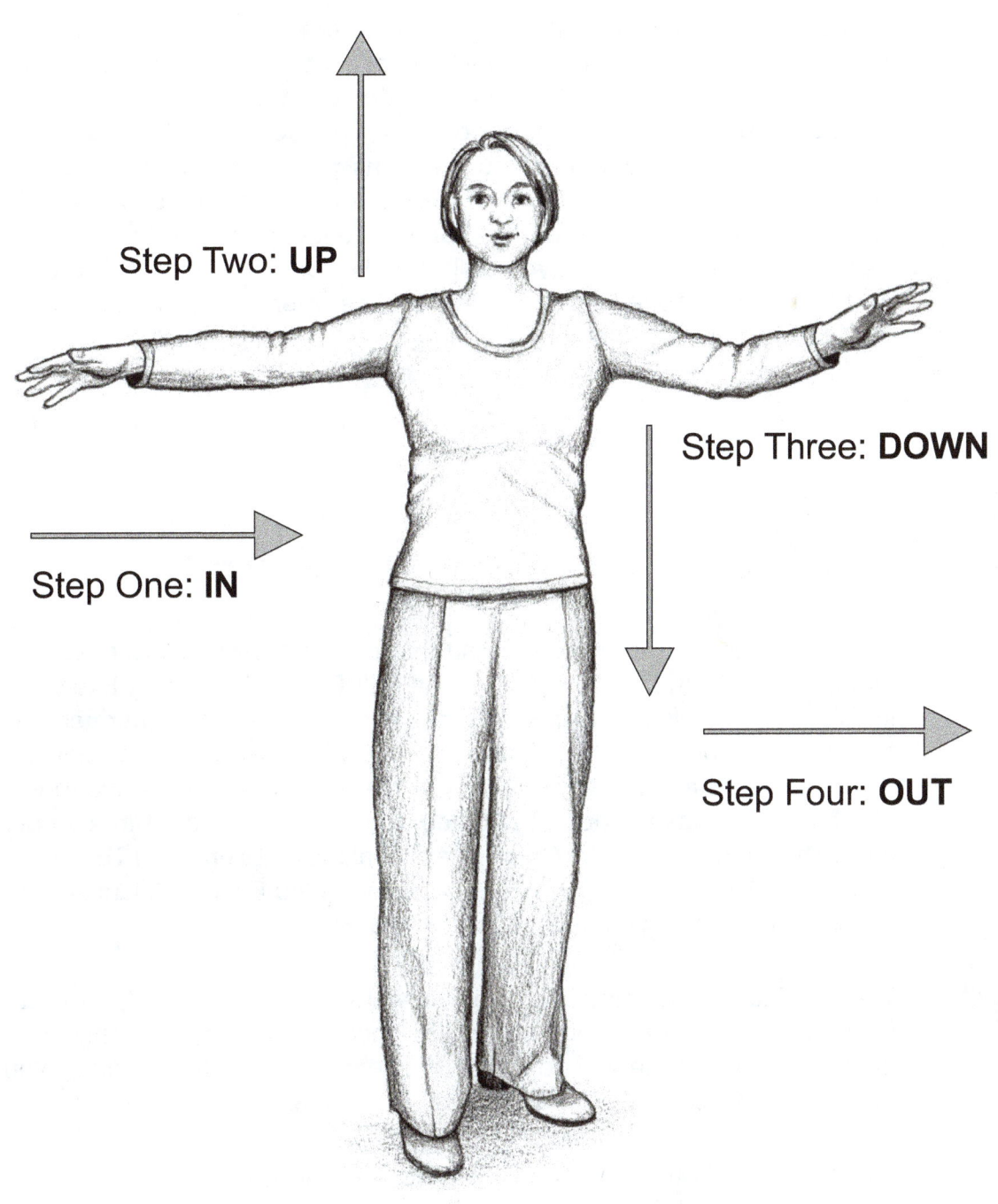

The circular flow of energy

Though this is happening in a larger time frame over the course of your lifetime, it's happening in a smaller level every day. Energy is constantly circulating through these four phases. For example, you get angry at someone. Afterwards, you reflect on this (IN). You realize that you were reactive and that you weren't as loving as you could be. You make a decision to be more heartful and gentle, instead of so reactive (UP). The next time you are in this situation you remember your decision and though you feel your anger, you deliberately work to contain it. (DOWN). And you then choose to express to the other more gently and respectfully, rather than just blasting (OUT).

* * * *

The Full Energy Balancing Exercise (FEBE)

We have created an energy exercise that covers the complete spectrum of IN, OUT, UP and DOWN. Called the Full Energy Balancing Exercises (FEBE), this exercise sequence vitalizes and balances your entire energy system. We abbreviate it FEBE and jokingly call it the Fun Energy Balancing Exercise. After all, getting energy brings a lot of fun and spice to life! The full version takes about 2 minutes, though you can do it in a longer form. The short version, the Quick Energy Balancing Exercises (QEBE) can be done in 10 seconds. There is also the Extended Energy Balancing Exercise (EEBE) which can take 10 to 30 minutes.

The Full Energy Balancing Exercise is powerful. Doing it regularly will clear your mind, center your emotions and balance your energy. Not only will it be effective each time you do it, but its effects are cumulative, taking you deeper and deeper into the richness of who you are.

We debated whether to put FEBE here, early in the book, or later. On the pro side, we felt that putting it here would introduce it to you early on and you could begin to get the benefits of it now. As you continue reading, subsequent chapters elaborate and bring depth and meaning to each phase of it.

On the other side of the coin we felt that until you have read the later chapters you would be just going through the motions without understanding how properly to do the exercise, and thus you wouldn't gain the full benefits from it. Our concern was you might you lose interest and think energy doesn't work because you're not experiencing anything yet.

Our solution is to mention FEBE and QEBE and EEBE now, and to provide a link to two online videos that will lead you through the exercises. In Chapter 18, you will see all the steps of the exercises written out.

Link to Video

You can find video clips of of The Full Energy Balancing Exercise (FEBE) and of The Quick Energy Balancing Exercise (QEBE) on our website at: *www.energybalancing.me*

Section Two

The Horizontal

The Plane of Action: IN and OUT

Part I - IN

6 Taking Energies IN

Vulnerability

An American working as a contractor for the US military in Afghanistan arrived here at our retreat center for a vacation. We were imagining him like a rather tough-looking military guy, but he was a man in his late forties who looked very ordinary, the typical "guy next door".

He told us about his work there in Afghanistan and what it was like for him personally. He was friendly but underneath we could feel his tension and a wall of protection. He confirmed this when he said; "I'm always on alert. I can never relax there. I always have the feeling I am in an enemy environment. Even though I am in a walled military compound, supposedly protected and safe, I can never sleep at peace. I sleep with my clothes on, because an attack could come at any moment."

Being here in a safe and friendly environment, and having a loving time with his wife, he was able to relax. After a few days his face started to change. A metamorphosis happened.

Towards the end of his stay we were surprised when he said he was eager to go back. "If I stay here any longer I'll never be able to handle being back there. I'd rather relax only a bit so I can toughen up easily again." His wife commented,

Walls protecting vulnerability
Our fundamental nature is vulnerable; we can be touched by life. To protect ourselves we build walls within our energy body that protect us.

half-jokingly and half-serious, that he can only take a safe and loving space for a short time before it gets too dangerous!

What we saw was that both were true. He needed to protect himself being over there by putting on a protective shield. Being here was so good for him to relax those walls, but he felt if he relaxed too much he would be too vulnerable upon arriving back there.

His wife's comment was astute; letting his walls down and letting himself be touched was both wonderful and overwhelming to him. He could only take it in small doses before the vulnerability became too much and his defenses wanted to reassert themselves. Her comment indicated that even without him being in a war zone, his pattern was to only let his defenses down for a short time before he would find an excuse to put them up again.

This man showed us a core truth about human nature – that we are all vulnerable. No matter how tough, strong or "above it all" one appears on the surface, underneath everyone is vulnerable. We are touched by everything around us.

Every human being is vulnerable

DEFINITION: **Vulnerability**
Vulnerability is our fundamental fragility, that capacity that makes us touchable and affected by a myriad of things

Vulnerability - our fundamental fragility

This is one of the most important insights that arise through understanding energy; that every human being is vulnerable. The term 'vulnerable' as we're using it here means touchable - we can be touched; things move us. It recognizes a central truth about the human energy system; that our energy body is fragile and affected by a myriad of things.

This man also demonstrated some of the ways we protect our vulnerability and how some of these are healthy and some not. His actions reflect one of the greatest dilemmas this core vulnerability poses for every human being.

- How much can we be open?
- Can we reveal our vulnerability?
- With whom and when?
- How do we protect our vulnerability?
- How much can we let our protections down after they've gone up?

The answers to these questions vary greatly by person and situation, but basically, with some notable exceptions, most of us have built protective walls within our energy field to survive. Some of these walls we take down when we feel safe; perhaps with our spouse or kids, a good friend, or maybe alone in nature. But many of these walls have become almost permanent protective layers within our energy body. Only on rare occasions do these walls come down, to then go quickly up again.

DEFINITION: **Walls**
Walls are protective layers of energy within the human energy field

Conscious Vulnerability and Conscious Boundaries

Two of the most important skills you can learn through energy work are conscious vulnerability and conscious boundaries. Conscious vulnerability is the ability to drop our walls and let our selves be touched. A conscious boundary is the ability to put up a protective wall and not let things come in that shouldn't.

DEFINITION: **Conscious Vulnerability**
Conscious vulnerability is the ability to drop our walls and let our selves be touched.

DEFINITION: **Conscious Boundary**
A conscious boundary is the ability to put up a protective wall and not let things come in that shouldn't.

This is important for several reasons:

1. There are things we want to be touched by. They are like energy food for our being, nurturing and enriching us. These are things like love, care, respect, as well as energies from nature, animals, etc.

2. There are energies that we don't want to come in because they are not healthy for us, things like aggression, negativity, judgment and disturbed emotions. We need to be able to "put on an energetic rain coat" at the right moments.

3. We can't experience intimacy if we are behind a wall. Two knights in armor can't get very close. Intimacy occurs when we take off our armor, open and let someone in.

4. Lastly, to be vulnerable is to be touched by life. A life lived behind walls is a very partial life. A life lived open means you are participating in the richness of That Which Is.

Section two of this book on IN addresses how to discern which energies are positive or negative, what it means to take energies in or not, how to repair energy leaks and the various skills to do all this.

This section also addresses the inner dimension of ourselves. There is a process of discovery that becoming energy aware initiates; what we could call "the journey inwards" to find our Deeper Self.

Taking the Good Stuff IN

Energies are coming towards us all the time. And when we say all the time we mean ALL THE TIME! Every second of every day an unbelievable amount of energy is headed our direction.

These energies enter our energy field, to then affect us in a myriad of ways. Some of these energies are good for us, providing "energetic sustenance" in the form of vitality or enriched feelings. Some of the energies are neutral; passing through our fields with no effect. And some of the energies are unhealthy, creating imbalance or disturbance.

One of the primary skills in Energy Balancing is discerning which energies are positive, which are neutral and which are negative. A second skill is to take in those that are healthy and to not take in those that aren't.

Energies to Let In

Person deflecting warm energy being sent to them

It's Monday morning. You'd rather be anywhere else, but here you are, walking into your work. A co-worker with whom you have a good relationship greets you with a simple, "Good morning". You grunt a good morning in return and continue on to your desk.

You just missed.

One of the primary skills in Energy Balancing is to take in the "good stuff" when the good stuff is there. Your co-worker just gave you some good stuff. Granted, not everyone saying good morning is sending good energy. They may be just going through a social ritual without anything behind it. But lets for a moment assume that this co-worker actually meant it; they were happy to see you and their heart had an upwelling of warmth and good will.

When someone cares they send us a stream of positive energy

When someone cares they send us a stream of positive energy. Those simple words, "Good morning", are more than words; there's also an energy transmission of care, respect and even love.

Love is energy. Care is energy. Respect is energy. These are all energetic substances vibrating at particular frequencies. They are substances a person sends out that then enters your energy field.

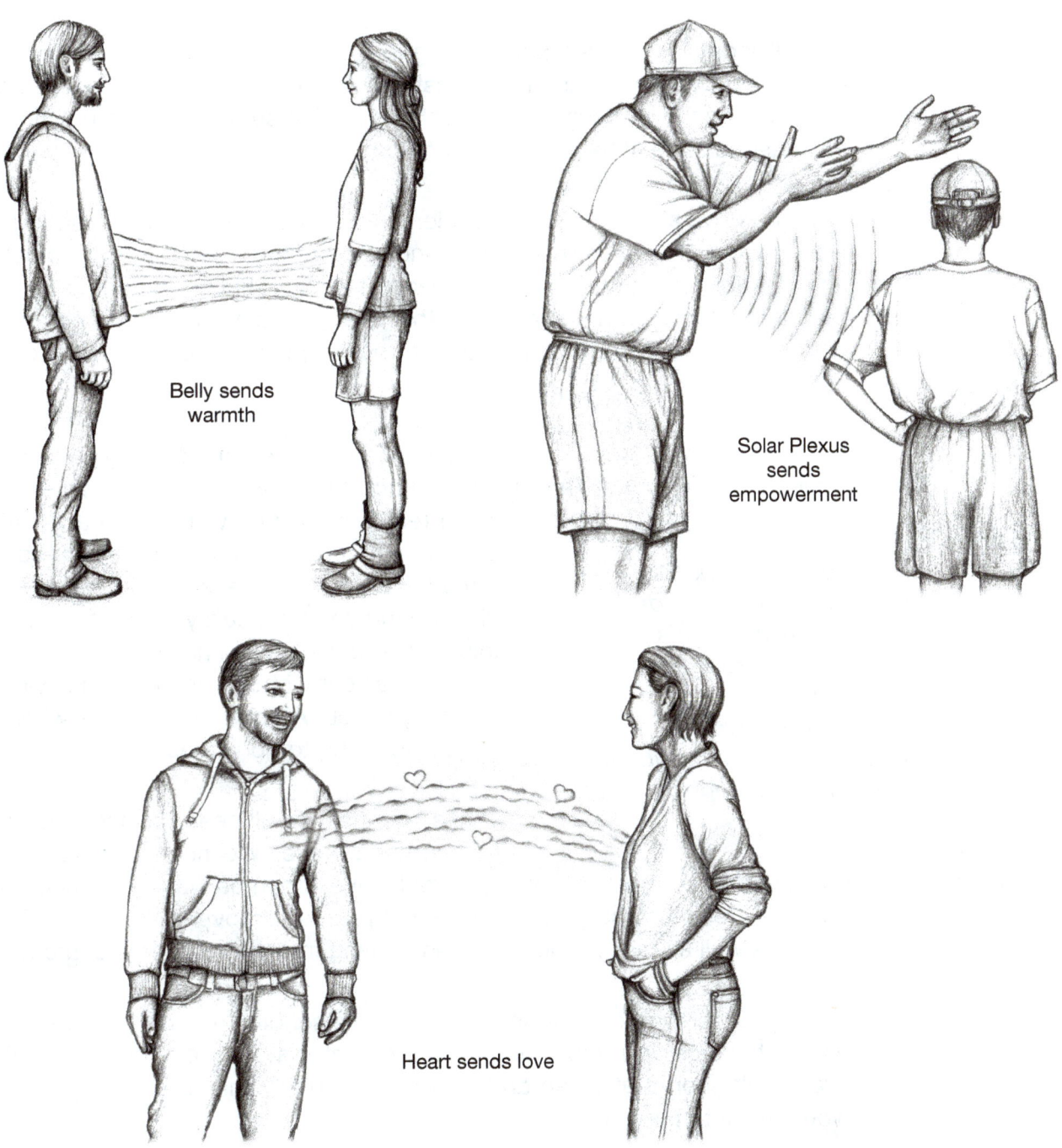

The difference in the type of thought or feeling is the difference in vibration. Some energies vibrate in the frequency we call emotion, some at the frequency we call thought. Some vibrate at very high frequencies we call inspiration, genius or enlightenment. Others vibrate at frequencies we call sadness or anger. Some thoughts and emotions are so-called negative because their vibrations are destructive and harmful to us. Others are deemed positive because their vibrations are life supportive and uplifting. All are substance at various levels of vibration.

Though we've already said this earlier in this book, we can't say it enough – energy is substance. This understanding is a magic key that can unlock an incredible new state of fulfilled living. It means that every thought and feeling is a form of energy and that this energy gets transmitted from one person to another and accumulates in rooms, places and in physical objects.

Some of this substance is energies you need. For example, imagine going through the day without any social contact. Now maybe you'd be in delight if the rest of your day were like that. That probably means then that you are over-saturated with too many energies or the energies around you are one's you don't want. If this is the case, then imagine a week, a month or a year with not one person saying anything to you. A point would come where it's just too long to go without.

Saying positive things to others can have a wonderful effect on them. There's a great video on YouTube that captures the essence of this; it's well worth watching: search YouTube for "Validation" by Hugh Newman.

That's because we all need positive energy from other people. We need warmth, respect and love. These come in different ways: It can be warm energy from the belly, respect energy from the solar plexus, or love energy from the heart, as well as many other energies coming from other energy centers.

When your co-worker greeted you, they were sending a stream of positive energy towards you. Assuming for a moment that their energy is "clean" (we'll look shortly at clean and unclean energies), this is an energy you would want to take in.

"Good Stuff" entering your field and nurturing you

What do we mean by take in? Let's use another example to highlight this. Someone you know compliments you. You can substitute your own words for our words here but imagine they say something like, "I really respect what you did back there. That was very loving and generous."

As part of an exercise in our trainings we ask a person to come to the front of the room. Members of the audience then say positive things to them. It's amazing the various colors of red that the human face can exhibit! You see people twisting and turning, hemming and hawing, and in general looking like they're being slowly tortured. Invariably we hear the words, "Yes, but…" as they deflect what's coming towards them. It's as if we just can't hear it when someone says something nice about us.

Exercise 6.1: An Experiment for today

We'd like to suggest an experiment for you to make today with people you interact with – it can be your partner or kids, a co-worker, or a clerk at the store. Say something positive about them to them. It need not be anything too sophisticated. It can be as simple as, "You look very nice today.", or, "I find you very skilled in how you did that."

Then watch what happens.

How many people really take in the energy?

How many deflect it?

How many contradict you with a negative, perhaps saying something like, "Well, I'm not really very good at this. It just looks that way."

I, Kabir, will never forget the first time I saw someone consciously take in positive energy. The opera singer Pavarotti finished singing and received a standing ovation from the audience. He opened his arms wide, leaned back, and drank in this energy.

How can you take in "the good stuff"?

There are several ways you can practice "taking in the good stuff":

- ***With a partner***
  If you are working with a partner, then have them say something positive to you.

- ***With situations that occur in your day***
  If you are doing this in situations that just occur in your day, then do this when someone sends positive energy your way via a look or words.

- ***On your own***
  If you are doing this on your own, do this in front of a mirror or just sitting with yourself. In this case, you would say something positive about yourself.

Working with a partner

In this book we're presenting Energy Balancing tools for centering yourself and for handling real life situations. You can also use these tools for helping a friend taking in the "good stuff".

Sit with a friend:

Person A:
1. Say something positive about person B to them
2. Imagine your heart sending this warm energy towards them

Person B:
1. Inhale the energy coming towards you
2. See this positive energy filling and nurturing you

Reverse the roles and do the exercise again.

Exercise 6.2:   Let Positive Energies – the Good Stuff - in

1. "See" the good stuff coming

Use your imagination to "see" the positive energy coming towards you.

2. Become receptive

Visualize your energy field becoming open and receptive. Try being like Pavarotti and open your arms to emphasize receiving.

3. Inhale

Inhaling brings energies IN to us. (Exhaling sends energies out)

4. Let yourself be filled with positive energies

As you inhale imagine these positive energies going deep into you. See them filling you, giving you vitality and warmth (or whatever the qualities are that these energies are carrying).

5. Be with it

Pause for a moment. Just be with the feeling. Let yourself digest what you just imbibed.

Quick Reference Points:
1. *"See" positive energies coming*
2. *Become receptive*
3. *Inhale*
4. *Let yourself be filled*
5. *Be with it*

So simple. And so effective. We are always amazed at just how powerful it is to take in positive energy.

We are also amazed at just how much good energy is available. There are so many moments with people where we can take in the beautiful energies people are sending us. And every time we walk by a flower or a tree, are outside in nature, or under the open sky, there is good energy to feed us.

> *I, Kabir, remember feeling exhausted after a seminar and going to a park that had beautiful flowers. I stood there and consciously opened to absorb the life force. I felt so quickly rejuvenated. Consciously opening your system and taking in exponentially magnifies how much good energy you absorb.*

Today, take a deliberate moment where you consciously open yourself and take in the good stuff.

Taking in life energy from nature

Building Charge and Potency by absorbing Positive Energies

Through absorbing positive energies you are building charge and potency in your energy field.

You've probably seen a demonstration of a martial artist punching through a thick board or breaking bricks. They do this through gathering energy and then releasing it in a concentrated blast. We can learn an immensely valuable skill from them - how to gather energies and make them potent.

Think of a piece of equipment in which the batteries ran out of charge, leaving it "dead". With a fresh (or recharged) set of batteries, it's up and running again. The

same happens in our energy field. Think of your field as a big battery carrying a state of charge. Your charge can be full and vital, or it can be depleted and flat.

DEFINITION: **Charge**
Charge is a state of fullness in the energy field - like a charged battery. Charge brings vitality to everything you do.

The key is in gathering and storing energy. The first step is in taking it in. The second step is not leaking it out. We'll deal with that in our chapter 8 on "Energy Leaks".

Good Energy Sources can be:

People

- Warmth, love, care and respect streaming from others
- Laughter, joy, a good conversation, inspiring ideas
- Heartfelt compliments, others' confidence or trust
- Value time with your partner, children or friends

Nature

- Walking barefoot on earth, being on the beach, lying in the grass.
- Standing in the middle of flowers and absorbing their beauty. Hugging a tree.
- Climbing a mountain, enjoying a grand view, inhaling fresh air.
- Standing under a waterfall. Sitting by the riverside. Admiring sunrise or sunset.

- Looking up to a starry sky, the moon, and the magic of the universe.

Animals
- The love and warmth from your pets; listening to a singing bird, watching a butterfly, smiling at the sight of a chipmunk – or swimming with dolphins.

Food
Food is energy and vibrates. What kind of vibration do you eat?
- High frequency food (fresh organic produce) radiates at a high level and enhances your vibration and vitality (Bovis Scale*). Low frequency food (artificial, old, processed, sugary or fat) lowers your vibration.
- These aspects also raise/lower the vibration of food:
  - Where your food comes from.
  - How it's processed.
  - The environment you eat in: Is it a beautiful place, an uplifting vibration?
  - The presentation it comes with: An aesthetic look and feel? Made with love?
  - The emotions you eat with: Joyful, relaxed?

Beauty
- In Music, Dance, Art, Literature, Architecture, Design, etc.

Meditation
- Connecting with your Deeper Self, with Life

And 1001 more that we haven't mentioned here.

Listen to your body and intuition. Trust it. It knows what is and isn't the good stuff.

What are your Good Energy Sources?

List things that are your good energy sources

Your personal list of good energy sources

_____
_____
_____
_____
_____

How much are you taking your good energy sources in?

_____
_____
_____
_____
_____

Which of the above (or others not on the list) would you like to add as a regular part of your self-nurturance?

_____
_____
_____
_____
_____

7 Not taking Energies IN

Healthy Boundaries and Protecting Yourself

There are many energies that we do not want to let into our energy field. Why? Because we could take almost everything from the "Good Energy Sources" list in the previous chapter and "turn it on its head", meaning, that most everything in that list can also be deleterious.

Love, care, respect from others can be deleterious? Yes, even those. How?

First, as you well know, you can just get too much of a good thing. If someone is looking at you with loving eyes, and then they say something positive about you, that's good. But if they keep looking, and keep saying positive things, how long can that go on? Even with love, there's only so much you can take in before you're saturated. After that, it starts disturbing.

But there's another reason why we can't always take in the positive energies; because there are often secondary energies that are coming in with the positive energies. For example, someone loves you and looks at you with love and genuinely says something complimentary to you. But they are also insecure and want your love and approval as well, and their compliment is tinged with a sucking, needy, dependent quality. Their love energy in that moment is not clean.

This happens a lot. In fact, it's rare that anything we do or any energy we send does not have other things attached to it.

Good energy with bad stuff coming along with it
A compliment that masks a sucking need for approval

Let's look at laughter. You know the incredible good feeling that happens from a good belly laugh. Laughter can be incredibly uplifting; really great energy. But now listen to the run of the mill jokes and the laughter that follows. A lot of laughter is because of someone's misfortune, or it's a put down of someone, a form of ridicule. There are often many negative energies that come with laughter.

Negative Energies

What do we mean by the words "negative energies".

Negative energies:
- Are destructive
- Cause damage
- Cause pain (though pain can also be positive – for example, speaking truth to someone that initially hurts them but causes them to change a limiting personal characteristic into something more life supportive)
- Are not life supportive
- Put a damper on the flow of life energy
- Inhibit positive energy

Negative energy limits the flow of positive life energy.

Mary was enthusiastic about her new plan to retire early from her medical practice and open a Bed & Breakfast in France. She was an excellent cook, she and her husband had studied French for the last 10 years and they had purchased a house near Bordeaux. Mary shared her plan with her colleague, but instead of meeting her enthusiasm, she just said: "Why would you give up your practice for this? Don't you know how the French make it difficult for foreigners? It will never work!"

You have most probably had this happen to you – or done it to someone else. You were enthusiastic about something. You shared it with a friend. Instead of meeting your excitement they told you why it won't work, why it's not good, and why you shouldn't do that.

That doesn't mean that people should always agree with you. You want people who can speak honestly to you; if your idea has flaws, it's good that they get pointed out. But a person can challenge the flaws in your ideas and still keep things positive. Unfortunately, how often does someone put the brakes on, find fault or squash the joy just because it's their habit to do so?

A person who is overly critical, fault finding, aggressive or belittling is negative. A person who is controlling and limiting is negative. A person who is depressed or heavy can be a negative influence. A fatalistic or pessimistic person is negative. A person who is fear-based and their basic attitude is 'can't' or 'don't' or 'won't' is negative. A person who lives in a victim attitude is negative.

Know anyone who's negative; perhaps that person in the mirror?

What's the affect of negativity on you?

Negativity limits the life flow. Life energy is a 'yes'. It wants to move, experience, explore, discover, create, relate and do. Negative energy breaks it, puts the brakes on it, limiting its flow.

There's a lot of negative energy around! But because it's around doesn't mean you have to take it in. You don't have to let it violate you.

Discerning what is Positive or Negative

How can you know what is positive or negative? That's not an easy question to answer. First because it takes becoming more sensitive and attuned, and that takes practice. And second, it's not easy because what might seem negative might be exactly what you need for your growth. For example, someone blasting anger in your direction would generally be considered negative; anger can rip and damage your energy body. But perhaps that person's anger is justified. Perhaps you need to be hit on the head for you to get something unconscious and unhealthy you are doing. In this case then their anger is ultimately positive.

Some negative energies we deal with:

From Others:
- Criticism
- Aggression
- Ridicule
- Control
- Depression
- Fear
- Victimhood

From the Environment:
- Pollution of air, water, earth
- Machines
- Electrical and electronic vibrations
- Noise and Disharmonic sounds from people, traffic, machines, planes and animals
- Tightness and Crowdedness
- Decay

There's a school of thought that says "Energy is just energy, neither positive or negative. It's just for us to learn to handle it." We would agree with that – up to a point. Ultimately it's all just energy, neither good nor bad. But being limited human beings, there are definitely some energies that are less healthy for us than others.

So how to discern which is which? There are no rigid and fixed rules. There are however a couple of useful guidelines.

- **Trust your intuition:** Learn to listen to your feelings and trust your intuition. Does something feel "off"? You might not be able to put your finger on it, but something in you feels there is something not right/unhealthy in the energies you are dealing with. Trust yourself. So often, things seem "nice" on the surface but underneath there are other not so nice things at play.

  There is something that grows over time in us called "truth sense". This is the ability to discern what is really going on, if something is true or not, and if there are secondary hidden currents or not. Though we can't say in a simple exercise "here's how you can train this", we hope that pointing out that such a sense exists will draw your attention to it and gradually you will learn to listen to it. In addition, there are a few awareness activities you can do to support this development.

- **Listen to your body:** Often you will get a tension, a "stumble", a knot, or some way that your body/psyche will tell you some something is off. Pay attention to these nuances. It's so easy to disregard these things. Don't! The moment that little bell rings inside, listen to it. Search for what it's telling you – even if it seems ridiculous – usually it's not.

- **Get the teaching:** If something seems negative, is there none-the-less a sense that there is a "truth" here that you need to learn? Ask yourself, "What might I need to learn through this?"

Energy Violations

Anything that enters your field without your willingness can be a violation. When someone is aggressive towards you and their energy hits you and collapses you – then they just violated you. If someone is too emotional in your direction, like Antonio was in the story earlier in this book – then that's a violation. Someone is controlling of you – that's a violation. Someone is very loving towards you – but in a moment when you do not want it or aren't open to it – that too can be a violation. Someone, with the best of intentions, is very caring towards you, like Kabir's mother at the dinner table trying to care for him, but with unconscious motives underneath - that can be a violation.

DEFINITION: **Energy Violation**
Anything that enters your field without your willingness can be an energy violation.

What that means is we are getting violated all the time. It's almost unbelievable just how often someone or something oversteps our boundaries. If it's not a person, it can be an animal or an inanimate object. Walk down a busy city street – traffic noises, voices, electrical radiations from machines, phones, computers – all these things are entering our field and violating us.

Taking care of your Personal Space

To protect yourself from violations is such an important energy skill. And it starts with understanding boundaries.

In the following section we'll explore ways to protect and strengthen your boundaries against violations. As you come to understand boundaries, you'll probably also recognize ways where you are violating others. We'll explore energy violations in more details in chapter 12.

Your energy field radiates out from your body about three feet in all directions. Instead of thinking about yourself as a body surrounded by an energy field, think of yourself as this six-foot diameter sphere of energy with the physical body at the center of it. Your field is YOU. You entire field is roughly six feet in diameter. This is your space.

DEFINITION: **Personal or "Sacred" Space**
The human energy field radiates approximately 3 feet in all directions around the body. This is your "personal space".

Let's call this sacred space, because it is sacred. Your energy is special and important. And it needs to be cared for and protected. It's like wearing beautiful, expensive clothes. You don't want a dog with muddy paws to jump up on you. Think of your energy field in exactly the same way. When you're centered and in balance, your field is beautifully bright, clean, clear and flowing. You don't want someone to throw a bunch of thick, muddy, yucky negative energy on you.

But that's exactly what happens. People unknowingly dump their negative energies into other people's energy fields. Sometimes they do it directly, such as when someone puts down your enthusiasm or aggresses you. Often times it's indirect; when a person is depressed or unhappy, it's like a dark cloud around them that sticks to whatever is near by. They're not trying to do something deliberate to you. But none-the-less, their 'dark cloud' has an affect upon you.

So what to do?

What you can do is define your boundaries, protect your energies and keep your space intact.

DEFINITION: Boundaries
The outer edge of our energy field that keeps energies from coming in our out

Boundaries – the Edge of the Field

DEFINITION: Conscious Boundary
A conscious boundary is the ability to put up a protective wall and not let things come in that shouldn't.

The human energy field is a bit like an egg, not only in shape, but also in the way that it has a distinct edge on the outside. Just as an egg's shell keeps the contents of the egg from leaking out and keeps destructive energies from coming in, so too does the outer edge of our energy field function like a boundary to keep energies from coming in or out.

The edge of the human energy field differs from that of an eggshell however in that our edge is changeable. Sometimes it can be soft and porous to let things in. At other times it can be hard and impermeable where nothing penetrates. You have the ability to control this.

Let's build a protective boundary to your energy field.

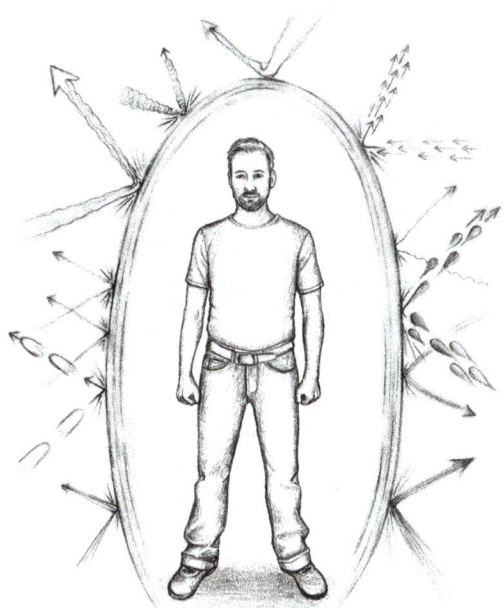

The protective boundary of our energy field
The boundary of the energy field keeps "stuff" from entering into us

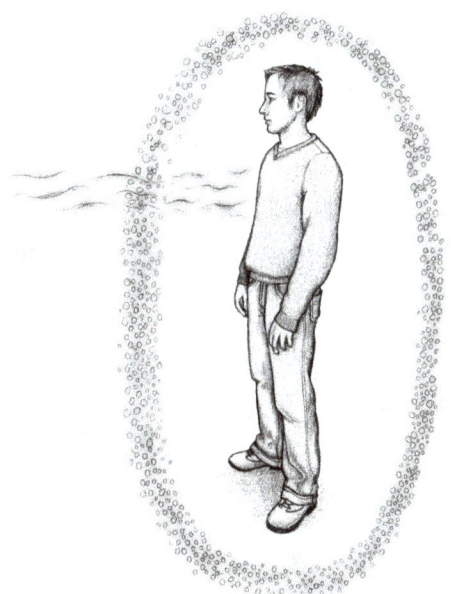

The Flexibility of the Field Boundary
The field boundary can open and become permeable to let things in, or it can close, becoming impermeable, to protect.

Exercise 7.1:   Protect Yourself

A: Preparation

1. Visualize yourself radiating Energy

Imagine your energy field radiating out about three feet in all directions

2. Tune to the Edge of Your Field

Tune to the outer edge of your field and imagine seeing this edge.

3. Close your Edge

Now imagine for a moment that you are closing the edge, hardening it and making it impenetrable.

B. Core Exercise

4. Build a Protective Boundary

Take your hands and hold them at arms length directly in front of you, with the palms facing outwards. Like a painter using their hands to paint, move your hands now from directly in front of you towards the sides, imagining as you do this that you are strengthening the protective edge of your field. Check your entire field edge all around you.

C: Completion

5. Let Energies bounce off

Once you feel done, in your minds eye, see energies coming towards you bouncing off your protective edge.

Quick Reference Points:
1. *Visualize yourself radiating Energy*
2. *Tune to the Edge of Your Field*
3. *Close your Edge*
4. *Build a Protective Boundary*
5. *Let Energies bounce off*

Great! And easy, too. It's not difficult to control the field. You'll get even more skilled over time, but already from the beginning it's amazing how much control over the field we can have.

Walling Yourself - A potential danger

A potential danger is that many of us have built protective walls within our fields and haven't let them down. You can be carrying a wall for years, even a lifetime. You probably know people who feel hard, tough, closed, or unavailable. There's a reason for that – because they are!

Energetically they've built a wall in their fields to protect their vulnerabilities. Maybe they let it down in some safe space – at home with a beloved, with their child, their dog, alone in nature. But for many people, not even then. Sometimes you can let these walls down for a second and then they just come right back up again; you open for a short moment, but the pattern of closing is too strong and it reasserts itself – even if you don't want it too.

Most of us (with some notable exceptions) have many walls within our field. Not only is our outer edge protected, but there are also walls at deeper layers of our onion. Many of these walls are there almost all the time, quietly but powerfully operating in the background.

We are mentioning this so that in this work of building a protective edge to your energy field you remain alert not to leave it there. If you close up deliberately, then make it a point to deliberately open up later when you feel safe.

Now let's open the edge of your energy field:

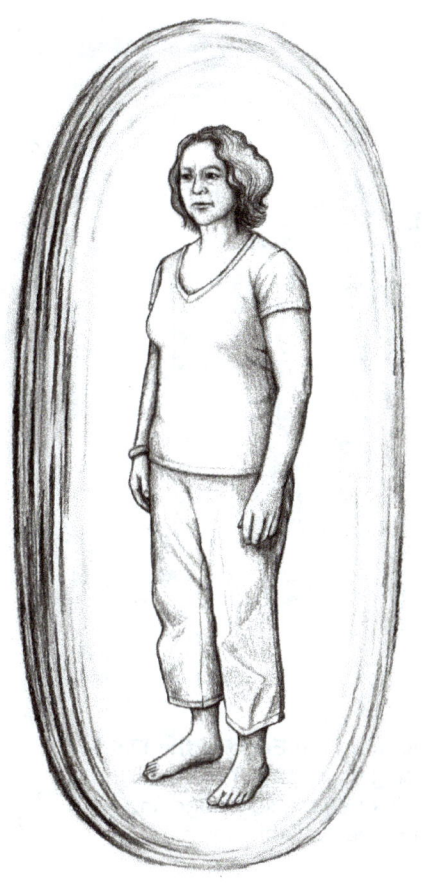

Walls in our Field
Walls in our field protect us – but they also make us unavailable. Walls can go up in a moment and stay up for a lifetime.

Exercise 7.2: Open yourself back up

1. Prepare your Hands

Place your hands at arms length out in front of you, with the palms facing inwards towards you, keeping your fingers relaxed.

Opening the Edge of the Field
Using your hands to remove the wall, open the field edge and become available again

2. Dissolve the Edge of your Field

Stroke the hands in towards you, each time moving them about 6 inches. Imagine the hands are dissolving the edge of the field and helping energies come in to you. Let the movement be gentle and soft. In your minds eye, see the hard shell becoming soft and porous.

3. Let Energies enter back in

'See' positive energies coming in through the edge of your field and entering deeper into you. Feel yourself like a sponge, absorbing it in.

Quick Reference Points:

1. Prepare your Hands
2. Dissolve the Edge of your Field
3. Let Energies enter back in

Open or protected – both have their right moments. The main thing is knowing which you need or want and having the skill to create that.

An Exercise for today 7.3: Open or Protected?

As you go about your day today, pay attention to the situations where you would want to keep your field open and those where you would want to protect yourself. Practice opening and closing your field as needed.

Stepping out of the Way

Energies can be omni-directional (going in all directions simultaneously) or directional (going in one particular direction). Directional energies radiate out from areas in the body and point in a particular direction, usually towards the front. Just as you can point a garden hose towards a particular plant, you can point energy in a particular direction.

Let's say you're with a person who is emotional, upset and angry. That emotion is both omni-directional because it is radiating out in all directions but it is also directional, coming from particular areas and streaming towards the front. If you are sitting directly in front of that stream of energy then your energy body is taking a direct hit. Ouch!

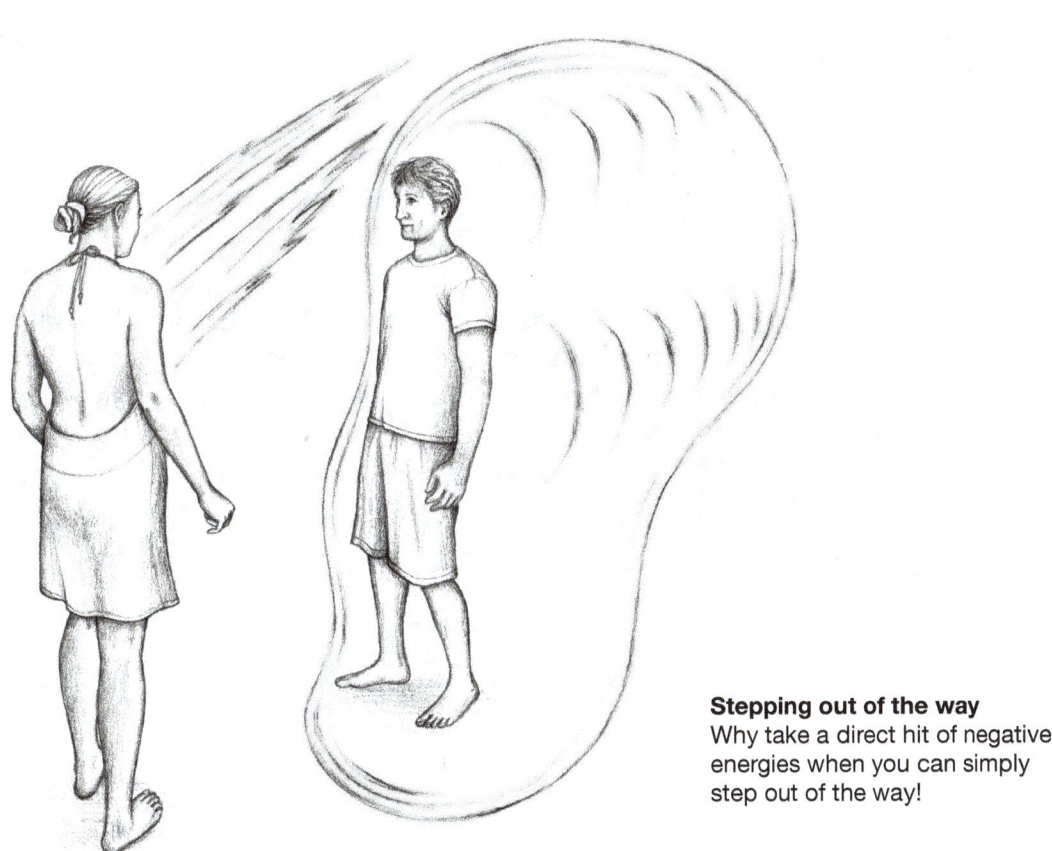

Stepping out of the way
Why take a direct hit of negative energies when you can simply step out of the way!

Simple solution – get out of the way! Step to the side of the person so you're not standing right in front of them. In addition, turn your body a bit so the more sensitive areas in the front of your field are not pointed directly towards them. The side of our energy body is not as sensitive as the front. Both of these things will lessen the impact of the energy on you.

When we have a fight (pretty rare these days but it still can happen!) we both know to turn sideways. Of course, the angry person usually has gone unconscious and wants to dump their anger into the other. So the recipient will say, "I can listen to your anger but don't point it directly at me. Turn away so I don't get hit."

Becoming Energy Space alert

It is an invaluable skill to become energy space alert. This means becoming aware of what's happening in the area around your energy field and the affect it will have on you.

Let's say you go to a restaurant and get seated with people sitting directly behind you with just a seat partition between you. You're sitting in each other's auras. That's hard on your energy field.

Sometimes you can't do anything about that such as on trains, busses and planes. Then you can use exercise 7.1 as a support to help you build a protective boundary to your energy field. But often times you can change the situation. For example, when being seated in a restaurant, look around and find a place where people aren't as close to you and ask to be seated there. Also, don't sit with a busy aisle behind you as people are walking through your field.

Bad space in restaurant

Be alert to the energies in places, and choose the most supportive space for

Good space in restaurant

Though the topic is too big for this book, learn to be aware of the Feng Shui (flow of energy) of the place you are in. Sitting in a room directly in the flow of a doorway means you are taking in disturbing and restless moving energies. Instead, find a place where the energies are more peaceful. As you start paying attention to the flow within buildings and places you will learn what feels good for you.

Saying "NO"

Though it's not our intention in this book to tackle the deeper psychological aspects that are behind many energy patterns, we wanted to draw your attention to what's operating behind the word "No". Many of us are simply "nice" people – too nice. We can't say no. There's a kind of moral and religious ethic about not being selfish or egotistical that makes it difficult for us to say no.

Someone asks us to do something. We often say yes, but underneath feel resentful because we really want to say no. Someone is excited or emotional and wants to tell you, and you think you have to listen. You don't' dare to say, "Sorry, but I'm not available to listen right now."

When we work with this in our trainings you almost can't believe how people stumble, struggle and almost gag on saying No. Being able to say no is necessary and healthy! Think about this: If you can't say a genuine 'No' then you also won't be able to say a genuine 'Yes'. Only when you can clearly take your space, can you then, in freedom and out of your own choice, make your space available to another. And that is so beautiful, for both yourself and the other.

Woman overwhelming and dumping energy into Man

Learning to say "No" to stop taking in energies that aren't good for us

Man saying "NO" to those energies and protecting his personal space

Saying NO to another is a YES to your personal space. This helps both of your fields come back to a "right space"

# Awareness Exercise 7.4: Saying "No"

We'd like to suggest a challenging exercise. Say NO to someone today. And if you can't yet do that, at least be honest with yourself that you want to say No, and take note of the effect an unhealthy, dishonest YES has on you. You can try saying NO internally without expressing it.

8 Energy Leaks and the Ring-Pass-Not

DEFINITION: Ring-Pass-Not

A ring-pass-not is a soft boundary edge that holds energies from going out and from moving beyond a certain point. A wall is a boundary that keeps outside energies from coming in. A Ring-Pass-Not keeps your energies from going out.

A 'ring-pass-not' is a soft boundary edge that holds energies from going out, from moving beyond a certain point. It's not so much a protective wall keeping things from the outside to come in but rather an edge of an energy field that acts to contain your energies from moving out. Though a ring-pass-not also works to keep energies from coming in, the emphasis we want to make in this section is on keeping your energies from going out.

A natural Ring-Pass-Not : A water droplet

Probably the best example of a ring-pass-not is one that you know well - a droplet of water. Surface tension holds the drop together and gives it its distinctive shape. Without that ring-pass-not the water would flow every which way and the drop would disappear. The ring-pass-not of a water drop is not a hard wall, but it does act as an edge to create a container.

The human energy field naturally has a ring-pass-not around it. This serves to keep you intact; it stops your energies from flowing too much out.

Not only does the entire field have a ring-pass-not, but specific areas of the field also have a ring-pass-not. Every energy center naturally has a ring-pass-not that contains the energy within it.

Violating our own Boundaries

The issue we all have with the ring-pass-not is that we unknowingly break this natural boundary. The result is that our energies flow out in ways that throw us off balance and where we violate our own boundaries.

We violate our own boundaries

I worked in an office with good friend who loved me deeply. When he arrived each day he would effusively greet me in his booming voice, "Good morning!" And I would just about fall off my chair!

When we spoke about this one day he pondered and then said, "My heart is like a big puppy dog. When I greet someone I love I jump on them. Now I see that I've been knocking people over my whole life! No wonder people have been running away from me!"

He commented, "Now that we're talking about this I realize that I always feel a subtle discomfort after I greet someone this way. Even though on one hand I feel happy, I feel this strange tension in my chest afterwards."

Not only was he violating my boundaries – he was violating his own boundaries. His heart was leaping so strongly in his chest towards the other that it was over-stepping the boundary of his own energy field.

What you learn is conscious containment. From a place of awareness you say to yourself, "Contain the energies. Don't let them jump on the other." You allow the enthusiasm to be inside but you don't broadcast it in too powerful a way to the other. You built a ring-pass-not in that moment to contain your enthusiasm and to let it express in a healthy way. This doesn't mean you don't express; it means you find a right balance of expression without over-stepping your field edge.

Once you understand this, you can consciously build a ring-pass-not. This will serve you in some very incredible ways. It is an important energy skill to learn.

Violating your own boundaries
You can easily violate your own boundaries when your emotions are too strong

The Benefits of a Ring-Pass-Not are:

- It contains your energies and allows them to build, creating potency and charge.
- It keeps your energies in a right balance, supporting the strengthening of your core.

A Ring-Pass-Not around the outer edge of our energy field
A ring-pass-not keeps our energies contained, from flowing everywhere

- By having a clear ring-pass-not, you have a clear space that is you. It's your sacred space, your Being space. Here you can allow yourself to be vulnerable. And in this vulnerability you also discover what we call the strength of vulnerability – the strength that comes when Being has room to Be and it can fill your field.

- And lastly, the best form of protection of all is when you are full and "filling your own space" with your core energies and you bring this to meet the present moment.

Lets try it:

Exercise 8.1:   Building a Ring-Pass-Not

A: Preparation

1. **Do a short version of the Tree Exercise (see exercise 4.3)**

Expand your roots, ground yourself, breathe up the core channel and expand your crown. Visualize yourself radiating out about three feet in all directions.

B. Core Exercise

2. **Condense the Edges of your Field to a Ring**

- *Extend your arms to the front. Have the palms facing in towards your body. Now move your hands slowly inwards towards your body about six inches. As you do this, visualize yourself condensing the boundary edge of your energy field and solidifying it.*

- *Do this around your entire field – front, back, side, top and bottom. "See" this ring being formed in the field acting as a boundary to keep your energies contained.*
- *When your energy field forms clear and well-defined boundaries, let your hands rest and relax.*

3. Imagine Ring-Pass-Not containing your Energy

Hold the picture of your Ring-Pass-Not in your mind. Imagine that the edges of your field all around you are well defined, but not walled or rigid. They contain your energy, so you won't loose energy.

C: Completion

4. Test your Ring-Pass-Not

Now slowly open your eyes. Is your Ring-Pass-Not still strong or did it weaken through looking outwards? No worries! Just visualize it again and remember its physical sensation

Quick Reference Points:

1. Do a short version of the Tree Exercise 4.3
2. Condense the Edges of your Field to a Ring
3. Imagine Ring-Pass-Not containing your Energy
4. Test your Ring-Pass-Not

Other Ways you violate Yourself

Sexual attraction rips
the belly area

Willing/doing rips the
solar plexus area

Thinking rips the
third eye area

A Ring-Pass-Not containing sexual energies
A consciously created ring-pass-not deliberately contains energies that would otherwise tend to overstep our own field boundaries. This does not repress the energies; on the contrary it is part of a larger transformation process that contains, controls, redirects and ultimately transforms them.

Energy Leaks

DEFINITION: **Energy Leaks**
One or several areas in our energy field, where energy can leak out

One of the benefits of a ring-pass-not is that it keeps your energy intact and available for you. Think of your energy field as a container. When a healthy ring-pass-not is not there, it's like having holes in the container through which we lose energy. We jokingly refer to this leaky state as the 'Swiss cheese energy field' – full of holes allowing energy to dissipate.

Large energy discharges are things like getting emotionally upset or stress. These burn huge amounts of energy. Small discharges we often don't even notice, but they leach away our energy; for example walking down a street and having our attention go all over, mental chatter, talking too much, etc.

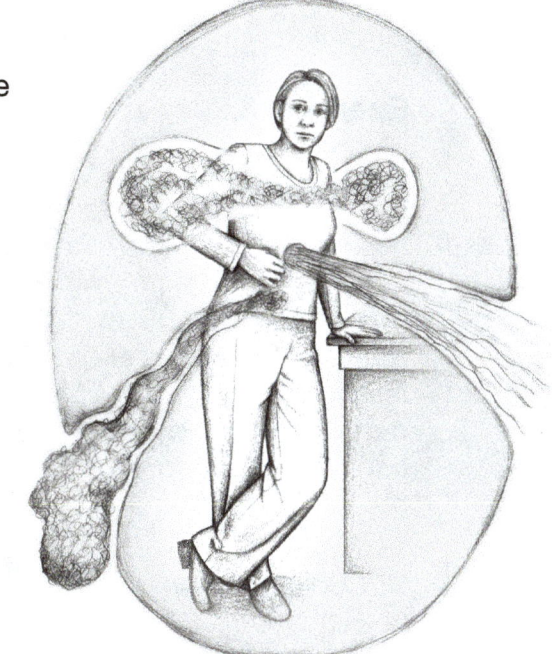

Energy Leaks

Examples of Energy Leaks

Large energy leaks
Emotional upset
Stress
"Bouncing off the walls"
High energy chaotic environments

Small energy leaks
Attention drawn this way and that way
Speaking too much
Overly focused outwards
Mental chatter

Exercise 8.2:   Seal your Energy Leak

A: Preparation

1. Tune into the Energy Leak

Stand with your feet about shoulder width apart. Start by tuning into the feeling of having over stepped your boundaries, of your energy being out too much. Pay close attention to the location where you feel you have over-stepped your boundaries, or where you're energy is leaking out

B: Core-Exercise

2. Re-collect leaking Energies

Focus on the place where the energies are too much out. Now use your hands to gather the energy back in, closer to your body. Trust your intuition to tell you the right distance, but start about an arm's length out and then re-collect the energy back to about half-arm length. After a few moments of doing this, you'll notice that area feeling different. It starts to feel more comfortable, more full of energy again.

3. Seal the Energy Leak

Imagine your hands could repair the leakage, smoothing out the edges of that area and putting an energetic band-aid on it. Now your energies can't leak so easily. Use the picture of an alive, nicely egg-shaped field all around you as a support.

C: Completion

4. Relax within your sealed Energy Field

Now let your hands rest and relax. Imagine that the edges of your field are sealed but not walled, and your energy contained, fully available to you.

Quick Reference Points:

1. Tune into the Energy Leak
2. Re-collect leaking Energies
3. Seal the Energy Leak
4. Relax within your sealed Energy Field

Exercise 8.3: **An Energy Leak Awareness Exercise for Today**

You can do a simple awareness exercise during your day today. Take note of the many instances where your attention and energy move outwards. Now notice – did this give me energy or deplete energy? Also, be alert that often times going out of ourself gives us energy in the moment – it may be exciting or engaging – but a bit afterwards our energy level significantly drops.

9 The Healthy and the Unhealthy IN

Healthy and unhealthy Ways of moving IN

"It is a call to move within, not reactively; not curling up like a dog in the cold, but soaring inwards like an eagle."

Jalal al-Din Muhammad Rumi

From an energetic perspective, there are healthy ways of moving within. Rumi describes it in his words, *"soaring inwards like an eagle."* A healthy way is when your energy is moving towards your center, your core, and you are attuned to and resting in you.

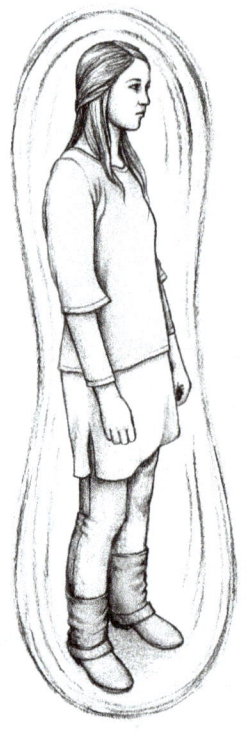

A contracted person
Unhealthy way of moving in

But Rumi also, in his words *"not reactively; not curling up like a dog in the cold"* addresses something else – unhealthy ways of being IN. In this kind of IN our energy field has become contracted, withdrawn, tight and small.

You may know this from when you've felt attacked and gotten hurt, and a part of you retreated inside. Or you may remember times when you've felt bad about yourself and have withdrawn.

Unfortunately, many of us have parts of our energy field that are withdrawn on an almost permanent level. Things happened earlier in our lives that made us retreat. Now, years later, we're still contracted, almost frozen into this position.

Contractions at deeper Levels of Yourself

You can be contracted at deeper levels of yourself, but you don't appear that way. Surface layers of your field may be bright and outgoing while deeper down parts are withdrawn and unavailable.

Not only are these contracted states not good for you because they make you small and restrict your flow, they damage your relationships. They are like closed doors that block intimacy. Secondary reactions to this are that others may feel rejected or unloved by you. Sometimes they'll withdraw and pull away. Other times this may draw out their neediness and make them knock more loudly on your closed doors. This can create a vicious circle of you closing more, them trying for more, around and around.

Outer bright person with deeper layers contracted

At the other end of the spectrum, these contractions can unconsciously invite others to take your space and do things that will make you contract even more. This mechanism works through the instincts. You've heard the expression, "the pecking order". The top hen pecks the ones beneath her. The next strongest in turn pecks those beneath her, etc. Everyone pecks the ones at the bottom.

When you contract your space you are abdicating your space; others will take it. Their instincts experience you as weak and vulnerable, thus peckable, and so you will get pecked, resulting in you contracting more. A vicious circle can ensue with you becoming smaller and smaller. This mechanism is often at work in situations of mobbing, hierarchy, power abuse and dominance.

Margaretha's story: "Open the curtain!"

The audience is on its feet, clapping and calling for an encore. "We did it!" Behind the curtain my New York pianist and I look at each other in delight. What a moment. My heart is beating with joy and gratitude; our recital "Moon*Night*Dreams" was a full success! The air still vibrates with the music. There was so much sync and flow… we were inspired.

Suddenly memories flash by…

…how music was my magical world already as a child. At age five I started playing piano and whenever I heard music I would start dancing on the spot… until one day at school classmates laughed at me and for the first time I felt ashamed…

… of being fourteen and at boarding school. I loved singing in the choir, playing piano for rehearsals and taking my first conducting lessons. But I felt so different from my classmates, the way they spoke, dressed and spent their free time. I started to hide in the dark library or in my little room, or drowning my solitude by playing on a tiny untunded house-organ…

… of the discouragement, when I told my favourite professor - I had just successfully finished my masters as a conductor and organist - I wanted to study voice. He just frowned and said, "I don't think you have either the voice or the oomph to become a singer on a professional level"…

But I still couldn't stop the longing in my heart, and I told myself, "I have to learn to sing freely – no matter what". I finally got accepted in the vocal education program.

And finally…

… of one of those many blissful moments in Cornelius Reid's vocal studio in New York City. I am holding a long high note. It first squeaks and squawks, until suddenly something in me cracks open and a beautiful yet so powerful sound is released that I hardly can believe it came from me...

My pianist's little nudge brings me back. Something I had dreamed of is now reality: I am here, a professional singer backstage, waiting to give Schumann's "Moon Night" as an encore. The audience is still clapping and calling. Let's go for it, now!

Of course my success as a singer didn't happen overnight. And it was not only voice training that got me there - it was also a journey of self-discovery. I came to realize that I was frozen; at school I had retreated, putting up walls no one could cut through to protect myself, but by so doing unconsciously tightening my energy system. This frozen state was blocking my core and making my energy dull. No wonder no one trusted me to become a marvellous singer!

In the inner work process I understood that only if I unfroze and opened back up to my feelings and my vulnerability would I liberate my true voice and biggest gift.

After many years of search I finally met teachers, who not only trusted my longing but also knew the tools for liberation. It took several years to free up my authentic voice energetically and psychologically as well as physically.

But once I had, I gained a whole new life. Today I am successful as a singer, as a vocal coach and as an energy therapist. I support people to open to their authentic self, free their energy flow, let their voice come from deep within their core and express themselves more spontaneously.

Opening deeper Layers of Yourself

If you feel frozen, contracted, and in hiding, that means you have retreated to the unhealthy IN. You are IN and imprisoned by it.

Here follows an exercise to open such an unhealthy IN-state. It gives space for your inner life to expand and breathe. This is not a quick fix. Each time you do this exercise you open up a little more. Doing this for a period of time will gradually open you out in incredible new ways.

Exercise 9.1:   Melting an unhealthy IN State

A: Preparation

1. Feel and be with the Contraction

Bring your awareness to where you feel contracted. You might feel it as a knot in the body, or as a numbness or frozenness, or you feel imprisoned in a tight energy field. Focus on this sensation in your body and/or in your energy field.

B: Core-Exercise

2. Melt the Contraction

Take some deep breaths into this place of contraction. Visualize your breath beginning to melt this frozen place. Feel the knots getting softer, relaxing the tight boundaries.

3. Expand contracted Energies with your Hands

- *Continue breathing and now put your hands on that part of the body where you feel the contraction.*

- *'See' your hands contacting this deeper place. Then gently move your hands outwards, opening that area of your energy field. Feel it as a delicate energy fabric that you gently with your fingers start pulling out.*

- *Visualize your core getting softer and expanding. You may notice your breath becoming easier and deeper. Let your energy field widen and getting fuller.*

C: Completion

4. Feel the Freedom to Be

Feel yourself having space again. Feel the freedom to be.

> #### Quick Reference Points:
> 1. Feel and be with the Contraction
> 2. Melt the Contraction
> 3. Expand contracted Energies with your Hands
> 4. Feel the Freedom to Be

Opening contracted energies back out

Opening the "unhealthy IN" opens your vulnerability. Deep feelings might come up: old tears that were hidden, sometimes even for years; fear that makes you tremble; even unexpressed anger - all might start vibrating in you. Dare to experience these feelings. Let them come up. This is a safe space now. Vulnerability is close to Essence. To open up is the most precious gift you can give yourself.

Opening the Unhealthy IN is an important step in coming back to your authentic self. One powerful method is "Energy Modelling" that helps you "see" the shape and structure of energy in the energy field.

Exercise 9.2: Opening Unhealthy IN with Energy Modelling

1. Step one: Diagnosing

- **Scanning: Finding where you are too much IN**

Scan your energy by moving your hands slowly through your field – up, down, front, side and back. At some points you'll want to perhaps slow down or stop, or your hands will different; dense, or cool, or hot or..?

- **Trusting your Intuition**

Listen to your hands, to the sensations in your body, to the thoughts that suddenly pop up into your mind. Don't filter, don't disregard; be open.

- **Finding the Right Spot**

At some point you will feel: "this is the spot" that is central to the energy being too much IN. If there's more than one spot, choose the strongest for now.

2. Step two: Energy Modelling

- **Finding the Energy "Shape"**

We're going to use your hands to sculpt or model the structure of the energy that's there. Keep your hands in this "off center" spot. Various qualities will begin to reveal themselves. Some examples are: collapsed, knotted, frozen, numb, heavy like a stone, empty, dull, spiky or sharp.

Try moving your hands and fingers intuitively this way and that. At some point a particular hand movement/position will feel 'right', as if you've found the shape or flow of the energy.

3. Step three: Opening the "Unhealthy IN"

- **Using Hands and Breathing**

Hold your hands in the position you've found in the Energy Modeling. Breathe deeply in and out here to charge this spot. The sensation will begin to shift.

Now slowly change your hand position into a new, more open position that feels healthier. Visualize the energy opening and flowing in this healthier way.

- **Coming open fully**

Continue this opening process and let it expand to other places in your body. Imagine your breath a bright light slowly melting knots within your system. Trust your body: if you need to shake or wriggle, let it happen.

- **Daring to open your Deeper Self**

Focus on the deeper self in your core. Let the energies of this essential YOU follow your hand movements. Dare to expand. Continue moving your hands and arms until they are fully open. Hold this expanded state for a few moments – the expanded, open YOU.

> **Quick Reference Points:**
>
> 1. Step one: Diagnosing
>   - *Finding where you are too much IN*
>   - *Trusting your Intuition*
>   - *Finding the Right Spot*
> 2. Step two: Energy Modelling
>   - *Finding the Energy "Shape"*
> 3. Step three: Opening the "Unhealthy IN"
>   - *Using Hands and Breathing*
>   - *Coming open fully*
>   - *Daring to open your Deeper Self*

DEFINITION: **Energy Modelling**

Energy Modelling helps you identify the flow, shape and structure of an energy that is throwing you off center

The Healthy IN – Essence and the Journey Inwards

Up to now we've looked at energies coming IN towards you and at how you keep your own energy contained IN within your field. There is another meaning we give to the word IN as well – your interiority, your inner world, as separate from the outer world around you.

One of the great steps on the inner journey of self-discovery is when you learn to go within. There are dimensions upon dimensions, worlds upon worlds of feelings, thoughts, and consciousness within us. This book supports the process of going within.

There is a beautiful song from the musician Donovan that so fully describes this.

> *There is an ocean of vast proportion*
> *And she flows within ourselves.*
> *To take dips daily we dive in gaily,*
> *He knows who goes within himself.*
> *The abode of Angels, the mystical Promised Land,*
> *The one and only Heaven, the God of man*
> *Is but the closing of an eyelid away.*

When I, Kabir, was a teen, I went through the typical teenage angst; the emotional rollercoaster, anger against the system, parents, school, and authorities, and the usual self-judgments and identity crisis. Like so many teenagers I thought, "If only I belonged to that in-group, had that nice car, got special attention from that pretty girl, then I would be happy." Of course, I had moments of happiness when I for a moment was at the top of the world, only to be thrown down again into the maelstrom.

In one of these darker moments of introspection and questioning I recalled the memory of a previous happy moment. For a moment, it was as if I was again living that moment and I was happy. A light went on inside me. I realized that if through a memory I could again be happy, then happiness was a feeling that lived somewhere inside my brain and could be accessed independently of what was happening in the outside world. It was as if there was a happiness button in my psyche and if I could push that button I could be happy.

As that insight grew in me I recognized that the outer things I had hoped to bring me happiness were ephemeral and changing. My car worked well when I bought it but then it broke. A friend I had last week was gone this week. Even people I had previously thought were happy because they had what I didn't, when I looked closer, also suffered the same disappointments that I did and were on their own roller coaster.

Happiness is a State of Mind, independent from Outside Things

I realized that happiness was a state of mind, independent from outside things, and that I could access it. Happiness lived within me, independent of the outer world. It didn't matter what I owned, who I knew, how much money I had or success I reached – what mattered was my access to the place inside where happiness resides.

This insight began an intense journey inwards. I desperately wanted to understand why I could sometimes find that button but at other times not. I wanted to find the source of these clouds of thoughts and feelings that would obscure the light of that inner Sun. I found that I was carrying a whole lot of feelings from my upbringing that were clogging me up. And I again and again experienced new facets of happiness, moments of greater joy and more profound insight.

I came to understand just how rich we are inside. What we contain within our bodies and minds is incredible; intelligence, joy, creativity, love and so much more. We just need to learn to access it.

I realized that the five senses – sight, touch, smell, hearing, and taste - are all focused towards the outside world. The continual input from them keeps us focused outwards as well. I saw that there is another sense that wasn't spoken of, that we could call the "inner sense", that allows us to tune to our interiority.

DEFINITION: **The "Inner Sense"**
The inner sense allows us to tune to our interiority

As this sense opens the inner world begins to reveal itself, and layer-by-layer, step-by-step, the deeper treasures of life are revealed. You discover the happiness you are looking for within you. A freedom emerges where your joy is independent of what is happening in your outer life. And you begin to discover your Essence, your essential Being, that which makes you uniquely you, the Golden Being at your center.

Section Two

The Horizontal

The Plane of Action: IN and OUT

Part II - OUT

10 Creatorship - Your Power to Create

The Power of Creatorship

Would you like to be more effective? Would you like to have more impact in your life? Would you like your relationships to be more fulfilling? Then you are ready for a next great step in handling the energies you send OUT. To have OUT energy flowing well is central to your life working well.

Creatorship
Energy flowing out to impact environment

We normally think of ourselves as expressing via words or action. But are you aware that there are powerful energies flowing out from your energy body? You are sending out streamers, radiations, cords and subtle vibes of all sorts. These outflowing energies affect the world around you in countless ways.

ENERGY PRINCIPLE 11:
We are powerful transmitters of energy

Every moment we send out powerful energies from our energy field

Your OUT energy creates:

- Self-expression
- Potency
- Connectedness
- Creativity
- Action
- Effectiveness
- Manifestation

Everyone shapes the environment through the energy they send out. We call this creatorship. It is one of the pillars of conscious living through energy.

DEFINITION: Creatorship
Our capacity to form and shape the environment through the energy we send out.

Sometimes it is only in looking back at a situation that you can see clearly the underneath energies of creatorship at work; in the moment the situation is happening we're too much in the heat of things to be objective.

During a project meeting I, Kabir, got upset with a team member. I met him the following week in another context. Next thing I knew we were in an argument.

As I reflected later in the day about what had happened, I realized that the argument seemed to be about some point of discussion relevant to today, but it wasn't – the argument was an expression of the unresolved anger I was still carrying from the previous meeting.

Though my words didn't obviously carry anger, the energy of anger was in my energy field and it had subtly come out and hit the other. He got hurt and frightened, then protective and aggressive. Though I had not been aware of it, I had attacked my co-worker and created an argument.

Conscious and Unconscious Creatorship

We refer to this as unconscious creatorship. Though Kabir was not aware he was doing it, he had created an argument.

Unconscious creatorship is where you are unconscious of the energies you are sending out and the affect they are having.

Definition: Unconscious Creatorship
You are unconscious of the energies you are sending out and the affect they are having.

How many things happen in your life that are the result of energies you broadcast unconsciously? You have certainly had an argument, or moments of friction or difficulty with another to later discover that undercurrents of emotions, attitudes or energies you were carrying had tainted your words or actions and were the real causes of the situation.

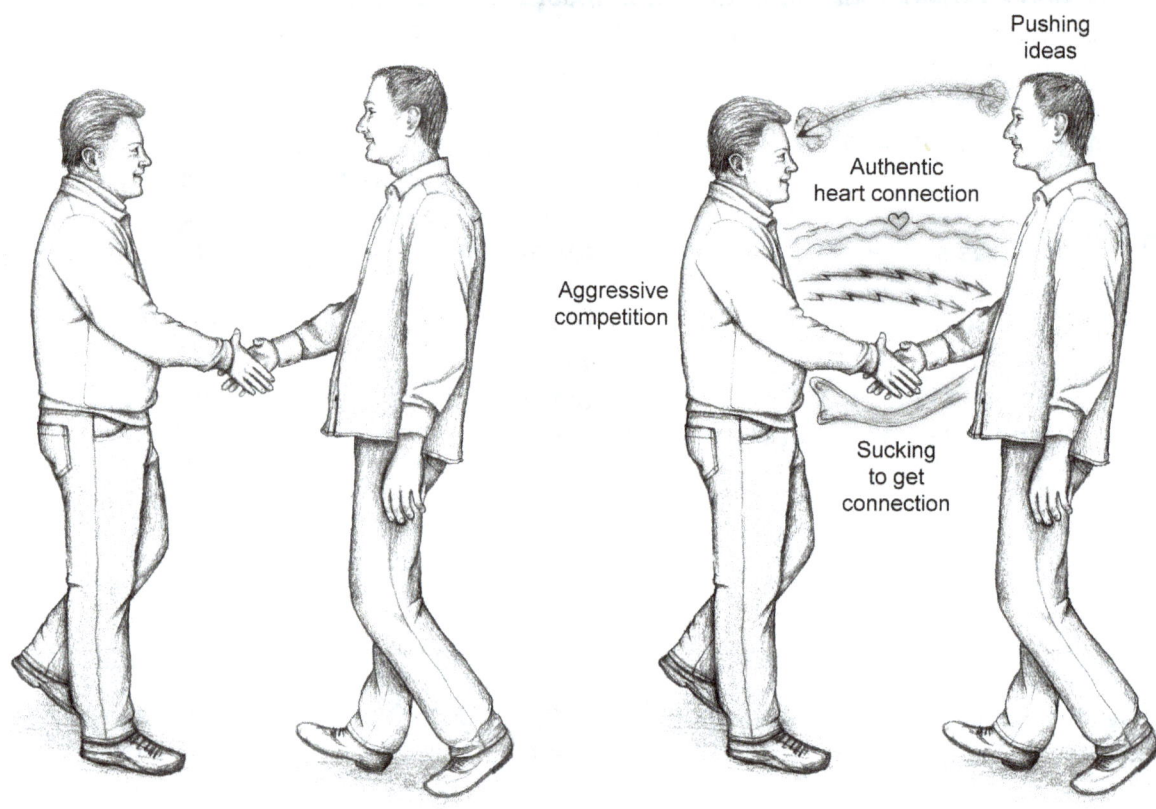

Unconscious creatorship
You think you are sending a warm greeting…

Unconscious creatorship
….but unconsciously you are doing something else.

 **DEFINITION:** **Conscious Creatorship**
You are aware of the energies you carry and send out and you become skillful in their usage.

Conscious creatorship is where you are aware of your energies and are deliberately using them to affect the world around you. The skill of conscious creatorship grows; once you start living with energy awareness and conscious creatorship, you become more and more skillful in your creativity.

We are creators learning to create.

As we create we learn. As we learn we create more skillfully. We enter a feedback loop of creatorship, learning and increasing skill.

"We are creators learning to create."

The Energy of Creatorship

Let's put this understanding of creatorship into practice as an energy skill.

Think of a person who you would like to give some advice to; it doesn't matter what advice, big or a small, profound or mundane. I'm sure you can think of someone who you have some words of wisdom for. For the purposes of our example, let's use something as mundane as, "You should buy a new car."

Let's apply our understanding of creatorship - it's not only the words that you communicate, it's the energies that come with them. To highlight this, we're going to say these same words using hand movements. Now in real life we don't normally use our hands in these ways, but underneath we are using energy in exactly these ways. So let's do the exercise with the hands to better illustrate the energy,

You can do this on your own, but if you have someone to do it with, all the better.

Exercise 10.1: Look into the Energy of Creatorship

*1. Hold your hands in front of your chest with the **palms facing upwards**. Now move them slowly forwards to the front whilst saying the words, "You could buy a new car." Take note of the feeling this brings.*

Hands with palms up

*2. Now again place the hands at chest height but this time with the **palms facing outwards**. Move them forwards away from the body with the words, "You should buy a new car."*

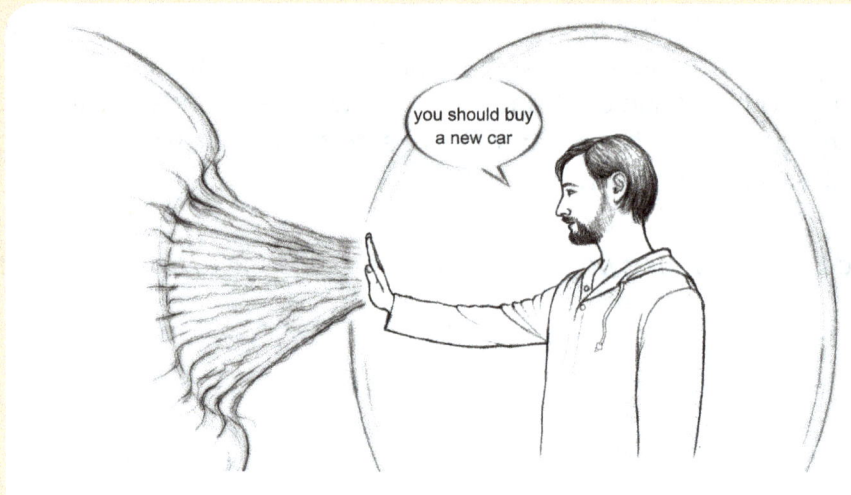

Hands with palms facing outwards

*3. And lastly, make your **right hand into a fist**. Put it up near your ear, as if you are holding a hammer. Now say the words, "You have to buy a new car", and at the same time strike the hammer downwards.*

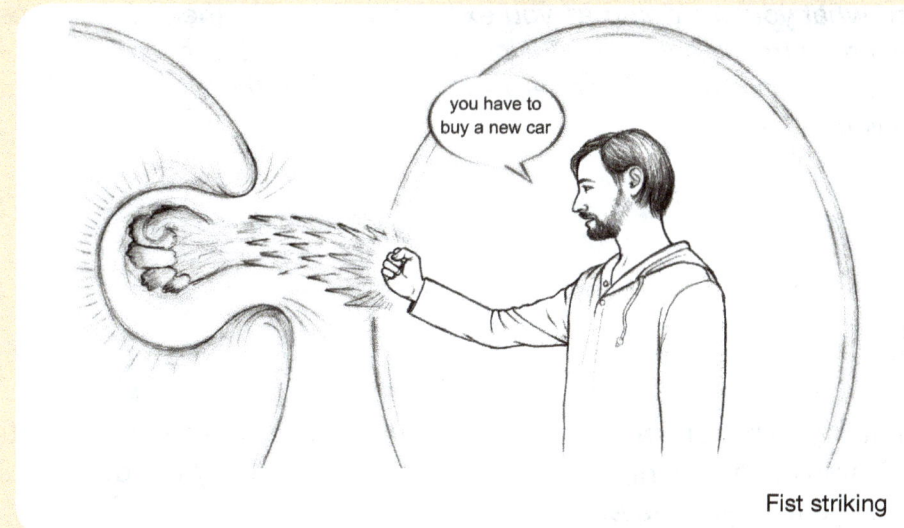

Fist striking

Notice any difference in the feeling of each of these?

Quite a difference!

The first time with palms upwards is gentle. It offers.

The second time with palms facing forwards pushes the idea onto the other. The third time with the fist striking forwards pounds the idea into them.

Each time we express ourselves to others we are sending the energy out in ways similar to those above, and people react accordingly.

> **Exercise 10.2 for today:** Watch Creatorship in Action
>
> *We'd suggest experimenting with this today as you interact with people. Watch what you are doing as you express yourself to them. How does the energy stream out of you? How does it impact the energy field of the other? Watch how their energies stream out of them and the affect upon you.*

Ownership - A shift in perspective with profound implications

Now that you're becoming aware of your creatorship, let's take a next step into ownership. Ownership is an attitude of responsibility or "owning up" to the things that we create.

Definition: Ownership
Ownership is an attitude of responsibility or "owning up" to the things that we create

This is an apparently simple change in perspective, but one that has the ability to profoundly change your life. Though there are many caveats, and certainly there is much that is not true in this, for now, take this statement as truth. "I create everything that's happening in my life."

Apply it to everything – your moods, your relationships, other people's behaviors, your health, your finances and your life situation. Even if a part of you says, "Well, I didn't create that. It's obvious it had nothing to do with me." Still for now, ask yourself "How am I creating this?"

Exercise 10.3 for the day: Take Ownership for your Creation

For the next days, with every interaction that happens between you and others, especially the one's that aren't all that you'd want them to be, look at your creatorship. Take ownership for your part of the creation.

Here's an example: referring back to the story above of when Kabir was carrying anger from a previous meeting, imagine if he had said to his co-worker, "I just realized that I'm angry about that situation we had last week, and that my anger came out and unconsciously aggressed on you." That's ownership.

The Different Layers of Energy

The way you say the word 'Hello' to your boss when you arrive late for work is different than how you say hello to your lover who you haven't seen for a week when you greet them at the airport. Saying hello has many layers besides a simple greeting.

Saying hello to your boss when you're late might also be saying, "I'm sorry I'm late. Please forgive me. Don't fire me." Or it can also be saying, even at the same time, "You don't own me. I can do what I want. I'm letting you know who's really the boss here."

Saying hello to your lover might be saying, "I love you." It might also be saying, "I missed you." Or perhaps it's also asking, "Do you still love me? Do you still want me?"

There are often many layers of hidden energies, each layer having its impact on the field of the other. As you become more energy aware you become aware of the multiple layers that are involved in situations.

Layers of energy

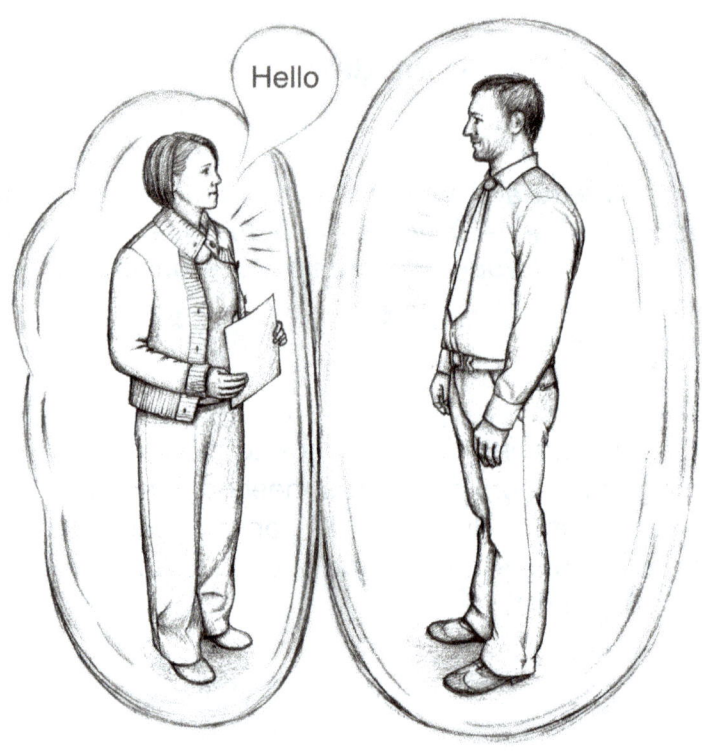

Hello to Boss
Though the words are the same, the energy in the way you say hello to your boss...

Hello to Lover
... is very different than the energy in how you say hello to your lover

ENERGY PRINCIPLE 12:
Every layer of the human energy field creates

Each layer creates and has its particular effect upon situations.

This is a big job. The ancient axiom of mystery schools, mystics and spiritual guides down the centuries has always been "Know Yourself". As you come to know yourself you come to know more and more layers and parts of you. Some of these are incredibly beautiful, and some are very disturbed.

We wish we could give you clear direction here on how to know yourself and become aware of your many layers, but in reality, this is a lifetime process that will take deep introspection and much wrestling with yourself. It's difficult because many parts are buried in our unconscious, and some have shame, fear, etc. around them, making our psyche resist letting them be revealed. If you want to go deeper in this type of self-exploration, then we'd suggest getting involved in serious inner work, or what we call "walking the path".

What we can do here is give you an understanding and exercises where you can learn to direct your energies more effectively to achieve the impact you would like to have.

11 The Art of Impacting

The Art of Impacting

Imagine Michelangelo sculpting his marble masterpiece, David. He has a hammer and a chisel. He places the chisel in a particular spot. He draws back the hammer and then brings it forwards with an exact amount of force, striking the chisel and chipping off precisely the piece of marble he intended.

Impacting
Just as a sculptor impacts the marble with a chisel to shape it, so are we impacting the world around and sculpting it through energy

Now imagine a new student of sculpture working on their first project. First, their placement of the chisel itself is questionable. Then, their first strike of the hammer on the chisel is tentative, lacking power and confidence. Very little happens. Their use of force was ineffective. Realizing they hit too gently, they draw back the hammer again and this time let fly with a real wallop. A large chunk of material flies off and a crack appears. Not the result they wanted either.

This is how we use energy – *we either send too little or too much*. Also, our "position of the chisel" –

where we send the energy, is not optimal. The result? Not usually what we were looking for.

The art then is in learning how to send energy out in an effective way to create the right impact:

- Sending the right amount of energy
- Sending it to the right location

DEFINITION: Impacting
The impact of the energy we send out on the world around

Creating the Right Impact – Getting the Effect you want

You send energy for a reason; you want to accomplish something. Everything we do comes from a desire with a particular outcome in mind.

Let's use some examples.

You say to someone, "Good morning". Your intention is to greet the other and acknowledge their presence. You are sending a stream of heartful, warm energy.

You say to your spouse, "Would you please pick up some bread when you're at the grocery story." Your intention is to create a specific action. Not only are you sending information, but you are sending a will stream to get him to do something.

In a meeting you say, "I think plan A is better than plan B." Your intention is to convince others to use plan A. In addition to the mental stream of energy that carries your idea, you are sending a will stream to convince others to your point of view.

In each of the apparently normal situations above, we are sending energy streams outwards that impact the fields of others. According to how we do this, so will be the reaction. Most of the frictions we have with people are due to our impacting being unconscious and lacking skill, with the result that we create reactions we don't want.

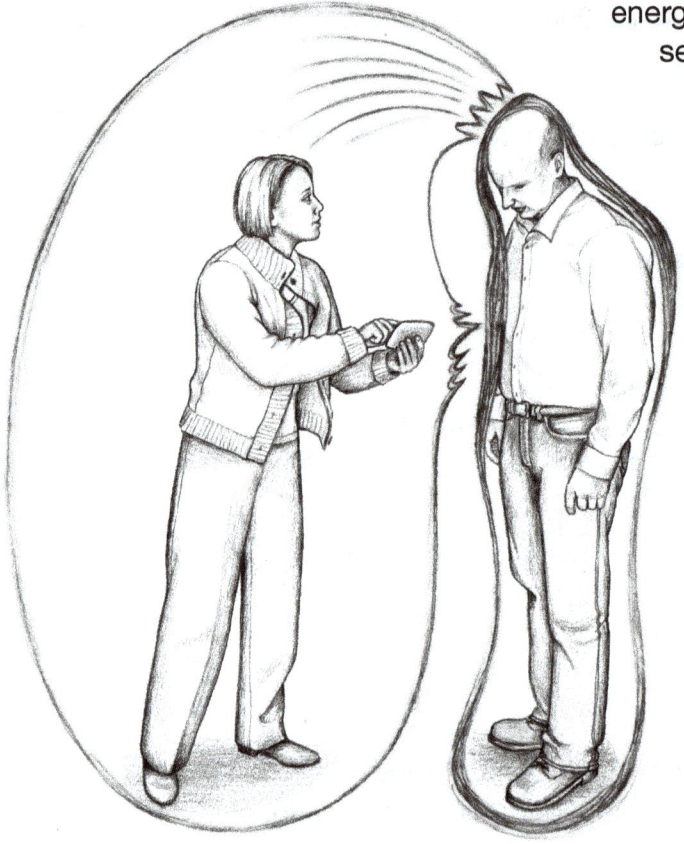

Asking and Willing
When you ask another to do something you are sending a "will" stream of energy.

Sending the Right Amount of Energy

Each interaction sends a specific amount of energy. There is a "right amount" to effectively get the result you want. Sending too much or too little energy won't create the optimum results.

Exercise 11.1: Toss the Energy Ball – Find the Right Impact

A: Preparation

- If you have a partner, have him/her stand across from you, about 6 feet away. Otherwise place a chair there as a substitute.
- Take your dominant hand, palm upwards. Visualize an imaginary energy ball there in your hand.

B. Core Exercise

Imagine the following situations:

1. **You are with a little Child learning something New**

- Speak out loud "No, don't do that.", as if you are speaking to a little child just learning to use a computer who is going to click the wrong icon.
- Now, imagining the ball of energy there in your hand, say the words again and simultaneously toss the ball to the child. Throw it with the amount of energy you are saying the words with.
- Do you toss it gently or hurl it forcefully? This ball toss illustrates the energy you are sending outwards.

2. **You are with a Person about to make a Mistake**

- Next, as if you are speaking to a person about to accidentally delete a document you've been working on for a week, speak out loud the same expression, "No, don't do that."
- Now say it again, this time throwing your imaginary energy ball to the person about to delete your important document.
- How do you throw it?

3. **You are with a Person about to have a Life-threatening Accident**

- Lastly, say the words: "No, don't do that.", as if speaking to a person about to step on a board you can see is cracked which will result in them crashing through the floor.

- *Again repeat the same words and toss the ball.*
- *How did you throw it this time? Softly, or with everything you've got?*

The amount of energy you are sending each time you speak is quite different. The first time is (hopefully!) gentle; you are sending a small stream gently. The second time is more urgent. You are sending a more powerful stream. The third time is with an absolute, life and death command. You are sending as powerful energy stream as you can.

4. The Right or Wrong Intensity of Energy Streams

- *To highlight the difference in energy, try speaking to the child learning computer with the same intensity with which you tried to save the person in the life-threatening situation.*
- *And now try speaking to the person about to plunge through a floor with the gentleness you spoke to the child on the computer.*

You can feel that the use of energy in both of these situations is not right. Unbeknownst to you, you are often using an incorrect amount of energy for the situation and therefore getting a result you don't want.

Exercise 11.2: Appropriate or Inappropriate Amount of Energy?

Let's put this into real life practice:

- Think of someone you want to do something for you. It could be anyone in your life. For our example here, let's say you are thinking of your spouse who you want to run an errand for you when they're out today.
- Think of the words you would say to them and imagine that ball of energy that you are about to toss when you say the words. Now speak the words and toss the ball.
- How did you throw it? Gentle or strong? Appropriate or inappropriate for the situation?

Sending Energy to the Right Location

Exercise 11.3: Sending Energy to the Right Location

Part 1: Just as you can throw the ball with an appropriate or inappropriate amount of energy, you can also throw it to the right or wrong place. The following example illustrates what we mean by right or wrong place.

1. **Nice Arc**

Again take an energy ball in your hand. Now toss it to the other in such a way that it goes directly to them in a nice arc; they almost don't have to move to catch it.

2. **Short Fall**

Now toss the ball without enough energy, so that the ball falls short and doesn't reach the other.

3. Complicated Wind Up

Now do a complicated wind up, one of these things you see a pitcher do on the baseball mound, but make it really complex, going this way and that, and then let it fly in such a way that you imagine the ball zigging and zagging. The other gets completely confused.

4. Great Force

And lastly, imagine hurling the ball with great force right at the person, as if you were trying to knock them over.

Tossing the ball in four different ways

Tossing the ball without enough energy

Tossing the ball in a gentle arc

Tossing the ball in a complex way

Hurling the ball with too much power

Part 2: *Now let's add some words to this as well. Use the same words you said to your spouse a moment before. If nothing comes to mind, then you can try this. "Would you drop off my computer for repair when you're at the mall today."*

1. Nice Arc

Now say your sentence and throw the ball in the perfectly appropriate way.

2. Short Fall

Now say it soft and tentatively, and throw the ball with so little force that it doesn't reach the other.

3. Complicated Wind Up

Now say it in an indirect, convoluted way. You can hem and haw, saying things like, "Well, maybe when you go to the mall, if you don't mind, I was kind of thinking that, you could drop by the shop…" Throw the ball in a convoluted wind-up as well.

4. Great Force

And lastly, again make the statement, e.g. "Drop off my computer for repair when you're at the mall today." Say it with a commanding, domineering voice that not so much asks but commands. Throw the ball with a lot of force, as if you would knock them over with it.

So now that you learned about the right amount and right location of sending energy, you can use those two criteria to evaluate your impact in any situation.

> **Exercise 11.4 for today:** How do you give Directives?
>
> *Think of a directive you gave to someone in the last days:*
>
> 1. **What was the amount of your energy?**
>
> - *Did you send the appropriate amount of energy?*
> - *Or did you send too little or too much?*
>
> 2. **Where did your energy go?**
>
> - *Did it come to the edge of their field?*
> - *Or did it enter their field and violate them?*
> - *Did it go direct to them, or did it waffle around?*
> - *Did it not have enough energy and not reach them?*
> - *Or perhaps you reached the other and then retracted the energy, as if it were on a string that you pulled back?*

Offering versus Imposing

Sending energy to the edge of another persons' field

Our outflowing energy is powerful. Many of the frictions we have with others are created because we unknowingly violate them by sending too much energy or overstepping their boundaries. You may be angry/ controlling/ emotional/ sharing/ loving or having a strong opinion that you want to express to another. There is a good chance you will violate them in the process. With awareness however, you learn to direct your energy rightly. You don't dump on the other and violate their field; you respect their space and manage your energies rightly.

This results in a *new mode of energy-based conscious communication* – an invaluable skill in relating to others. Lets say a person is speaking about doing something and your first impulse is to say, "Don't", with a bunch of good reasons why not. But instead, you contain your impulse behind a ring-pass-not. Then, instead of imposing your impulse into their field and violating them, you present it to the edge of their field as an offering.

It might sound verbally something like this. "My first impulse when you were speaking was to say, "Don't", but I stopped myself. Instead I'd just like to share the concerns that come up for me. Even though I have these concerns and feel I should share them with you, I trust you to make the right decision for yourself. I don't want to impose on you."

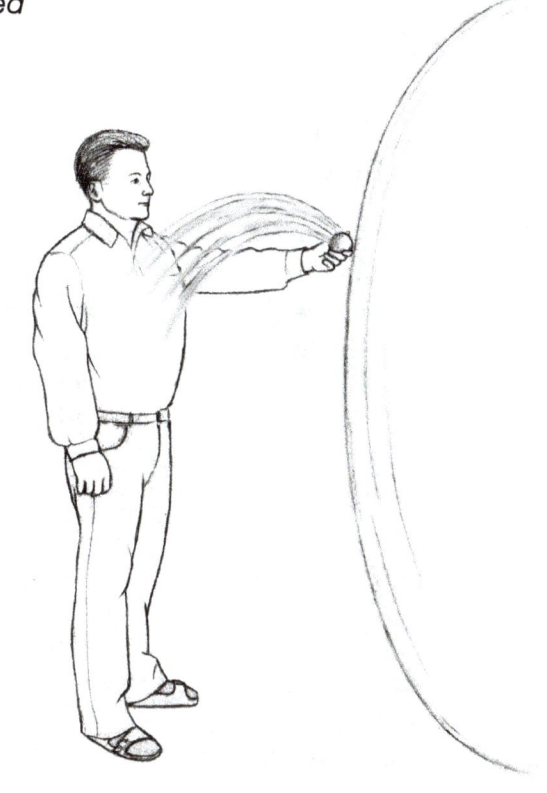

Offering something to the edge of another person's field

That's the verbal part. These words reflect a deeper energy dynamic. You have a concern. Fine – we all have responses to what others are saying or doing. But you now respect their space, and offer them your thoughts, presenting them to the edge of their field, instead of pushing your thoughts into their field.

Let's try this.

Exercise 11.5: Offering versus Imposing – Send Energy to the Edge of Another Person's Field

A: Preparation

Think of a situation where your will was involved and the communication wasn't all that you would have liked it to be; perhaps there was friction or resistance from the other, or you were disappointed, angry, frustrated or upset. Perhaps you wanted something from another, or you might have been giving a directive, "Do this", or you were giving advice, or simply passing on some information. It could be with anyone - family, co-workers or even a stranger. Choose one situation where you would like to get more clarity or improve the communication and we'll work with this.

B: Diagnosis

Visualize what you were trying to transmit. Imagine that information is a substance. Take a sheet of paper, crumble it up and let it represent that substance. How you were giving the other that substance? How did it enter their field?

- *Did you throw it at them?*
- *Did force it on them?*
- *Were you angrily smashing it into them?*
- *Were you insecurely dropping it on the floor in front of them?*
- *How does this affect that communication?*

C: Try Offering instead of Imposing

Let's try something new. This time gently offer this paper to the edge of the other person's field. Give them the choice to take it or not. Be alert to not violate their field.

D. Completion: Task for real life situations

Now that you practiced this on your own, we would invite you today to bring it into real practice. If there's something to share with someone in your life, see if you can offer the substance of communication in a conscious way.

Heaven and Hell in Relationships

Energy flowing OUT improperly is a big issue. It easily violates others and causes them to react. Or it can be unclear, confusing, indirect or impotent, with the result that you don't get what you want. We so often unconsciously use our OUT energy incorrectly on others, and others are doing it to us. We are all suffering as we continually step on each other's energetic toes.

The right use of OUT energy and how it connects to another person's energy field is the difference between heaven and hell in relationships, as well as in effectiveness vs. impotence in getting things done.

What would relating be like when we don't violate each other? A whole new dimension of relating would occur. We call this conscious relating. It's based in respect for each other's field, and it creates the most fulfilling and productive type of relationship you can ever imagine.

Conscious relating creates heaven in relationships

Why? Let's refer back to the example of you wanting someone to do something and what we learnt about offering vs. imposing. You can will them to do it, or you can offer to the edge of their field. Offering is respectful. It honors their space, their free will and their choice. In this honoring you don't get the resistance, pushback, sabotage or resentment that normally occurs when you overstep another's boundaries. And amazingly enough, when you relate like this, people are even more willing to do what is being asked, because they are being asked instead of being told.

Sending Energy from Center

The theme of Center is central to Energy Balancing; one we return to again and again, each time adding new aspects to help your center deepen. Each section of this book explores a particular direction of energy flow that adds to our experience of center.

OUT energy holds an important key for holding center. When we can be in our center and send energy OUT in a balanced way, the results are incredible.

The problem however is the very nature of outflowing energy; it takes us out of ourselves and in the direction we are sending the energy. Unless we have learnt to hold our center while in action, outward flowing energy sends our energy outwards and therefore takes us out of our center.

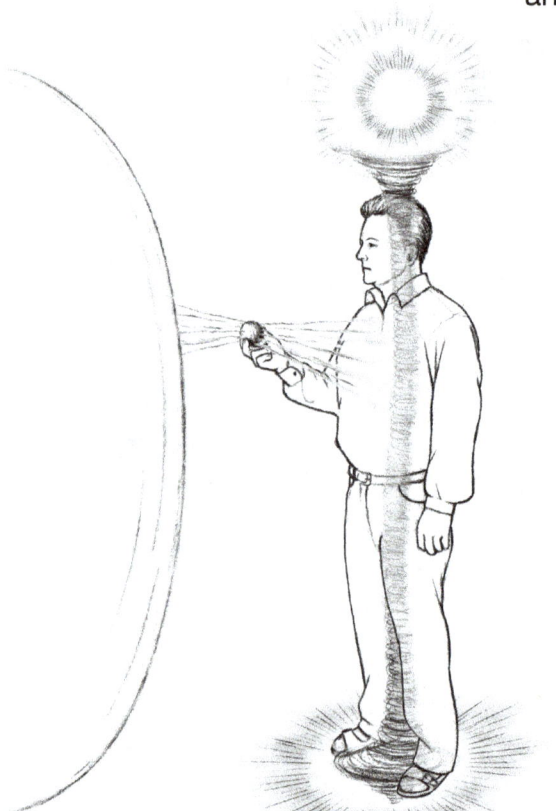
Sending energy from center

This was the essence of Ritama's experience in dance that she shared with us earlier – she was too much in front of herself. The art we need to learn here is to find center, extend energy outwards from center, and then return back to center.

Holding Center in Action

We had a staff meeting in which one of our staff was presenting an idea. She began speaking to the group, getting more enthusiastic as she warmed up to her subject. As she got going she extended her energy more and more outwards towards us. She was not only sending energy forwards to reach us; her energy body extended towards the front of herself as well and brought her out of center. The other members of the meeting became restless and uncomfortable, started fidgeting and became progressively more non-responsive. The result of this person's being out of center was to throw all members of the meeting out of center.

There are two aspects to holding center in action. The first is keeping in center whilst being in action. The second is extending energy outwards and then bringing it back in again.

The first part of keeping in center we have already begun in chapter 4 on centering. You connect to your center and then, it's as if you are keeping one eye on center and one eye on your activity. You stay connected inwards even whilst focusing outwards.

What you do next is extend your energy forwards, release, and then bring the energy back in. The more you practice the more you find a right rhythm of center, extend, release and return.

Exercise 11.6: Release the Arrow – Come back to Center

Imagine yourself in a situation similar to our staff meeting where you are speaking to others.

1. Charge yourself

Gather energetic charge in your core channel

2. Extend yourself

Extend this vital charge into your energy field.

3. Let the Energy fly

Potently extend the energy out of your field towards the others, aware of the right impact.

4. Let go

Disconnect! "Release the arrow" so to speak - let go and let the energy move on its own. No need to stay connected to it. Trust that you have set the energy in motion.

5. Come back

Whilst keeping one eye on the energy you have sent out and the impact it is having, let your main focus be again inwards, on your center.

6. Center

Breathe into center. Bring your energies back to your center.

> Quick Reference Points:
> 1. Charge
> 2. Extend
> 3. Let the Energy fly

> 4. Let go
> 5. Come back
> 6. Center

Think of a tennis player playing a match. They don't take one powerful swing with their tennis racket and then continue to hold the racket in the extended position. They swing and then return, swing and then return.

The same move out/return cycle is applicable to anything you do that flows your energies outwards. In some cases you can make just one extension, one impact. If you say to someone, "Would you please not leave your dishes in the sink but put them in the dishwasher", you can say that once, let go and then come back to yourself.

But lets say you are presenting a concept to another that has many pieces to it. The tendency is to start talking and then talk more and more and more, taking your energy further and further away from your center. Some possible results of this are that the other stops listening, pulls away or gets reactive. You may start asserting more, controlling or even become aggressive with how you bring your energy across.

Instead, imagine that your communication, your idea, has many pieces. Each piece needs to be sent outwards with right impact, and then you let go and come back to center; you gather energetic charge, to then again send the next piece. Like a tennis player, you hit one ball, then reset yourself, then hit the next ball. You center, extend from center and then come back to center.

12 Energy Violations

Energy Violations

You're now beginning to understand that much of our use of energy is unconscious. And not only unconscious, but we're also not in center when we're using energy. The result is that we do things to each other that are not very nice, often violating people with our energies. We overstep their boundaries, bombard them, hit them, send them energies they don't want, control, manipulate and suck on them - not a very pleasant state of affairs.

Remember, we are not talking about physical violations; we are referring to energies radiating OUT from your energy field that enter into another's field without their permission and overstep their boundaries. As energy is substance, these violations are just as real as physical ones.

We spoke of violations earlier in chapter 7. But let's refresh our memories and then add to our understanding of violations.

DEFINITION: Energy Violation
Anything that enters your field without your willingness can be an energy violation.

We often recognize being violated by others – how about recognizing ourselves as violators? Now a part of you might say, "Not me; I don't violate others. I'm loving, kind, generous and considerate." Yes, we believe you are. And we also believe that unbeknownst to you, even in your very lovingness, you often violate people in powerful ways.

Violations are a big issue. They are going on all the time between us. They are the major cause of frictions in relationships and the number one reason for hurt and anger. To understand how others violate you and to be able to handle this will give you a whole new peace of mind in relating. And to become aware of how you violate others and learn to not do that is not only a major step in your own maturity; it's a step in your capacity to love as well as your creatorship towards creating more fulfilling relationships.

In chapter 7 on boundaries we looked at how you can stop yourself from being violated. Let's now look at how you can be more aware of other's boundaries and stop violating them!

1. Aggression Violations

We all know the obvious type of an aggression violation - when you burst out with anger or rage onto another. But are you aware that when you get angry towards another, even without expressing anger, there's a very good chance that your energy hit them? Or are you aware than when you are irritable or grumpy, that that too is sending out spikes from your energy field, like the spines of a cactus, that are entering the other and violating them?

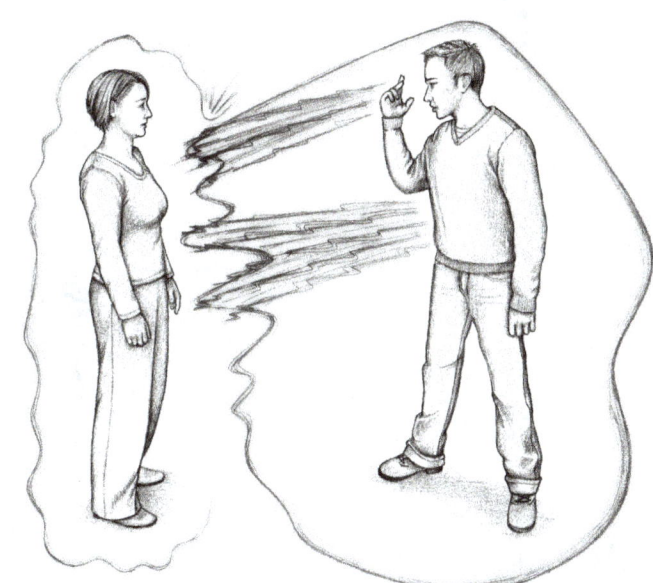

2. Will Violations

Will violations occur when you "will" someone, putting your intention, your will onto another - pushing them to do something. Though will violations often occur with words, they can just as easily be done without words. A person can send a powerful stream of will energy, wanting a person to do a particular thing, without speaking at all.

Here are some different types of will violations. Though these types overlap into one another we'll list them separately to highlight their specifics.

Willing

"Let's go to the store. They've got a great sale on today."

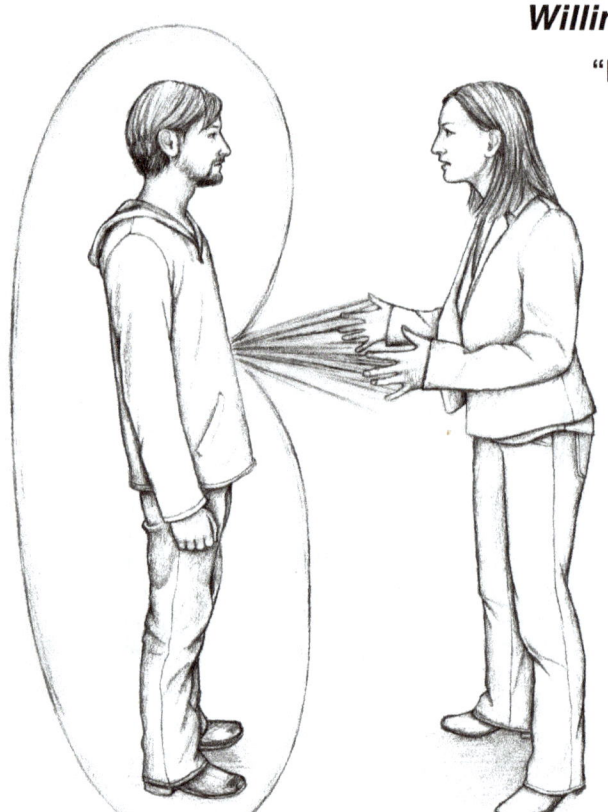

Sounds like an innocent invitation. And sometimes it is. But this can be a powerful will violation depending on how it's said. I, Kabir, have had this done to me so strongly I've been almost yanked out of my chair. The person unknowingly in their enthusiasm powerfully grabbed me with their will.

Battle of Wills

Imagine a tug of war with people pulling a rope in different directions. You might have been in a meeting where you had strongly different ideas about something. Instead of it being a co-creative discussion to look at the pros and cons, each party was trying to will the others to their point of view. This becomes a tension-laden situation with powerful will streams pulling that pull the lines of energy in the room tight.

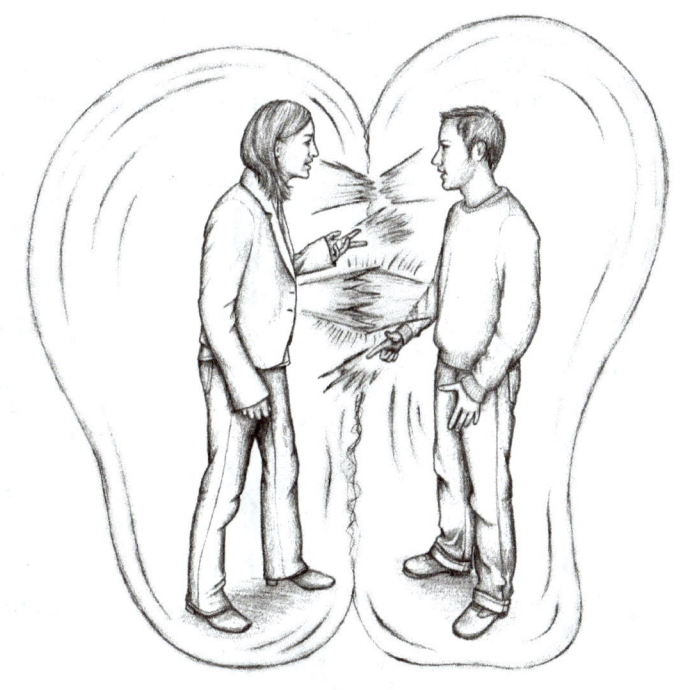

Controlling

Control violations occur when you try to control another person. Often they are done with the best of intentions. The energy pushes on the field of the other with the intention that they do/act/be a certain way.

You may have seen a dog's owner grabbing the neck of the dog and forcing its head. That's what control energy does.

Though control violations can be done in an obviously authoritative and domineer-

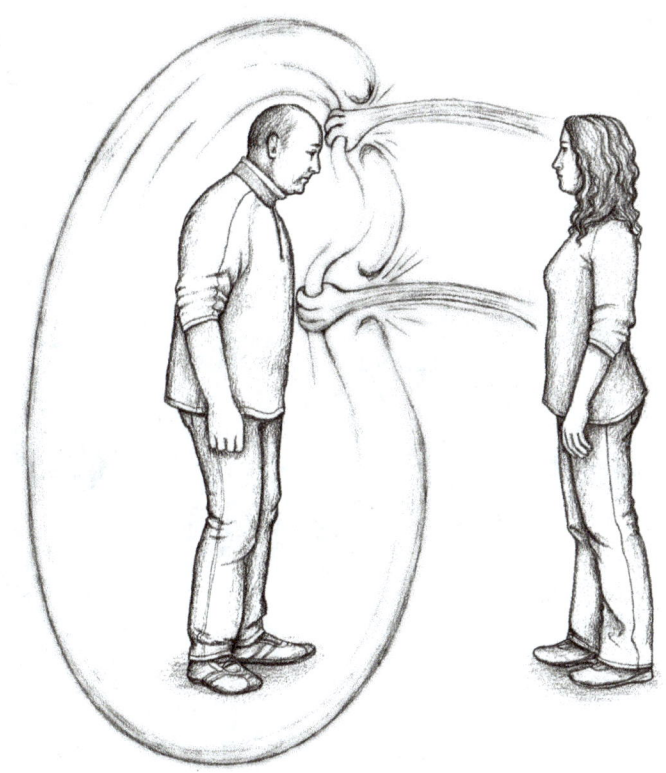

ing tone of voice, they often occur in a much friendlier tone. With the best of intentions you give a person advice. In German they understand this. The German word "Ratschlag" means advise. "Ratschlag" is composed of two German words. "Rat" means "advise". "Schlag" means "to beat" – you beat with advise.

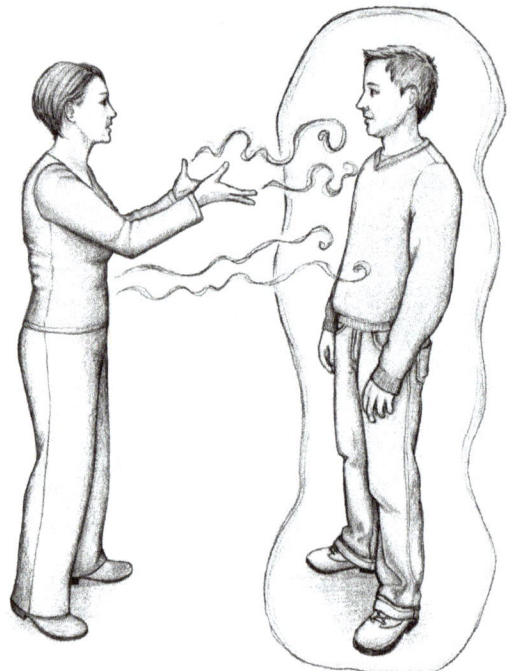

Manipulation

This is a form of control violation but it's done more subtly, not so obvious. The intention is hidden behind something else.

Back Seat Driver

A 'back seat driver' violation is a form of manipulation. Usually fear-based, it uses the will to grab another's energy and try to make them do something. Ever sat in a car with an-

other who wants you to slow down? They might not say a word but they can sure push on you with their fear. Ever been a back seat driver?

Domination

Domination pushes down on another. You feel you have the hierarchical right to make the other subordinate.

3. Overwhelm Violations

Overwhelm violations are when one person's energy is simply too much.

Emotional Overwhelm

You have probably sat with someone who is bubbling over with feelings; happy, sad, angry, it doesn't matter. Their emotional geyser is erupting on to you! When you are very emotional, your geyser is erupting on others. It might have been a pleasant experience you are sharing, depending on the emotions, but it can easily become too much.

Thought Overwhelm

Ever had the sense of being hit by a mental tidal wave and talked into the ground? You were! Thoughts are energy. A person can flatten you with thought energy. Can you also remember a moment where you flattened another with your thoughts?

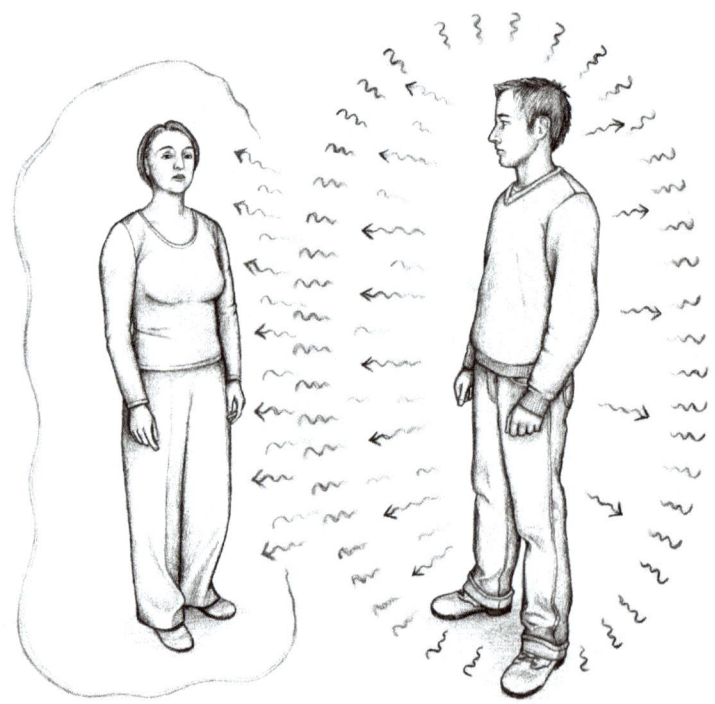

Energetic Charge Overwhelm

A person can be charged with energy. They might be potent and vital, perhaps nervous, aggressive or restless. They might simply be standing near to you, doing nothing in particular, but their powerful radiation can knock you over or make you feel restless for no reason. When you carry a lot of charge, this radiates out and effects others.

4. Care Violations

We've often heard one partner in a relationship saying to the other, "Please stop mothering me". And how often have you seen a parent caring for a child and the child resisting? In situations like that you care for others, want to make them better, or give them something. But in that very action you might overstep their boundary, pushing your care onto them.

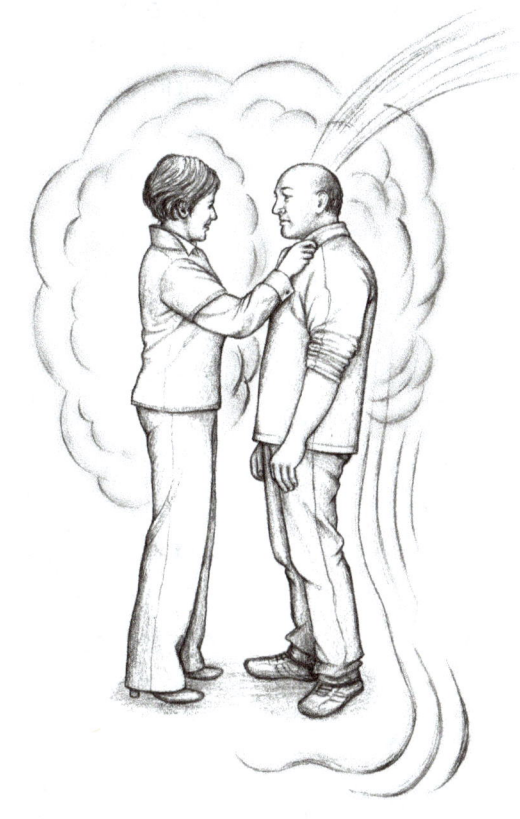

5. Love Violations

The daughter of our secretary said to her, "Mom, would you tell me you love me only once a month please." Our secretary's need to love her daughter was so great that she was overwhelming her with love.

Love violations lead to much pain in relationships; one partner "over loves" the other with the result that the other closes up, pushes them away, or becomes irritable or angry.

Love violations are complex because often, in addition to the "pure love of our heart", there are other energies woven in with the love such as neediness and dependency, attachment, holding on or control that taint the love and violate.

6. Sucking Violations – Energetic Vampirism

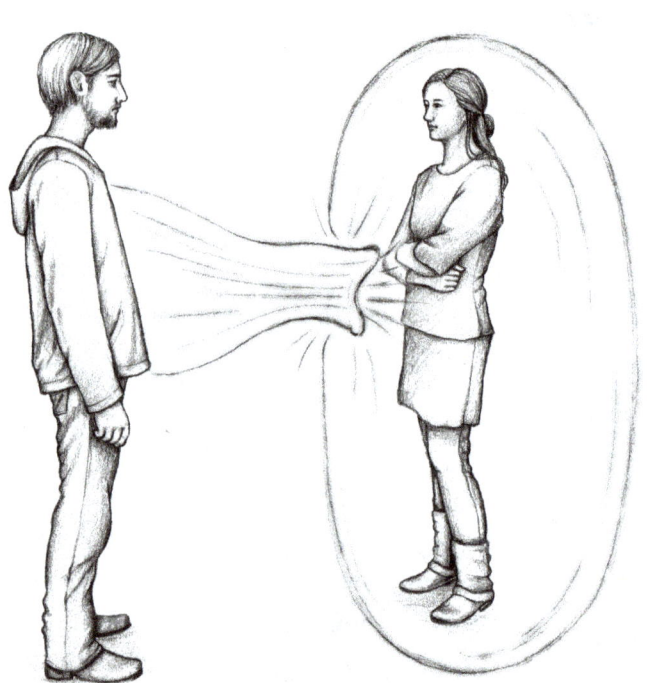

One of the more uncomfortable forms of violation occurs when you try to "suck" energy from the other. This commonly occurs when feeling needy. As the needy person you send a powerful energy cord out from your belly, attaching yourself to their energy field and pulling on them to get connection, security, closeness, protection or belonging.

Sucking violations are often masked. The sucking can appear to be giving, caring, friendly or pleasing. The person being sucked on gets confused, as they have mixed feelings arising. On the one side, they might feel flattered that you find them so desirable to be around, or want to care for them. And yet they feel strangely ambivalent in your presence, often drained after being with you and often relieved when you go apart.

Sucking violations occur all the time in normal situations. They also occur in situations of illness, both physical and psychological. An ill person needs energy and will draw it from those around them. Many nurses and doctors suffer from this.

7. Taking Another Over via Energetic Resonance

A subtle yet powerful form of violation occurs through the energetic principle of resonance. In this case, if you are strong in your feelings about something, you will radiate this energy outwards. It's kind of like playing music with a strong beat in the background. Though one is not really listening to the music, their foot starts bouncing to the rhythm. Through resonance one person can take over another person. The 2nd person loses touch with him or herself in that moment.

13 The Art of Bringing Your Essence Out

Allowing GO and Being Total

In the last section of chapter 11 we used the expression– letting go. Imagine now a person who wants to jump from a high cliff into the waters below. They climb up a narrow path to then precariously inch their way out to the jump off point. And then they get stuck. Fear has taken over and now they are hanging on to the side of a cliff. Friends nearby are yelling, "Let go, it's safe. Jump." Finally, the person on the cliff releases their grip and they get that incredible adrenalin rush as they plunge downwards into the waters below.

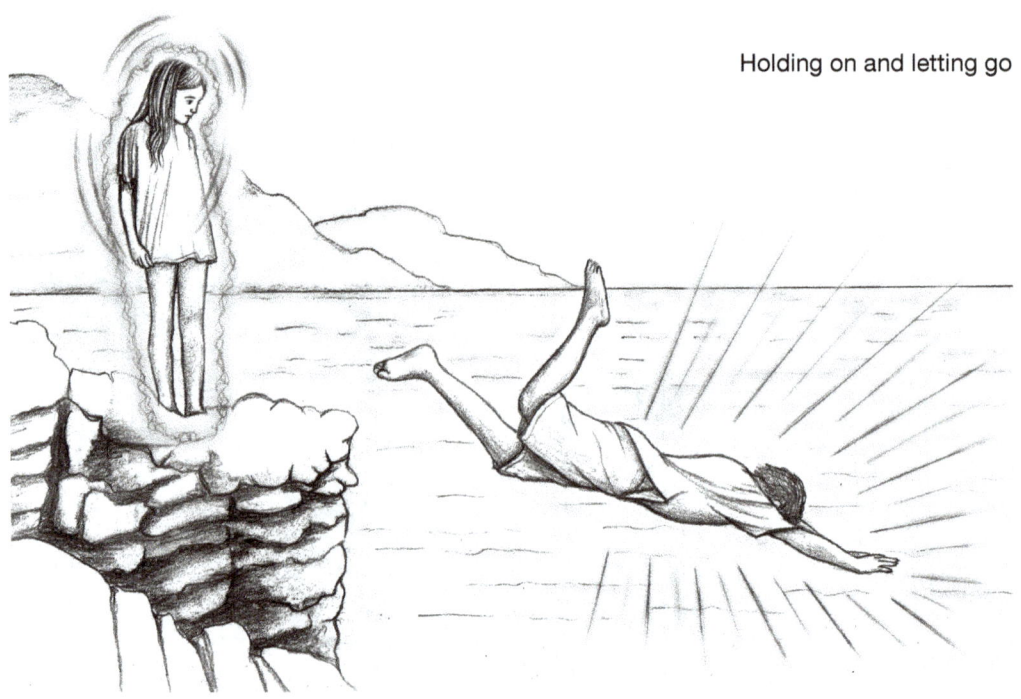

Holding on and letting go

The emphasis in this situation is on the process of releasing the hands – letting go of something that is holding on.

Allowing GO – getting the green light

There is another way of viewing this. Imagine a racecar waiting behind the red light at the starting gate. The driver is revving up his engine waiting for the light to turn green. There is a count down – 3, 2, 1, and the light turns green. He takes his one foot off the brake and slams his other foot onto the gas and the car surges forwards. The emphasis here is on going, on moving forwards.

Think of letting go as meaning "Allowing Go", a forwards movement, a surge forwards, allowing going. It has a whole different feeling than the previous example of releasing something that's holding on.

Totality means allowing your energies a full go

Let's apply this to the art of bringing our energies out. We'll use the example of telling someone you love them, but we could substitute any other expression as well. Let's assume you want to tell someone you love them. Sometimes that's the most easy and natural thing in the world to do. Other times it's very difficult, as if the words just won't come out, and our energy just won't extend forwards.

What's happening in those moments is that something is holding back. Something is not allowing GO. To return to our racecar image, imagine the driver only partially takes his foot off the brakes and only partially puts his foot on the gas. There is a forward motion but it's inhibited, strained and partial.

This is what happens a great deal of time with our energy. We want to bring our energy out but we put the brakes on it. Whether it be telling someone we love them, asking our boss for a raise or expressing an idea we're enthusiastic about - we brake ourselves and in so doing break our energy flow.

So here's an exercise you can do to learn the art of letting GO and being total.

Exercise 13.1:   Allowing Go and Being Total

1. Bring your hands in front of your chest at about the level of your heart, palms facing in.

2. Now inhale, and with your exhale, open your arms outwards, towards the front and sides.

3. See the energy reaching way out towards the front of you, as if there is no friction, nothing to inhibit it, so the energy can extend effortlessly far forwards.

Using the hands to GO

4. Focus on the exhale and let your self relax. Imagine the energy flowing outwards easily and fluidly. Visualize in your mind's eye 'Allowing GO'.

Allowing GO is related to an understanding we call totality. Being total means to give it your all. You've certainly had the experience of doing something that your heart's not in. You kind of go through the motions but you're not really present – there's no energy really behind, or worse, your resisting and putting the brakes on even whilst doing it.

Now imagine a moment in your life where you were total. Perhaps you were competing in a sports competition and you were going 200%. Or maybe you were working at your computer and you were completely engrossed in the project at hand. Being total can happen with anything – it's a state of presence; full energy, no holding back, allowing a full GO.

Exercise 13.2 of Today: Totality Inventory of your Activities

- *Do a short inventory of your activities today and in the recent past. How total were you? How present? How much were you giving your all? Some areas of your life probably rank higher than others.*
- *Now imagine everything you do being total. If you're doing it, then do it right. If you are there, then really be there. What a great way to live, and it's so effective and joyful too.*

Being total doesn't mean exhausting yourself with too much inappropriate energy. Lets say you're driving on a beautiful winding road through the mountains. You can drive at breakneck speed as if you're on a rally. That's total. You can also drive at a relaxed and easy pace but be really present. You are alert to the car and the road; you are taking in the scenery. You are present, here and now, at one with the car, the road and the environment. This is also total.

So total doesn't mean using too much energy; it's a state of presence with the right amount of energy. Now imagine living your life being total with everything you do; every moment the appropriate amount of energy, every moment being present and alert. Now you've got the art of letting energy flow.

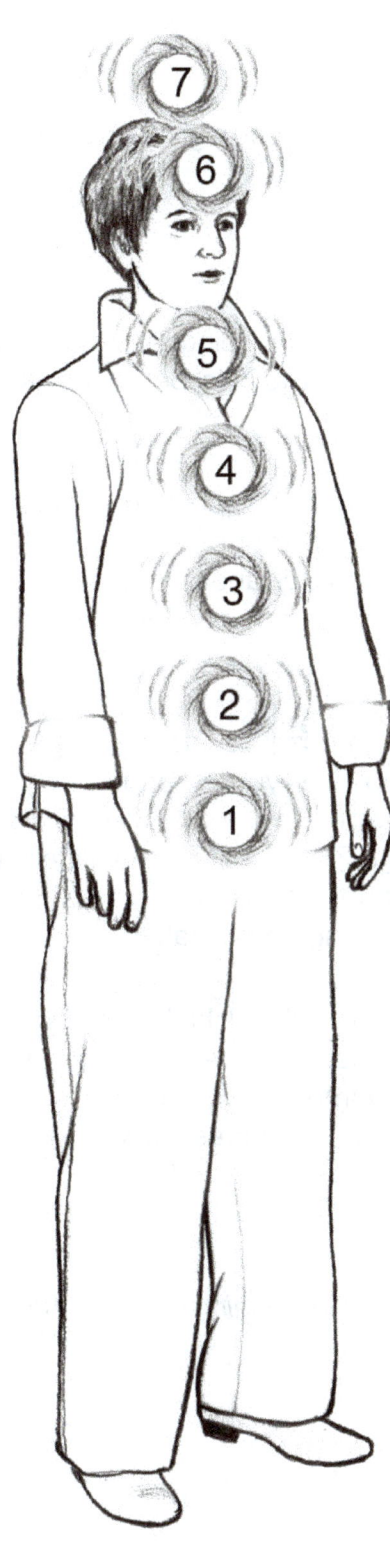

7 - Crown
Purpose, Meaning, Inspiration, Unity

6 - Third Eye
Vision, Understanding, Intelligence, Holistic Thought, Intuition

5 - Throat
Expression, Creativity, Truth

4 - Heart
Love, Compassion, Empathy, Openness, Gratitude, Service, Generosity

3 - Solar Plexus
Identity, Worth, Strength, Self

2 - Belly
Connecting, Caring, Sensuality, Warmth, Play, Pleasure

1 - Base
Abundance, Aliveness, Grounding, Manifestation

Essence Qualities

Our Essence is uniqe and individual, and simultaneously universal. Essence unfolds through the chakras as distinct "flowers of being". Some Essence qualities are listed above.

Living your Essence - Dare to Be You

The last thing we'd like to mention here is the deeper significance of the out flow of energy – bringing your essence out.

What do we mean by essence?

There is something that is fundamentally you – your Beingness, the most essential part of you. This is something that just IS. No one can take it away, no one can alter it – it just is.

To touch your essence is one of the most joyful of all experiences. Doubts and insecurities fall away. The noise of the mind disappears, and you shift from the tumultuous outer layers of the personality and energy field into that deep and profound contact with that which is really you – your essence.

Your essence is like a diamond in that though it is just one diamond, yet it has many facets. You might touch your love or your strength, or your clarity or your playfulness. There are many aspects of your essence. Each is different and yet each is you. The changing light will refract differently through the facets of a diamond at different moments to create those beautiful and varied effects of light shining through a crystal.

Your awareness has the same function as the light: it highlights certain aspects of your essence and makes them shine. Just like the diamond, so does essence reflect differently in different moments, with so many different aspects of who you are. Yet, all are aspects of your essence.

DEFINITION: Essence

Essence is the most essential, fundamental YOU; the shining qualities that every one of us is born with.

To know and live your essence is one of the most important things you can ever do. Yet most of us don't feel we can bring our essence out. Maybe you don't feel safe, or you expect others to reject you, not really be present, or use your vulnerabilities against you. And you're probably right – all those things can happen.

It takes courage to be true to yourself and to express the deeper you. This is the higher meaning of OUT; bringing your essence out. You give yourself more space, pushing back those energies that infringe upon you. You give yourself room to be big. You expand – living from your center, in touch with your essence, and radiating you outwards as you go forwards with your life.

You expand – living from your center, in touch with your essence, and radiating you outwards as you go forwards with your life.

Exercise 13.3: Bringing your Essence OUT

A: Preparation: Tune into Your Essence

Let's begin by thinking of a moment where you were "rich in your self". That might have been moment of love, where you heart was open; or a moment of strength, when you were really in your energy. It could have been a moment of clarity, where you really saw. Essence has many qualities, but what distinguishes them is that there is something fundamentally You – rich, full, and fundamental to who you are.

This moment of essence might have been a feeling, a thought or a sensation in the body. Whatever form that moment of essence took, be with that now.

1. Tune into the Physical Sensation of Essence

Give it a couple of moments for it to come as alive as possible. Notice that this thought or feeling has a distinct physical sensation somewhere in your body or your energy field. Take a moment to be aware of the physicality of Essence.

2. Tune into the Energetic Level of Essence

Now shift your awareness to the energetic level of this feeling or thought. This state has an energetic substance to it, and sits somewhere in your energy field. That substance has a distinct quality and specific flow to the energy.

3. Model the Energy of Essence

Put your hands where you feel that energetic substance sits: for a moment open and close your hands there, move them in or out, change their shape, until your hands find a shape that reflects the energy there. You have now modelled this energy and helped it become more tangible.

4. Expand your Essence

Now let this state become even larger in you. Use your hands to expand it. Imagine the energy field opening outwards, radiating more into the environment. Take a moment to let essence "take space".

Bringing your Essence out

Perfect. Now we're going to take a more challenging next step.

5. Find your Appropriate Expression

Imagine yourself expressing this state of Essence in whatever way might be appropriate for you. Perhaps it's words you speak, or the exuberant expression of a feeling. Perhaps it's something you would do, an action you would take. Or it might be simply standing there and "being" in a particular way, carrying a particular posture, a look on your face, a certain radiation.

6. Express your Essence in the Matrix

Lastly, and here's the really challenging part, see yourself doing this now with people around. We call the environment around the matrix - the web of energies, people, things, vibes, etc. that compose your environment. Imagine expressing your Essence in the matrix.

Quick Reference Points:

1. Tune into the Physical Sensation of Essence
2. Tune into the Energetic Level of Essence
3. Model the Energy of Essence
4. Expand your Essence
5. Find your Appropriate Expression
6. Express your Essence in the Matrix

Live your Essence amidst the Storms of Life

There is a good chance that there are people who won't be so in tune with your essence. They might judge your essence, be threatened by it, or simply be too much in their own thing to take notice. Perhaps they're just in a different space and their vibes and yours are not in sync.

These energies affect you. They can inhibit you and make you keep your essence more private. They might even actively attack you and try to shut you down.

Being bright amidst dense energies

This is a key thing in life – that our essence, our deeper and more precious thoughts and feelings won't always be supported or understood, and might even be aggressed on in subtle or not so subtle ways. So for us this is one of the most important skills we can learn:

- to have the courage to dare to let our selves live our essence, and then to have the skill to hold our center in the midst of what we might encounter.

> *For a moment, let yourself dare. Feel the energetic presence of your essence. Let it be big and radiant. See yourself in real life environments. Imagine yourself acting and expressing this essence. And even though there might be dense energies that are not supportive, you feel your center and the preciousness of who you are and what you carry. Really hold true to that energy. Let your essence become stronger, more anchored, and able to withstand the storms life brings.*

This is the real art of living:

- being in touch with your essence, with your deeper self, and letting it shine.

Allow yourself to have an effect on the world around you. Create and sculpt and shape it based on your essence, the highest in you, the Golden Being in your center.

Section Three

The Vertical
The Plane of Consciousness: UP, BEYOND and DOWN

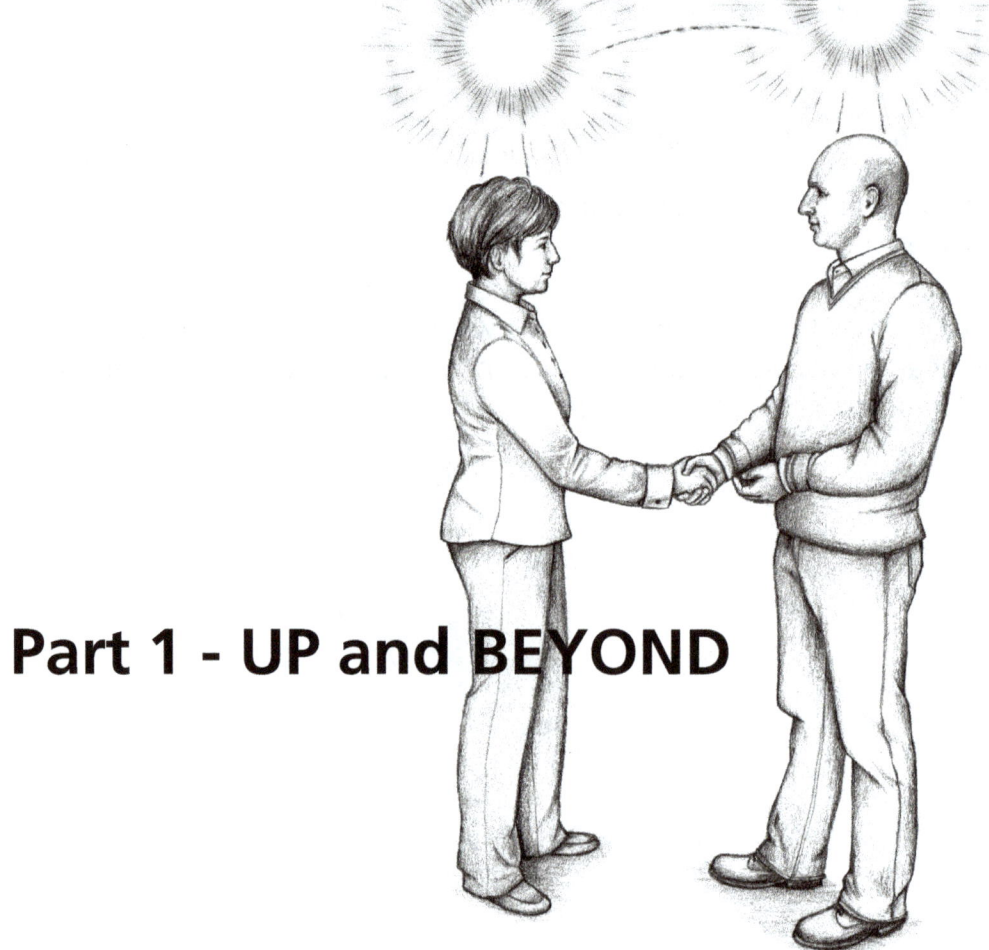

Part 1 - UP and BEYOND

14 UP - The Shift in Consciousness

Up - The Shift in Consciousness

"The mind can proceed only so far upon what it knows and can prove. There comes a point where the mind takes a higher plane of knowledge, but can never prove how it got there. All great discoveries have involved such a leap."

Albert Einstein

This saying reveals a profound insight into the human system – that we have different levels of knowledge and thinking. And there is a second insight hidden behind this that has immense and immediate significance for us – that we can deliberately shift to a higher level of thought.

ENERGY PRINCIPLE 13:
Energy lifts consciousness

The process of moving energy from a lower to a higher state lifts the level of consciousness

Once you understand this you have a master key for living. It not only provides the most potent Energy Skill of all, it takes you to a level where you are not just living, you are thriving - living abundantly in joy and well-being.

An objection might come up; *"Well, that's fine for Einstein to say, he's a genius, but I'm just an ordinary guy."*

Wrong!

- You are much more than you recognize or give yourself credit for
- You are accessing places of higher consciousness all the time, though you may not notice that you are doing so
- There are ways to deliberately access this higher level

The way is via the core channel of energy and the vertical flow within it that we call "UP and DOWN".

Up And Down

We've spoken about the core channel and its importance in centering. It holds another significance as well. Connected to the core are the seven energy centers called the chakras. A chakra is a vortex of energy, a powerful point of swirling energy. Each chakra is related to a type of thought and feeling, or what we refer to as a level of consciousness.

The best way to understand what we mean by a level of consciousness is to imagine a totem pole, the type you see in the culture of various indigenous people's. Visualize this imaginary totem pole with seven faces upon it. The full spectrum of evolutionary time is represented, each face representing one of seven evolutionary phases. The face at the bottom of the totem pole looks the most primitive. It represents our earliest evolutionary origins and corresponds with the most primitive parts of the psyche.

As we move upwards, each face represents a next step in evolutionary unfoldment and is correspondingly more sophisticated.

At the top of our imaginary totem pole are our most recent and advanced evolutionary unfoldments, corresponding with the heights and greatness of the human spirit. The face there is the most refined. This is how the chakra system works. It corresponds with evolution.

The face at the bottom of the totem pole corresponds with the base chakra at the bottom of the spine and our earliest evolutionary drives and instincts.

The face at the top of the totem pole corresponds with the crown chakra at the top of the head, the last of the chakras to develop in the human energy system. It's the most advanced and refined, and corresponds with the most elevated qualities of consciousness, intelligence and the human spirit. It represents our potential, our future, for it's a center that for most of us has only begun to open.

The totem pole is an excellent representation of the chakra system because each face on it appears to be an entity in itself. This is exactly how the chakras work. Each center or chakra represents a level of thought and feeling that operates almost autonomously. One chakra might be thinking one thing, and another chakra might be thinking something else - at the same time.

Totem Pole
Many Indigenous cultures have expressed Man's multiple dimensions through the symbol of a totem pole

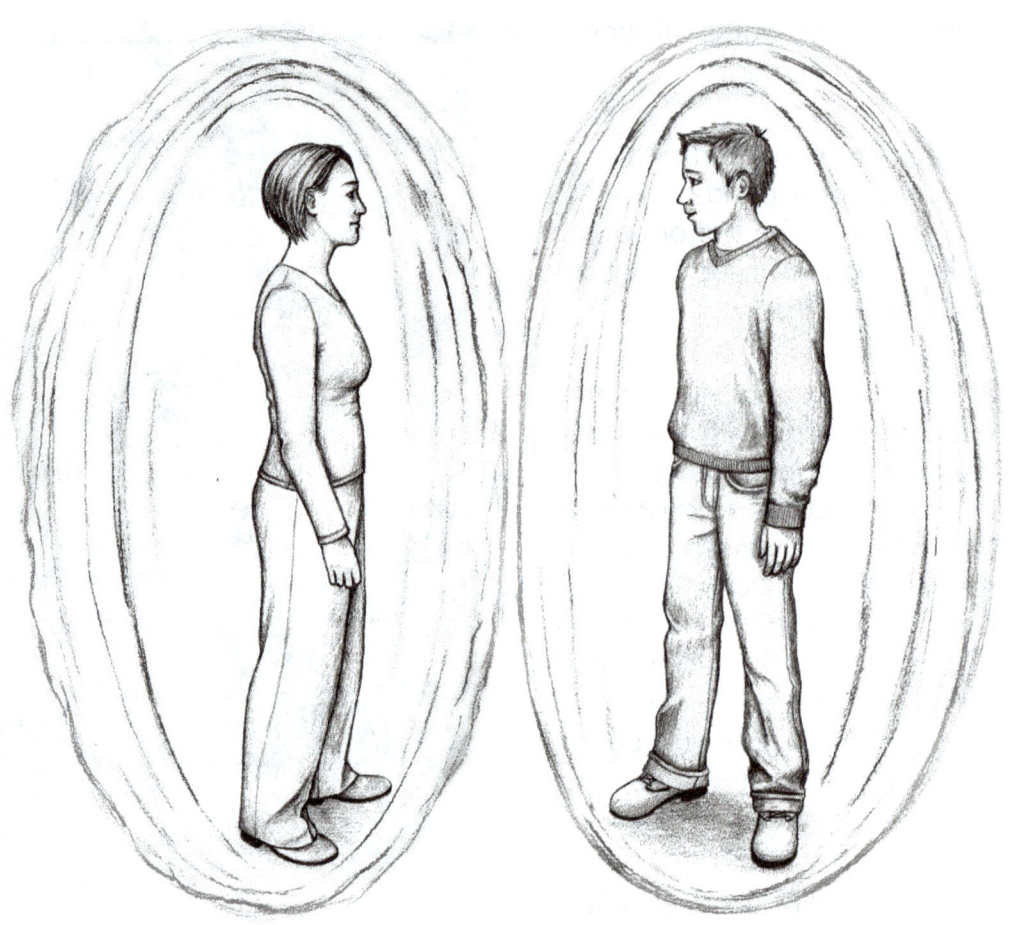

The Seven Levels of Consciousness

A level of consciousness is like looking through a lens that "colors" reality a certain way. The examples below show how each chakra would "see" another person.

	Center	Level of Consciousness
7	Crown	Sees the other as a divine soul
6	Third Eye	Sees a sophisticated and intelligent person
5	Throat	Sees a creative person
4	Heart	Sees a loving person
3	Solar Plexus	Sees someone to compete against
2	Belly	Sees the other as a sexual object
1	Base	Sees the other as a threat, someone to fear

Love versus Sex

Let's make this real by an example you are familiar with - having sex. The genitals are at the base of the spine and they correspond with the base chakra, the center from where the sexual drives originate. Though this may not be true for all of us, most of us have had sexual experiences which were pretty much that – a sexual experience – lustful, passionate and raw. It wasn't about love. It wasn't about intimacy or deep soul connection. It was about sex.

Now you have probably had the experience of having sex with someone you love; you were in love, and from this love connection you made love. What a different experience! Your hearts meet, there is an attunement with each other, a melting and merging and opening that lifts you both into the most exquisite intimacy.

Both experiences are sexual. What's the difference? And why can the same act be so radically different?

Understood energetically, just having sex involves primarily the base chakra (and a bit of the second chakra just above it at the belly). These centers are raw and instinctual, their drives powerful and consuming. Have you ever heard two cats having sex? Are they making love or killing each other? It can be hard to tell.

Now contrast this with the sexual experience of making love with someone you really love. You can feel your heart; it's almost palpable in the middle of your chest. There's such warmth that opens there. Along with these physical sensations come the most wonderful feelings of tenderness, respect, care and attunement.

What's happening is that a center higher up in the chakra system is now involved in the sexual act – the heart center. Its vibrations are more refined and its consciousness greater. Though the base center is still involved because the sexual act is connected to the base, because the heart center is now also involved, a new quality is brought into play.

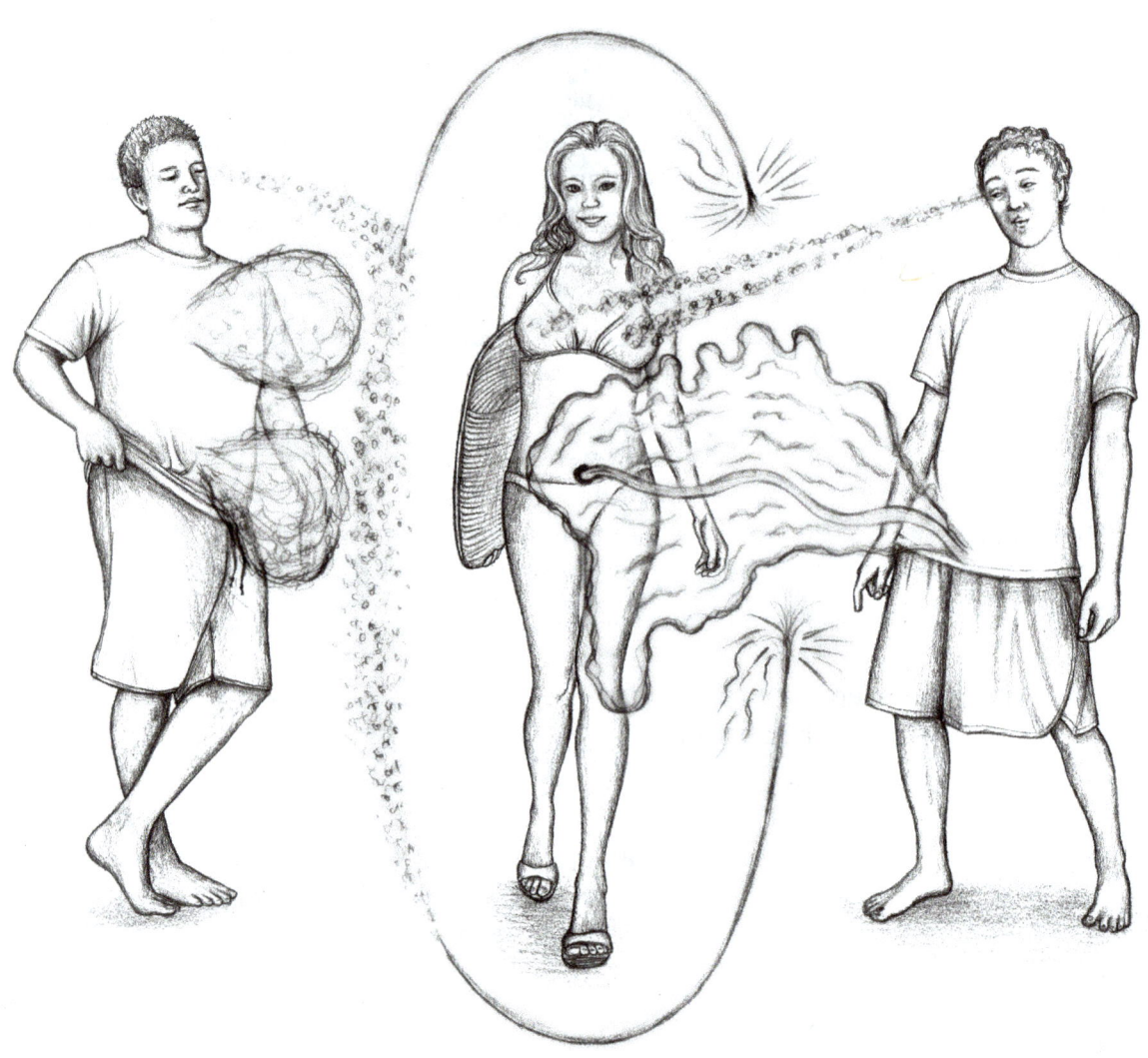

Two types of sexual energies

Left: Sexuality present but refined, heartful and respectful
Right: Sexuality out of control – raw, penetrating and violating

The energy of the heart lifts and transforms the raw sexual energies to an entirely new plane.

When you make love versus have sex you've lifted your level of consciousness up the core to a center higher in the chakra system. This higher level now acts upon the lower level to change it.

When you make love versus have sex you've lifted your level of consciousness up the core from the base center to the heart, a center higher up in your energy system.

We are lifting consciousness all the time. You've certainly had a moment of anger where you wanted to lash out with words or even strike out physically but you didn't. Why not? Because another place inside stopped you. A higher center (in this case your third eye, a decision making center) stopped the emotions of aggression that live lower down in the base and solar plexus centers.

Both examples illustrate shifts in consciousness and energy due to movement along the core channel. Why this is important is because you can deliberately move the energy up or down, effectively changing from one emotion to another, from one type of thinking or consciousness to another.

You can deliberately move energy up or down to change from one emotion or thinking to another.

Lets look at Einstein's quote again now in this context.

There comes a point where the mind takes a higher plane of knowledge, but can never prove how it got there. All great discoveries have involved such a leap."

He refers to 'higher plane of knowledge'. 'Plane' implies higher and lower, something above or below something else. It also implies superior and inferior, not in the sense of good and bad, better or worse, but in the sense of more or less refined, sophisticated and potent.

DEFINITION: **Level of Consciousness**

A way of looking at the world that includes feelings as well as thoughts. The levels of consciousness are connected to evolution and reflect earlier and later developments in the capacity of perception.

This is the magic key that understanding the "up and down" dimension of the core channel and the chakra system reveals – that there are higher and lower planes or levels of consciousness, of thought and thinking. Also, that there is a continual movement of energies, thoughts and feelings up and down within our system. Normally this happens unconsciously, but, and this is the big but, once you understand these "locations of thought" and you learn how to move energy, you can begin to take a more active part in determining the "center where you are thinking from".

Breathing it Up

Let's now add a new dimension to our work with the core. We will build on one of our earlier energy principles, "Energy follows thought" - where our thought goes energy flows.

In addition to directing our thought, we can also use our breath to direct the flow of energy. Breathing is one of the most powerful tools in energy work because when we breathe we are also inhaling and exhaling the life force. Directed breathing uses the imagination to "see" the breath moving in a particular location.

We'll try this with the heart center, as this is an easy center to feel.

Exercise 14.1: Turn on the Flame of Your Heart

Do the exercise below slowly. Take a moment for each step to open.

1. Vitalize your Heart

Imagine your heart center becoming more vital and radiant.

2. Tune to Love

Tune to the feelings of love that reside in your heart. If you want, you can tune to a person you love or a moment where your love was strong.

3. Fuel your Love

Breathe in and out of your heart. Imagine your love being fueled by the life force that's contained within the breath, and your love growing stronger and brighter.

4. Let Love flow out

Now that you've built a potency of loving energy in the heart, as you exhale, see this love flowing out of you.

Quick Reference Points:

1. *Vitalize your Heart*
2. *Tune to Love*
3. *Fuel your Love*
4. *Let Love flow out*

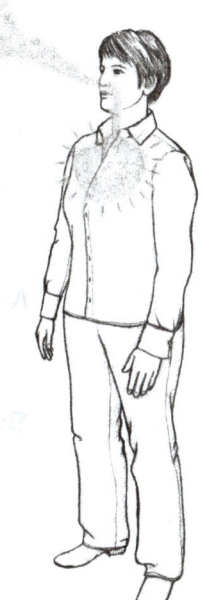

Directed breathing - in and out of the heart

As you can see, directed breathing when used with the intention to change feelings, to open types of thoughts and to move energy can be powerful.

We'll do this exercise for you to get the feeling of moving energy in the core up to the heart. Afterwards, we'll begin to work with shifting consciousness to even higher levels.

Exercise 14.2: Ignite more Love - Breathe Energy to Your Heart

A: Preparation: Awaken the Base Center

1. Breathe through the Base of the Tree

Let's go back to our image of the tree. Start by inhaling and exhaling through your base center in your pelvis area.

2. Ground Yourself

Now, visualize the energy of each breath moving down from the base, into the roots of the tree below the base and into the earth.

B: Core-Exercise

3. Vitalize the Base

Then, on the inhale, breathe the energy from the earth up the roots and into your base. Each breath brings vitality to the base. Imagine the charge growing greater, the reservoir more full. Do this breathing of the earth energy into the base 10 times; 10 deep, full slow breaths here.

4. Suck Energy up to your Heart

Now on the next inhalation breathe this charge up the spine to your heart. You can imagine the way you suck liquid up a straw – using the breath to suck the energy from the base up the spine to your heart. Do this three times.

5. Breathe through the Heart

Now, as we did in the previous exercise, imagine for a moment that you are inhaling and exhaling through your heart in the center of your chest. Visualize the energy of each breath moving in and out there. Each breath stimulates the heart center, bringing vitality there.

C: Completion

6. Tune into your Heart

When you tune into your heart now, you might notice that there is a different quality to the feelings in the heart than after the previous exercise where we only did heart breathing without bringing the energies up.

Quick Reference Points:

1. *Breathe through the Base of the Tree*
2. *Ground Yourself*
3. *Vitalize the Base*
4. *Suck Energy up to your Heart*
5. *Breathe through the Heart*
6. *Tune into your Heart*

Shifting Consciousness through moving Energy upwards

Now that we have the basics of moving energy up the core, let's put this into practice in using it as an energy skill to shift consciousness.

The lower three centers, the base, the belly and the solar plexus, are generally the most active in us.

> **Typical thoughts of the 1st three centers**
>
> ***Base***
> Will I have enough money?
> I'm worried
> I'm scared
> I don't trust him/her/it
>
> ***Belly***
> Do I belong?
> I'm not going to get my needs met
> I want to be close to him/her
> I have to get more
>
> ***Solar Plexus***
> Respect me!
> He's more successful/richer/more important than me
> I want to be number one
> I'm so stupid/dumb/inferior/etc.

They dominate us with their emotions and thoughts, which can range from 'very bright' to 'extremely dense'.

We're not going to go into the full spectrum that these centers contain except a brief mention in the sidebar to the right. But we will focus upon some of the more challenging things you might encounter here in the lower centers and what to do about them.

There are many levels we can shift to, many different floors within our building of consciousness. We are going to focus on four different movements upwards. We have chosen these four because they are central for everyone in the maturation process.

Four Primary Shifts in Consciousness

Shift Up #1: From Dependence to Empowerment
Moving from the belly to the solar plexus

Our first movement is from the belly center upwards to the solar plexus center just above it. This is one of the most important shifts in consciousness that every person must go through to become an empowered individual.

The belly center has to do with your inner child. It represents your emotional attachments to others and things. When it is not healthy or out of balance you carry the emotions and thinking of a child. You become dependent, needy and overly emotional and attached.

The solar plexus center sits just below the V of the ribs. When healthy, it gives access to the mature adult in you. You have a feeling of autonomy, of standing on your own two feet. You feel competent, independent, empowered and strong.

You might want to use this Energy Skill when you're feeling:

- Needy or dependent
- Caught in "I can't" attitudes
- Feeling like a lost child
- Emotionally overwhelmed
- Slothful, "blobby", muddy

> **Exercise 14.3:** **From Dependence to Empowerment: Moving from Belly to Solar Plexus**
>
> **1. Awaken the Belly**
>
> *Begin by inhaling and exhaling through your belly. Visualize each breath moving deep into the belly, filling this center with energy and awareness. You might feel your belly becoming quieter or warmer. Take at least 5 full slow breathes here.*
>
> **2. Breathe up to the Solar Plexus**
>
> *Now on the next inhalation, breathe the energy from the belly up into your solar plexus under your ribs and visualize the solar plexus filling up with energy. Do this three times.*

3. Open the Solar Plexus

Now breathe in and out through the solar plexus. With each exhale imagine the solar plexus relaxing and opening up. Your body might subtly change its posture. You might notice shifts in your physical sensations and emotions. Do you feel more empowered? Check whether your outlook has changed.

4. Test your Empowerment

Think of a situation where you had previously not been feeling empowered. Now, continuing to breathe in the solar plexus, do you now feel more confidence, strength or capacity to act in that situation?

Quick Reference Points:

1. *Awaken the Belly*
2. *Breathe up to the Solar Plexus*
3. *Open the Solar Plexus*
4. *Test your Empowerment*

Shift Up #2: From "Animal Man" to "Divinely Human"
Moving from the lower three centers up to the heart

Though we have already been working with breathing into the heart, we're going to bring in now the "heart consciousness" that will add a whole other dimension to it.

Your heart is one of the most powerful and important centers in you. Not only does it open you to love, it opens a new way of seeing and feeling the world that contains compassion, empathy, unity and oneness.

The purpose of breathing to the Heart

The lower three centers, the base, the belly and the solar plexus contain powerful instincts connected to our evolutionary past. Though these centers are vital for living, to only live in them keeps us in "animal man", where our concerns are survival, procreation and social position. Breathing to your heart lifts you to a higher level of consciousness. It opens the "divinely human" in you, where you recognize your interconnectedness with all things and come to experience the unity of life. As part of this experience there is the emergence of altruism, empathy, generosity and compassion.

> **Exercise 14.4:** From Animal Man to "Divinely Human": Moving from the Lower to the Heart
>
> **1. Awaken the Lower Three Centers**
>
> - *Turn your attention to your base, the root of your tree. Breathe vitality in there, filling your reservoir.*
> - *Let the vitality reach up to your belly center, until it feels full and warm.*
> - *Now suck the energy upwards to the solar plexus.*
> - *Visualize the connection of the three lower energy centers like a column full of vitality, warmth and passion. Imagine those energy centers aligned and centered.*
>
> **2. Soften and Lift Energy up to the Heart**
>
> *Now let your breath become softer and finer and lift the energy to your heart, stimulating the energy in your heart to glow brighter and be more radiant.*

Moving Energies up to the Heart

> ### 3. Radiate Love
>
> *Let love and gratitude overflow. Let them radiate out to the world.*
>
> ***Addition:*** *If you had been busy with issues or problems before this exercise you can use this shift to look at them "through the eyes of the heart". You might be surprised at how your heart can give you a new perspective and insight.into those issues.*
>
> ### Quick Reference Points:
>
> *1. Awaken the Lower Three Centers*
>
> *2. Soften and Lift Energy up to the Heart*
>
> *3. Radiate Love*

Shift Up #3: From Drama to the Watcher
Moving from the lower five centers up to the awakened third eye

Your third eye is a miracle of consciousness. It gives you the powers of thought, intuition, vision and insight. Accessing your third eye is an essential Energy Balancing Skill because it takes you out of the "noise" of emotional drama.

The purpose of breathing to the Third Eye

Breathing to the third eye opens one of the qualities that is most essential to holding center - we call it 'the watcher'. The watcher is a place of detached, objective observation that simply watches the emotions or thoughts that are moving in you. It doesn't analyze or judge them. It doesn't try to change or alter them. It simply steps out of the drama and becomes an alert and present bystander.

The following exercise is one of the outstanding gems of Energy Balancing, a bright diamond that you can carry in your pocket wherever you go. It is so simple to do and can be used anywhere and anytime, and yet its effects are just amazing. We invite you to let it become a treasure for your life as it has for ours, and to remember it in situations where you feel tense, overwhelmed, lost, scattered, or simply out of balance.

The third eye tends to tense up due to how we think. We use this exercise to relax the third eye and to help it to expand its state of consciousness. It will also relax stress in your physical eyes and your forehead.

We suggest you read the whole exercise first so you understand it, and then we'll guide you into a simple 4 step version of it.

Exercise 14.5: From Drama to the Clarity of the "Watcher" – Moving from the Lower Five Centers to the Awakened Third Eye

A. Preparation

1. Relax the Third Eye

First rub your face with both hands to wake it up. Then with three fingers slowly massage your forehead from the bridge of your nose up to the hairline. Follow this movement with your eyes and your breath. Let your hands and your eyes rest at the hairline for a moment and feel the shift. Do this 3-5 times.

B: Shifting of your energies

2. Vitalize the Lower Centers

Turn your attention to your three lower energy centers, base, belly and solar plexus. Take note of any motions or emotions there. Then with several strong in-breaths breathe vitality into all of them.

225

3. 'Sweep' vital Energy UP the Core Channel to the Third Eye

Suck the vitality of the lower centers into your core channel and all the way upwards to your third eye in the middle of your forehead. Use your hands in front of your body with a sweeping up motion up the core channel to support the movement of energy upwards.

4. Expand the Third Eye

Continue doing the upwards sweep several times until you feel your head lighter, vibrating and shining with energy. Use your hands to open the whole area around your head, as if you have a halo glowing around you.

C: Core exercise

5. Resting in the Watcher

Connect to the watcher in you. Imagine in the very center of your head a glowing place of intelligence and clarity and let it shine more brightly with every breath.

6. Let the Watcher look down to the Lower Centers

Resting your awareness on the sensation of expansion and clarity in your third eye, now look down from the watcher to your lower centers. Let the watcher take note of what is moving there. A great spectrum of possible feelings exist there; perhaps excitement, sadness or anger; warmth, tension, restlessness or tiredness; an energy flow at one place and an energy leak or a block somewhere else. These are just a few words to help you focus and "watch" what is uniquely moving in you.

D: Completion

7. Here and Now

Whatever you "see" – just be with it. Don't change it. Don't judge yourself for it. Just watch it. Stay present in the "here and now". This is the gift of the watcher.

> **Quick Reference Points:**
> 1. Rub your forehead to awaken the Third Eye
> 2. Sweep the vital energies all from the bottom up to the Third Eye
> 3. Connect to the Watcher deep inside the Third Eye
> 4. Let the Watcher look down and take note of what is going on in the body

Shift Up #4: From Personality to Wisdom
Moving from the lower six centers up to the crown

The crown center at the top of your head opens a wealth of wisdom, understanding, and bigger picture thinking. Here you step beyond the limited self into an awareness of the bigger universe of which you are a part. You become aware of the many forces that shape things, and you have an encompassing time reference that sees your current situation in the context of both past and future. You become aware of yourself as a spiritual being, a being of vast energies and consciousness.

The purpose of breathing to the Crown

The purpose of breathing to the crown is to open this higher dimension of consciousness and from it to bring new direction, purpose and new perspective to the challenges you face.

Exercise 14.6: From Personality to Wisdom – Moving from the Lower Six Centers to the Crown

A: Preparation

1. Ground and align like a Tree

Let's go back to our image of the tree. Take a moment to inhale and exhale through your base center at the bottom of the spine. Visualize the energy of each breath moving down the base, into the roots of the tree and into the earth. Then on the inhale breathe the energy from the earth, up the root and into your base. Each breath brings vitality there. Imagine the charge growing greater, the reservoir more full. Take 10 full slow breathes here.

2. Fire Energy up to the Top of the Head

Now on this next inhalation strongly breathe this charge up the spine to the top of the head. You can imagine the way you suck liquid up a straw – imagine using the breath to suck the energy from the base, up the spine, all the way to the top of the head, filling the crown. Do this three times.

B: Core-Exercise

3. Visualize glowing Light in and around your Head

Now breathe in and out of the crown. Visualize a sphere of glowing light around and above the top of the head. This is the crown chakra, the highest part of our tree. See this sphere growing brighter and more vital.

4. Vitalize Wisdom

Imagine the quality of wisdom here. You are accessing your own wisdom, the collective wisdom of humanity, and the wisdom that is fundamental to life. Let each breath "vitalize wisdom", helping you touch the immense consciousness that you hold.

People practicing meditation will repetitively breathe up the base to the crown and then meditate on the crown for an hour or longer, so spend as much time here as you're comfortable with.

C: Completion

5. Come back and enjoy the "Glow"

When you feel complete, open your eyes and look around. You might notice your eyes are clearer, or there is a sparkle to what you perceive. Take a few moments to enjoy the "glow" of this type of powerful energy exercise.

Quick Reference Points:

1. *Become a Tree*
2. *Fire Energy up to the Top of the Head*
3. *Visualize glowing Light*
4. *Vitalize Wisdom*
5. *Come back and enjoy the "Glow"*

If you feel ungrounded after this exercise you can take a few moments to breathe the energy from the crown down the spine to the base and into the earth. See yourself 'grounding' and anchoring in the earth. Check chapter 16 for more on grounding.

We spoke earlier of "not just living, but thriving" to indicate another dimension of living that brings us joy and wellbeing. The movement of energies UP is the ultimate Energy Balancing Skill. UP raises your vibration and lifts your consciousness. It takes you out of emotions and thoughts that cloud and clog you, and gives you new insights and a higher perspective. UP changes dense energies into something more life supportive. Ultimately, UP transforms the simply mundane or even negative into something of meaning, significance and something, that is profoundly uplifting - the higher dimensions of thought and feeling which are inherent to you.

15 Beyond - Meeting the Magic of the Higher

Beyond – the Magic of the Higher

Ocean swells gently roll across the calm sea, and the waves break softly upon the beach. A warm breeze caresses my skin. Above, a clear and starry sky - the vastness of the universe. My thoughts rise; to the wonder of this planet we call Earth; to billions of years of evolution, never stopping; to the millions of stars shining brightly and to those that have already turned to stone eons ago. The Big Bang theory, Quantum theory, Parallel universes – my mind can't grasp it! But Eternity shivers through me. Who am I? I am connected in mysterious ways to something bigger.

I'm a grain of sand in the desert, a drop in the ocean, ever moving with the flow….

We have all touched "something greater". That touch takes us beyond the familiar into the extra ordinary. You might have experienced it in a moment such as described above, or being on your own in nature. Or you might have felt it in a moment of bliss while making love, or looking in the eyes of another or in the togetherness of community. However it happened, you have had moments that have lifted you out of the normal and connected you to something greater.

This "something greater" is the ultimate goal of working with Energy. Here, energy uplifts us and takes us to a place of consciousness, wisdom, connection, clarity, purpose, dynamism and love. It's the same goal and promise as religions and spirituality; to open us to a higher dimension of life. Energy becomes a Path to the transcendent.

All Spiritual Traditions point to the same Thing – there is "Something More"

In all cultures and ages there are, as the Zen masters say, "fingers pointing towards the moon" - **indications that "something more" does exist and that it is the birthright and destiny of all**. And almost all cultures provide paths and practices to get there. Whether it be the stately rituals of organized religions, or the trance-like ecstatic dance of native people, cultures everywhere provide means through which we contact this other dimension.

Our modern age brings many unique contributions in this direction. One of these is so significant, yet so non-phenomenal, that we don't even recognize its importance. That contribution is the ability to access all of the worlds' spiritual teachings and the resultant study of comparative religion.

In the past, each culture's spiritual beliefs and practices existed within the confines of that culture, with little contact to the outside world. Due to limited trade routes and dangerous waterways, little interaction and cross-pollination occurred.

Though this provided relatively undisturbed environments for each culture's spiritual traditions to grow within, it also created distortions due to cultural limitations and biases.

Suddenly, in just a single century, the world has opened up. Go to any large bookstore and you will find spiritual texts from every culture and age. What shaman, monks, mystics and medicine men once kept as their most precious and often guarded secrets in monasteries and mystery schools is now publicly available, neatly stacked next to each other and searchable via a web browser.

On the surface the forms of these many spiritual traditions seem to differ; each is wrapped in its unique cultural garb. But when you put them side-by-side commonalities emerge, as if all these many traditions grasp the same universal truths and principles, the differences being mainly due to the form of cultural expression.

Something significant opens at the Top of the Head

One of the most central of these recurring threads is that something of great significance opens at the top of the head. The most common symbol that almost all cultures use to indicate a person of spiritual attainment is a special head garb. Whether a golden crown or a feathered headdress, cultures down the ages have placed something on top of the head in connection with spiritual attainment. And if you look at religious art, Saints and Buddha's are portrayed with a halo of light around or above their head.

And these are just the external representations. If you look into the practices used for spiritual development across these many traditions, you see again and again methods that focus on the top of the head.

Contemplation and meditation, the use of special substances and objects, and energy work are just a few of them.

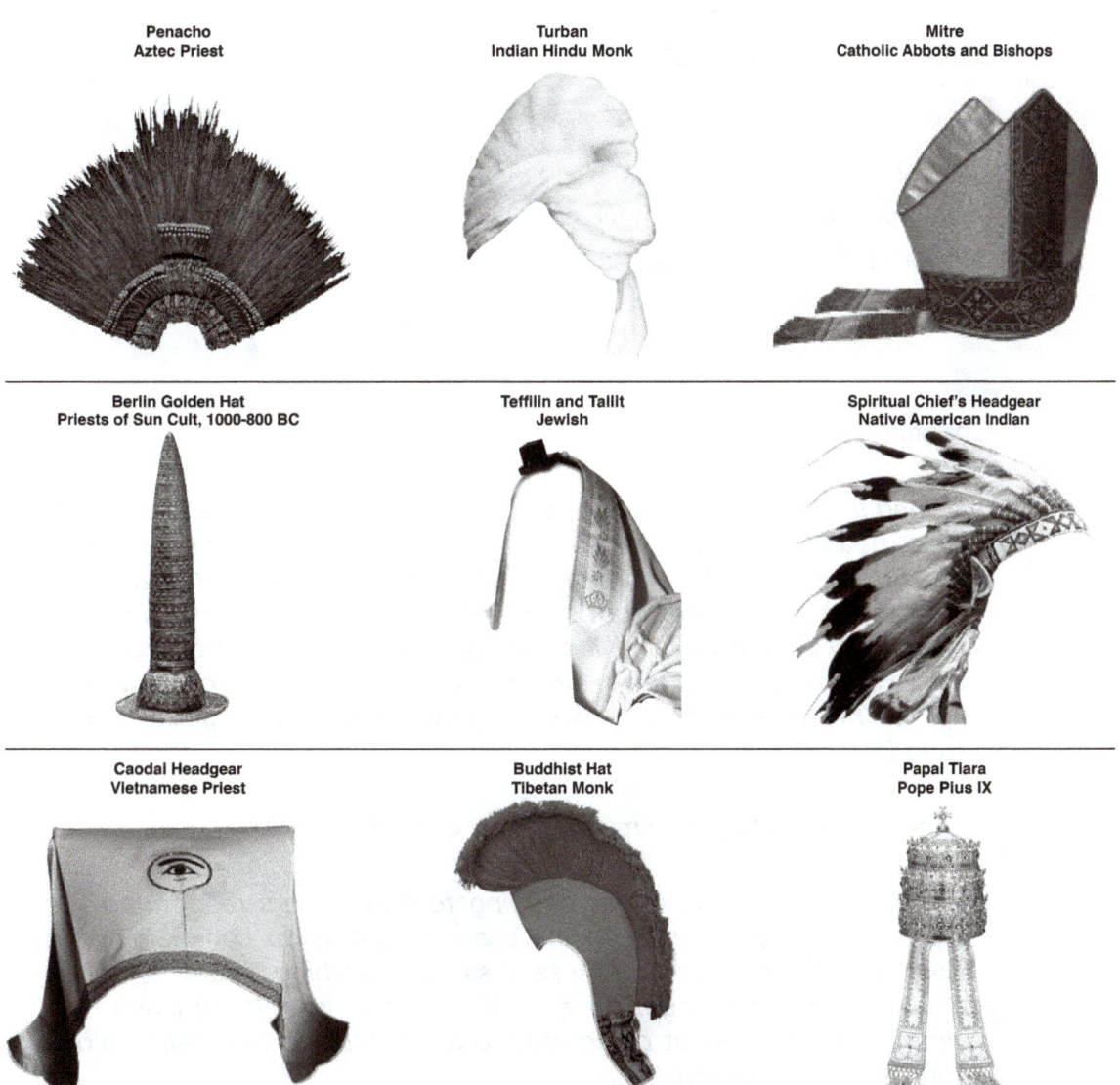

Spiritual "headgear" indicating spiritual attainment
Most cultures have indicated spiritual attainment with some sort of headgear

When you strip away the mystical and religious wrappings what stands revealed are ways of stimulating higher consciousness through directing energy and awareness to the top of the head.

ENERGY PRINCIPLE 14:

Higher consciousness opens at the top of the head

Directing energy to the top of the head stimulates higher states of consciousness

Christiane's story:

I "had it all". I was in a loving relationship with a wonderfully compatible, beautiful and successful man. I was CEO of my own company, leading national and international projects in marketing research for fast moving consumer goods. My life was also fast moving: I played field hockey in a top first league, loved freeride skiing and surfing, and I spent my vacations in far and beautiful places. It looked and felt great: being successful, enjoying good times, having good friends and love in my life.

And yet, something was missing. How could that be?

When I tried to share that nagging feeling, others responded like "What's your problem? You have everything. Stop complaining." It was hard to describe that I was missing something "more" although I couldn't put the finger on what that "more" was. It felt like a hole inside of me, and not being able to share this left me feeling alone and somehow wrong.

I kept looking in different directions, became a Feng Shui consultant, did relationship and communication trainings and took classes in chakra work and energy healing. And then one day I walked into an Essence Training workshop. During a guided exercise, with eyes closed, I heard the words: "Breathe your energy up above your head, breathe into your crown". I tried hard, but all I felt was a headache. How was this sup-

posed to work? I cracked an eyelid open and peeked around at the group. Everyone else was sitting with eyes closed, seemingly very concentrated. Was it only me feeling clueless?

"And now take your awareness further up". Further up? Is there anything at all there? I doubted it, as my headache got worse. I didn't really see the point. Yet, something urged me to keep going.

For a long time "going up" and the transcendent just remained a mystery. I thought I just wasn't talented for this. I'd so much love to say that "a boom-bang enlightenment experience" happened to me and the world was never the same again. But it didn't. What did happen is my headaches slowly became less painful and I started sensing a prickling on top of my head. This special type of "Beyond" meditation became an increasingly peaceful and at the same time exciting experience.

Though it seemed like little or nothing changed, my system slowly started to transform. My consciousness just didn't yet perceive the subtle shifts in my energy field that were preparing me for something bigger. And then suddenly, a greater space opened. A new realm, a larger perspective unveiled. Over the course of time this happened again and again, and each time I was in awe as I gained such new insights and new levels of happiness.

The Higher Self
A profound state of higher consciousness opens at the top of the head. We refer to it as the Higher Self

Out of the World's "Normal Madness"

Anyone who has opened to higher states of consciousness indicates that these states lift you out of the ordinary. They bring a clarity and wisdom which takes you above the "normal madness" of the world. You are connected to a larger sense of life; they give meaning and purpose, and they put you in touch with what could be called the spiritual, mystical or transcendent. These states open the most desirable qualities of

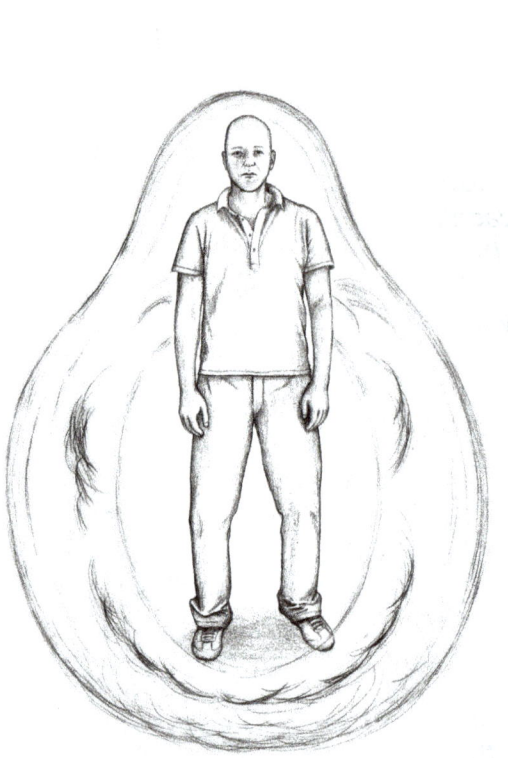

The "Normal Madness"
Normal state where most of us live -
with energy polarized downwards

Going Beyond
Lifting the energies to higher
consciousness

human nature such as love, wisdom, compassion, altruism and power or vision.

In Energy Balancing we call this simply Beyond. Whatever name is used, whether it be Soul, Higher Self, Enlightenment, or Higher Consciousness, is not important; what we care about is directly entering the experience of the transcendent that opens here.

Energy Balancing is not clothed in religious garb. It distills down many methods into one basic practice to help awaken in you this higher dimension of who you are – through bringing energy up the spine to and beyond the top of the head. Energy Balancing offers a scientific approach to the spiritual.

You have already had experiences with the higher through the Core Channel Experience and the Tree Exercise in chapter 4. Here we'll look at the deeper significance of why we're doing it, and we'll add some things to make it more powerful.

Invocation and Evocation

To better prepare you for the next exercise, we'd like to explain some of the terms we use:

DEFINITION: **Eighth Center or Higher Self**
A higher part of your self about one foot above your head, a vortex of energy carrying a high frequency vibration, containing higher aspects of consciousness.

DEFINITION: **Bridge**
The bridge is part of the core channel. Imagine the core extends from the base of the spine through the top of the head and continues upwards another foot to the Higher Self or Eighth Center.
This bridge links the crown to the Higher Self. By directing energy up through this bridge we are stimulating and opening the bridge and creating a more direct connection.

DEFINITION: Invocation - The process of reaching up

To invoke is what you do; it's your way of calling out and saying hello: "Hello Higher me/ Wise part of me/Higher Self/Existence/Spirit /God, be with me now." You send words, intention, emotion and a stream of energy upwards to create an energetic pathway.

DEFINITION: Evocation - What's evoked is the response that comes back

It's the magic. It might be a feeling, an insight, a picture or a vision – we never know until it happens. It might be as subtle as the fragrance of a tiny flower that's just barely sensed on the breeze, or it might be as powerful as a lighting bolt. The main thing is trust, surrender and letting go.

ENERGY PRINCIPLE 15:

Invocation and Evocation

The relationship of invocation and evocation is one of cause and effect. When you reach up, the energy world will respond back.

The Magic starts

Through invocation and evocation the magic starts. The higher dimension becomes more active. In fact, the higher has always been active. Though it is trying to reach down, the lower is so busy and noisy, so focused elsewhere, that we often don't notice and the higher has more difficulty penetrating. The moment you deliberately bring your energies up you are paying attention and have begun to open the channel. Whether you are generally opening upwards or asking specifics from the Beyond; you are becoming available for the magic.

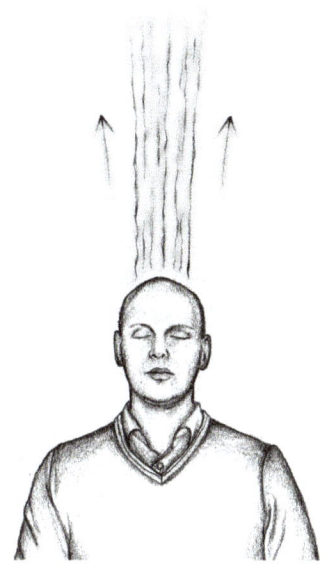

Invocation
Invocation is a "calling upwards" to the Higher Self

Exercise 15.1: Accessing the Beyond – Meeting the Magic

1. Go UP via the Bridge to the Higher Self

When you bring the energy to the top of the head on the UP movement, visualize it going through the top of the head and above it through the bridge. Imagine a ball of light about one foot above the head. See it as an extension of the core channel: imagine the core extends from the base of the spine through the top of the head and up to this ball of light. We can think of it as an eighth center or a Higher Self.

2. Make Contact with the Beyond

Imagine that you are making contact with the Beyond, the transcendent. You might visualize qualities here such as wisdom, love, compassion, vision or power. You might see it as your real home, your ultimate self or a doorway to the Spirit.

These are all different names to address different aspects of the rich spectrum contained here. Let the experience be yours; don't get caught by the names we call it, again, find what works for you. What's important is that you are open to access something higher.

3. Invoke – Call out to the Beyond

You might simply say, "Hello Higher me/ Wise part of me/Higher Self/ Existence/Spirit /God, be with me now." Or you might be more specific, holding the intention to get guidance, support and help on a particular subject, "Higher Self, help me understand _____."

Evocation
Evocation is the response from the above to our call

4. Evoke – Become receptive to the Response

As much as possible, be without expectations or demands. This is not a process of will or doing. This is not up to you now. You've done your part. You've sent the energy upwards. You've authentically asked and sent forth an invitation and intention. Now let go and be available. In its own way and time the magic from Beyond begins to work in you. It's begun.

5. The Higher responds

It is just amazing the things that start opening. It's not always immediate. It may not come in the same moment as your movement upwards, but the flow starts. The response might come immediately or in a day or a week or a month. But as you start invoking, something is evoked.

Quick Reference Points:

1. Go UP via the Bridge to the Higher Self
2. Make Contact with the Beyond
3. Invoke – Call out to the Beyond
4. Evoke – Become receptive to the Response
5. The Higher responds

When you listen to the Beyond, be open with all your senses. The response might come as a picture or a feeling. It might come as a physical sensation or in words. You might hear or see. You might get a sudden knowing, or even a smell or taste. Some of these signs might not make sense to you right away. Be patient - it's like learning a new language. Over time you will learn to understand and translate your perceptions.

To recognize "a Touch from the Beyond" be alert for some of the following:

- A sense of a higher vibration
- A feeling of being lighter and brighter
- Insight, clarity or information
- Unusual feelings or sensations in your body
- A bigger picture of yourself and the situations you are in
- More detachment from your own thoughts and emotions
- So called "coincidences" that occur bringing connections, information or people that have a special significance

- An awareness that you are more than the "little self", the personality, with all it's patterns, noise, busyness and thoughts
- A sense of deeper significance, of greater things at work
- A sense of purpose
- And many more ways that the Beyond may make itself known to you that we haven't thought to mention. Be alert for the 'Touch of Magic.'

Your practical mind might say, "these beautiful and insightful states are fine for a blissful meditation. But what about my daily life, my job, my family duties?"

Imagine having this at work in your daily life. Talk about the ultimate energy skill; these states of higher consciousness are it! You start living at a high level of intelligence, love and power that overflows into every area of your life, and you handle all these areas in entirely new, life supportive

The Higher Self present in normal life
Through working with the Beyond the Higher Self becomes more and more present in your daily life

and positive ways.

Christiane:

In fact, these higher spaces had an immediate effect on my daily life. Meeting another person became more exciting. My experience of nature became richer. Meditations became a joy. And access to what we call the Higher Mind offered continual guidance in my life. I now take wiser decisions. I feel in a better flow at my work.

My happiness becomes increasingly independent from outer circumstances and other people's actions. My life is so much more fulfilled life than ten years ago.

What's most important to me is, I found my purpose: to help others find this connection as well. That has become both my central-most drive and my peace of mind. I have a deep sense of why I'm here and what this life is about. I feel connected to something bigger and sense that I am not doing it on my own - a higher force is supporting me.

Today, 'Beyond', the transcendent, is a very natural part of myself and one of my greatest treasures. I lead seminars to support others to re-connect with their Higher Self, to access the Higher and gain intuition and inspiration. Life is really exciting now! And though in the process it sometimes seemed to take forever, that connection is the most important thing I have ever achieved in my life: I have found myself - my true Being.

This is the real goal of Energy Balancing – to awaken to this wondrous YOU.

Section Three

The Vertical
The Plane of Consciousness: UP, BEYOND and DOWN

Part 2 - DOWN

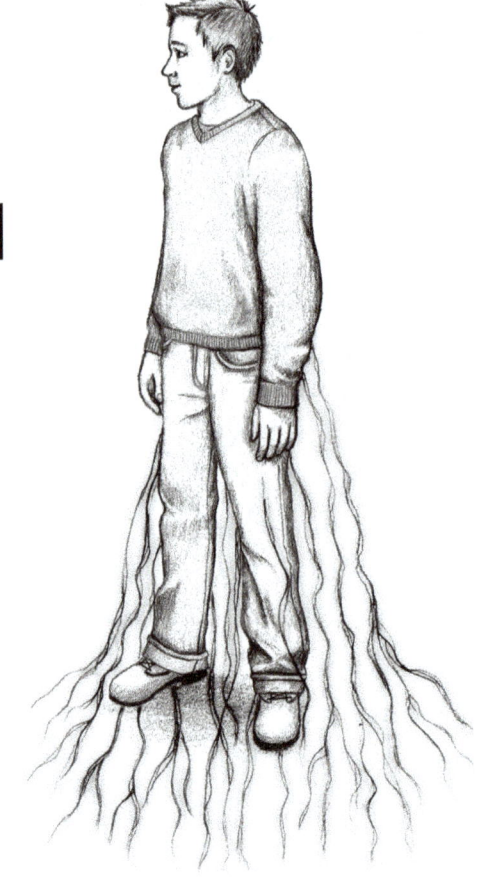

16 Bring the Higher Down - Make it Real

Spirituality is tangible

Margaretha:

I am seven years old and sitting in church. My father delivering his Sunday sermon is a faint murmuring in the background; my attention is elsewhere - I'm fascinated by the huge colored stones through which the light falls into the church. The colors are so intense, sparkling like the facets of over-sized diamonds. Looking at this wondrous play of light gives me continuous shivers down my spine and a strong tingling on my head. There is the presence of something higher. I don't give it much thought. It just feels natural and tangible. God - the higher - is an experience in my body.

Although I would, from time to time, touch these elevated states while listening to music or being with nature, this experience slowly faded and was nearly lost. 27 years later my connection to that Greater opened back again, but this time so much stronger. In an energy session suddenly my crown center popped back open and energy flooded into my system. It was so strong my arms were lifted up wide to the side - I just couldn't help it. Like Michelangelo's Vitruvian Man I stood and started laughing and shaking, losing all sense of time and space. Powerful energies streamed like bubbles of champagne through my whole body. From that moment on my life has never been the same...

ENERGY PRINCIPLE 16:

The physicality of spirituality

Spirituality is an experience in the body

To experience the Beyond is one of the most significant and uplifting experiences that can ever occur for a human being. It opens dimensions of intelligence, love, power and purpose that are truly extraordinary. This experience forever alters you. You have a new energy, a wider vision, and an insight into life and its many situations. You literally begin to live on a higher dimension of consciousness that alters everything else in your life.

But even this is not the end goal. In fact, we call it only the halfway point. The second half of the journey is to bring this consciousness back down, to live it in your body and mind and emotions. As we see in Margaretha's story above, this downpour of energy becomes a physical and tangible experience. It starts to live within your body. You learn to put it into practice, to express it in your actions, and to let it transform your life. Every single aspect of who you are and the life you live comes to carry this experience.

ENERGY PRINCIPLE 17:

Manifesting the Higher

We are here to bring down the higher energies of our soul and give them form in our body, mind, emotions and actions

As the Beyond opens you awaken to a higher sense of purpose. You know that you are here for a reason, and that all that occurs has a deeper significance.

Having this connection to purpose challenges you to live this purpose. It's one thing to envision a better world. It's another thing to get out there and effectively do something about it.

This is the challenge of DOWN – to make it real. Good ideas are generally useless if you don't do anything with them. As the old saying goes, "The road to hell is paved with good intentions." Good ideas without a grounded and realistic application can be not just useless, they can even be destructive.

> DOWN means to bring down the higher frequency energy and consciousness of the Beyond into this world, into this body and this personality. It's to live your soul here on earth.

Every one of us faces the challenge of living the higher aspects of our self that we occasionally make contact with here in this world. Who has not wrestled with having a beautiful thought but not being able to express it well? Or having an intention but being unable to execute it to the fullest of what you intended? Or having an addiction – food, cigarettes, alcohol, drugs – or even simply a bad habit, that you set about to change, only for it to get the upper hand again? In all these cases we were unable to ground our higher knowing.

Being Grounded

This word "grounded" is a keynote of Down. If we use the word "transcendent" as a keynote of Beyond, indicating something that gives us wings and lifts us to a higher dimension, so grounded is the opposite end of the pole. It keeps us real. It connects us to the body. It puts us in touch with nature and the natural world. It deals with practicals and tangibles, not as something mundane, or drudgery, but rather as the embodiment of something higher, as the expression in form of the

Grounding
Higher energies coming down, infusing the
body and grounding

formless. It's the ability to bring down this more ideal You, these higher thoughts and feelings, and being really able to live You, this big, wondrous rich You, here in this world.

Let's explore this state of being grounded. You have certainly had the experience of feeling dizzy and lightheaded. Whether it came about because of standing up too fast, of having been ill, or having ingested a mind-altering substance, in that moment you were not grounded. You were unstable, wobbly and fragile.

 **DEFINITION: Grounding**

Grounding is the ability to bring down higher vibrational energies, thoughts and feelings and ground them here in this world. Grounding keeps us real, connects us to the body and puts us in touch with nature and the natural world.

Now contrast this with a moment when you were grounded. Perhaps you were playing a sport and were really "on" with your game. Your feet anchored you firmly into the ground. You placed your steps flawlessly. You were agile, dynamic and balanced, each movement coordinated, using the earth to jump, run and push forwards potently. Nice feeling, wasn't it?

Sportsperson being dynamic and grounded

Person being grounded whilst writing a check

Let's look at another aspect of being grounded; the sense of being practical and realistic. It might have been in a very ordinary moment such as balancing your checkbook or paying the bills. In that moment you were on top of things; your cash flow was clear, you were responsibly taking care of your commitments, and you had that good feeling that comes when you have a handle on things.

Now let's look at one more aspect of grounding; whether it be digging in your garden, hiking in the mountains, or burying your feet in the sand on the beach; you have certainly had moments when you were in tune with nature, where you were in your body and your senses and you felt an at-oneness with the natural world. What a wonderful feeling. It leaves you so satisfied and full.

Though the three examples above address different aspects of grounding, there is a common thread: you are present, here and now. You are connected to this moment and what you are doing. With each example you are flowing with it, in tune with it, balanced, connected and centered.

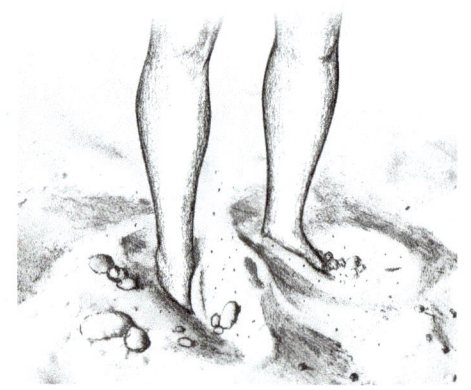

Person being grounded through having their feet in the sand

Here some key points to describe being grounded:

- You have your feet on the earth, in reality or metaphorically
- You are practical
- You are here and now
- You are realistic
- You are connected to the earth, this moment, the energies around
- You are anchored solidly in your body

Why would you want this? Why is it important to you? And why is it an energy skill?

When you are grounded you are in touch with this moment and the world around. You are not somewhere else in your mind. You are present and alert, and this makes you effective. To give you an example, have you ever driven while having a conversation on your cell phone? Or even worse, have you ever tried dialing a phone number while driving?

This is a moment when you're not paying attention to the car and the road. Your attention is elsewhere. Did you know that a staggering 28% of car accidents are due to talking or texting on the phone?

Being Ungrounded

With driving, the results of not being grounded and present can be catastrophic. With most other activities, the results are not so obvious but still destructive to us. At the minimum we simply miss the moment. Have you ever been in a beautiful place in nature but were so busy in your mind with something else that you hardly noticed the beauty around you? More frequently, when we're not grounded we make mistakes; we're clumsy, we don't think things through, or we end up trampling on others or the situation because we're not attuned.

Another example of being ungrounded is a person who has their head in the clouds. You may have known someone (or yourself) being enamored with a great idea and it really was a great idea. But it wasn't realistic; it wasn't down to earth or practical. Not that ideas have to be practical. In fact, most good ideas start as dreams, far removed from reality. But someone then takes these ideas and brings them down and begins to build them. You are probably familiar with the expressions, "an air head", or a person living in "la la land". They refer to someone whose way out there, not realistic, not connected or grounded. They feel like they're living in a fantasy world, divorced from reality.

Ungrounded person with energies swirling around their head

Or have you ever asked someone how they're doing and they start telling a story that goes on and on and on, like you really need to hear every single nuance for you to get it.

And actually, a two-word answer like, "I'm sad" would have said more, been more grounded, and more effective? We refer to this as "story". People spend a lot of time in story.

Contrast "la la land" with a person who is grounded; they are here, connected and in touch with the now. A grounded person is an effective person. Not that being grounded is about doing. You can simply be, doing nothing, but you are effective in that you are here and present. And because you are in touch you are also effective in your responses to the now.

Here's a simple exercise: Try saying to someone who is in story, "I really want to hear you but I'm getting lost in all the words and details. Can you instead tell me in three words, what are you really feeling?"

How can you know when you're not grounded?

Here are some key points to describe not being grounded:

You might feel…

- Clumsy
- Disconnected
- Mental - in your head, thinking about something else, past or future
- Not in your senses
- Overly fragile
- Lacking earth strength, vitality, endurance

Situations where you might be ungrounded:

- In Meetings
- Being fragile due to illness, lack of sleep, drugs
- After long hours at the computer
- Waking up and not being in your body

I, Kabir, had to laugh when I first heard the expression "death by meeting". I have sat through all too many meetings that were a living hell. There's something about a group of people all going mental, then feeding on each other's mental until you are so ungrounded, so in your head that you just want to scream.

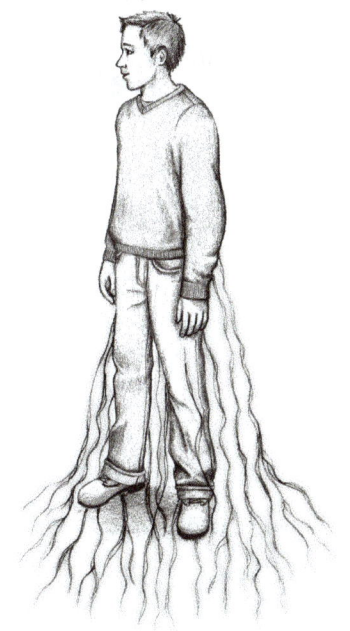

The Energetics of being grounded
When you are grounded the energy is flowing in your core and anchors through the bottom of the spine, your base, into the earth

Four Easy Ways to ground Yourself

So what can we do about it? You can simply bring the energy down. Being grounded is a state of energy flowing downwards and anchoring via the base at the bottom of the spine, through our legs and into the earth. It's an energetic state that is easy to reach.

Exercise 16.1: Breathe it Down

1. Take a full breath in and then emphasize the exhale. As you exhale visualize the energy flowing down your spine to your base, located at the coccyx, the bottom of your spine. The base contains a great reservoir of life energy called the Kundalini energy.

2. Imagine your base as a basin holding life force. Let your breath fill this basin until you feel it full and charged with life force.

3. Then let the breath continue down to the earth. Feel yourself connecting to the earth. Ground to the earth.

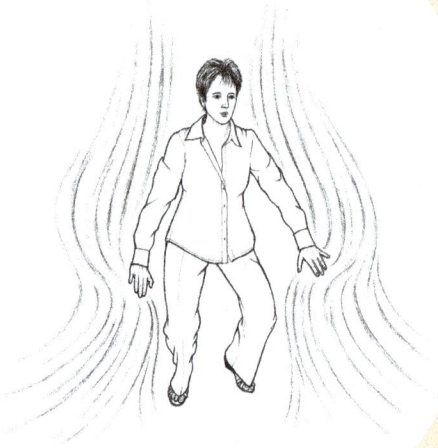

Breathing energies down

Exercise 16.2: Bring your Energy Down

1. Lift your arms up in front of your body and, palms facing down, slowly sweep energy down to your base. Do this several times.

2. Now go to wherever your hands can reach in the upper area of your energy field – way out in front of yourself, to the sides and above the head - and repeat the down movement. Imagine bringing yourself out from your mind and down into your body.

Bringing your energy down

3. With your hands open the energies around your base, widening this area.

4. To ground, continue the down sweep towards your feet. Take time to feel the flow through your legs and through your joints into the earth.

5. Imagine a point some feet into the earth – like an imaginary gravitational center - that you can relax and anchor into.

Exercise 16.3: Grow Your Roots

1. Take one hand in front of your body and one behind, palms facing down, and gently move the hands downwards to your base and below. Imagine that your hands are helping to open the energies of the base downwards.

2. Connect to the earth. Imagine yourself like a tree and see your "roots" anchored deeply within it. Feel the grounding, solidity and nurturance this gives you.

Grow your roots

Exercise 16.4: Pump Your Base

1. Stand with your knees slightly bent, and hold your hands next to your hips, palms facing down parallel to the ground.

2. Now begin to move your body down as if you are pushing the air towards the ground. Come back up with your inhale and push down with your exhale. Start slowly and then intensify the movement.

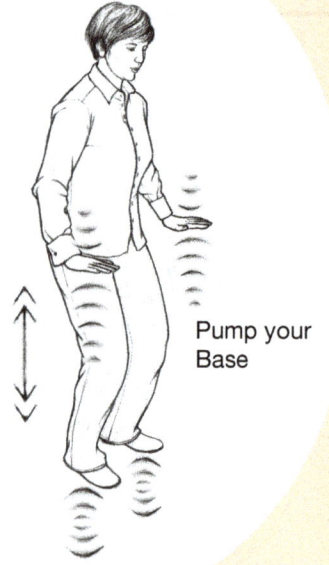

3. To this rhythmic motion add a deep sound "HUH", everytime you pump downwards. Let it come from deep in your body.

4. Relax and feel the vibration of energy heated up.

Pump your Base

Four Quick Ways to ground Yourself

And if you really only have a few minutes to ground yourself, you can choose one of the following quick versions.

Exercise 16.5: Drop your Arms

Bring your arms over your head and hold them for a moment. Breathe. Then let your arms drop to your sides. Feel the gravity.

Exercise 16.6: Stamp the Ground

Stamp your feet into the ground as hard you can. (if you wear high heels, you might take them off before ☺). Kick against the ground until you can feel your feet warm and charged with energy.

Exercise 16.7: Simply Move

Move – simply moving the body brings you back into it

Exercise 16.8: Tune to the Physical

Connect to the physical world around you, even if it is an artificial plastic business room. Just feel the earth that this room rests upon, even if it's 20 stories down.

And if you are courageous, you can do a more advanced intervention in an ungrounded situation, where others are involved:

Exercise 16.9: Advanced Grounding Intervention

If you feel you can, tell the group that they all need to get back in their bodies and ask everyone to stand up, move the body and do the arms dropping exercise. Try something like, "Guys, I need to stop for a moment. I feel so in my head and disconnected from my body. I need to ground again. I think we all do. Could we all stand up for a moment and do a short grounding exercise together please?"

17 Energy and Consciousness – Your Higher Calling

The Higher Purpose of Energy Balancing

The World of Energy is incredible! The moment you begin to open your eyes and understand what is going on, an entirely new dimension of life emerges. It's wonderful, magical, wacky and sometimes plain weird. But whatever it is - the awareness of energy alters you forever. For once you "get energy" you have forever stepped into another dimension of living; you have an x-ray insight into what's really going on in situations and you have new skills to handle things.

Now that you're living in the energy world, you realize that it's not just another, more interesting place, but that you've set foot on a Path that is taking you somewhere. Opening yourself to the world of energy begins a journey. Where is it leading you?

As you've saw throughout this book, there are the various layers of energy and at the center is your core, the Golden Being of your Essence. Energy reveals that you are an immense being. Your potentials of consciousness, love, intelligence and creatorship are incredible beyond measure.

ENERGY PRINCIPLE 18:

The higher calling of energy
Energy seeks to unfold higher vibration and higher consciousness

The goal of Energy Balancing is to unfold and live the immensity of your consciousness - and to live it in the most immediate, down-to-earth and practical ways possible as you relate, work, communicate and create.

Entering the world of energy you recognize that this unfoldment of consciousness is a learning process. You come to see the "learning universe"; that the entire universe is evolving and that existence is taking you to greater and greater heights of consciousness and unfoldment of Being.

You recognize that you are in a unique classroom in the learning universe, what we call the "Earth School". Here you get specific teachings on life, consciousness and who you are. Understanding energy is one of the foundational teachings here, one that gives you a key to getting many other teachings. Through getting energy you have a framework that shows how and why things are the way they are, gives you direction on how to proceed, and the tools to do so.

Now it's the walking – using energy day-to-day, moment-to-moment as you dance with life and the myriad situations you are in. This is where consciousness comes in – becoming more and more aware of what is going on. The journey into energy is a journey into consciousness. As you become more conscious you become more aware of energy. As you use energy, you become more conscious. They are two poles of the same phenomena.

How can you proceed?

If you've read this far then energy has spoken to you. It has become more than a concept, it's a living spark that is alive inside and is seeking to burn brighter.

How can you proceed? Of course, we'd be remiss if we didn't tell you about the Energy Balancing Institute and the full Energy Balancing

Training. This is a unique entrance into the world of energy. You can take a basic program that will give you the ABC's of energy, and you get advanced training to become a Certified Energy Balancer for working with others.

We'd also be remiss if we didn't encourage you to get to know the 'Essence Training Inner Work School', where you can do the deep work of awakening. Essence Training is a powerful transformation process. Based on the Science of Human Potential it combines energy, inner work and meditation in one of the most powerful programs available for personal transformation. Both the Energy Balancing programs and Essence Training are amongst the top trainings in the world on energy and consciousness. For more on both of these, see chapter 20.

Of course we would like you to come and work with us. But we're realistic. Readers of this book are spread out all over the planet. And right now there are many great teachers and programs. So whether you do this work with us or someone else, there are three things we would like to encourage you towards.

1. Meditation

The first is meditation. Meditation is the process of turning your awareness inwards and coming attuned to your inner life.

We can't sing the praises of meditation strongly enough. For us, it's an absolutely foundational practice that quiets the mind and emotions, clears the noise of the inner and outer world, helps us find center and balance, and ultimately unlocks the doors to higher consciousness.

We also know that most people who try meditation don't stick with it. That's because in the beginning the chaos and tensions of the inner life are

A group meditation on the beach

so uncomfortable that we'd rather not face them and instead we run away through distracting ourselves with other things.

Definition: Meditation

Meditation is the process of turning your awareness inwards and coming attuned to your inner life, particularly your higher aspects. Meditation is also a powerful methodology that guides energies through certain channels to open higher levels of energy, consciousness and perception.

Energy Balancing plays an important role in meditation because it aligns and integrates the many unbalanced energies inside of us. Through creating balance Energy Balancing creates the foundation upon which meditation is built.

We can't encourage you enough to learn to meditate and to make meditation a part of your daily life. A half hour a day of meditation is one of the greatest gifts you can give to yourself, and one that grows and bears fruit forever.

The Latin root of the word meditation is mederi or medicare – the same root for the word medicine – meaning to heal, to cure, to get better. Meditation is a form of medicine for the soul. Just as there are different medicines for the different needs of the body, so are there different meditations for different needs of the psyche. You'll need to experiment to find what works best for you. If you find someone who understands the science of meditation and can help "prescribe" the right meditation for you, all the better.

There are many people and organizations offering training in meditation. You can also join us for our regular 10-day meditation retreats at the Esencia Retreat Center in the Caribbean.

2. Inner Work

In addition to meditation, we'd like to encourage you towards inner work. Inner Work is the process of maturing yourself. You work on the whole spectrum of you who are; from the physical, through the emotional and mental to the spiritual. You work to release unhealthy emotions, thought patterns and energetic disturbances you are carrying from your past. Most importantly, you come to recognize the many strengths and qualities you have, and what it means to mature and live them.

Inner work means to grow up. When we say "growing up" we are referring to the process of growing into a mature, conscious, potent and whole human being. It's a deliberate undertaking – you choose to grow, and you deliberately "till and plant and weed" the garden of your psyche.

The Soul and the Essence

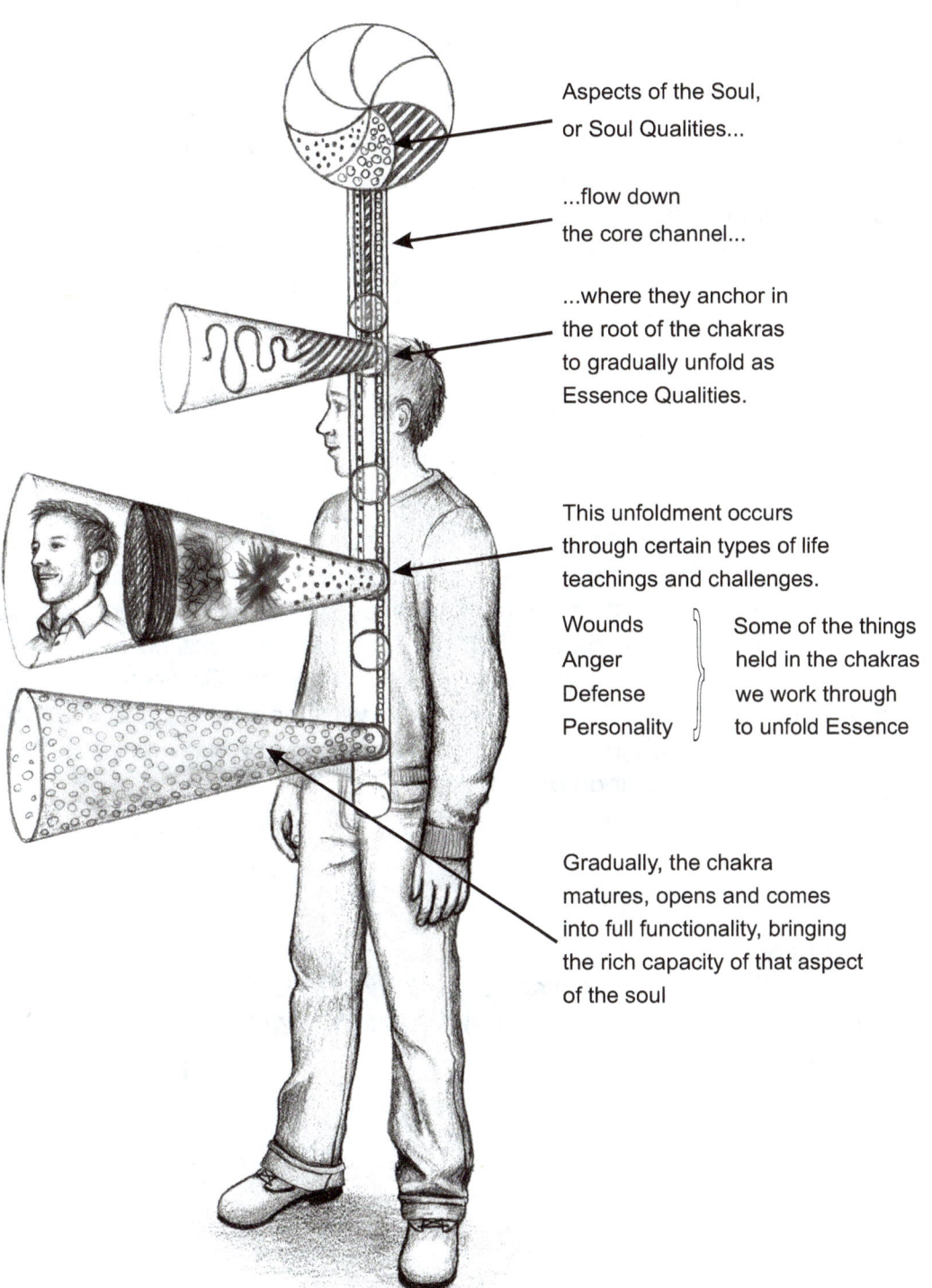

DEFINITION: Inner Work
Inner Work is the process of deliberately maturing yourself by directly 'working on' the various components of your psyche

There are a lot of good people and programs around today. You'll have to experiment a bit to see what works for you and to sort out the fluff from the good stuff, but jump in and begin. A good starting point is inner child work and working with your family past. We say this because so many of the issues we carry stem from childhood. Healing your family past (even if you come from a so-called "good" family) is essential for inner development.

3. Chakra Psychology

The third thing we would encourage you towards is in-depth exploration of the chakras. The chakras are an important aspect of our energy body. They are central to "getting energy", to inner work and meditation. As we mentioned in the beginning of this book, chakra work is so broad that we've decided to dedicate an entire book just to this. Some of the more advanced Energy Balancing trainings work with the chakras and Essence Training is completely based upon the chakras, each module of its programs being focused upon one chakra.

DEFINITION: Chakra Psychology
The emerging field of chakra psychology charts the full spectrum of consciousness from our earliest evolutionary origins up to and beyond the greatness of our soul.

The emerging field of chakra psychology charts the full spectrum of consciousness from our earliest evolutionary origins up to and beyond the greatness of our soul. To understand the chakras is a master key to unfolding our fullest potential. If you want to know yourself, come to know your chakras.

These three things – meditation, inner work and chakra psychology - together within the framework of energy will take you to places you've never even dreamed of, and will give you a fulfillment in life beyond anything you thought possible.

We would like to encourage you to go deep into this journey. We see each human being as point of light within the bigger tapestry of Life, and when one person lifts their vibration, it radiates out to affect the greater whole. Imagine our planet with millions of people, someday billions of people, becoming energy aware, conscious and mature human beings. This is ultimately the goal of this book – a mature and enlightened planetary civilization. Play your part.

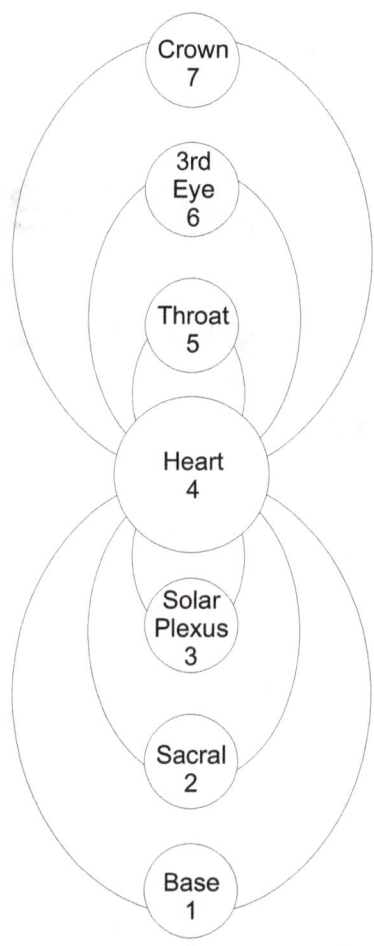

Chakra Psychology
The Chakra System

Enlightened Group Work
An Essence Training module - a group of people working together and building a group field that lifts everyone

Section Four

Orchestrating your Energies

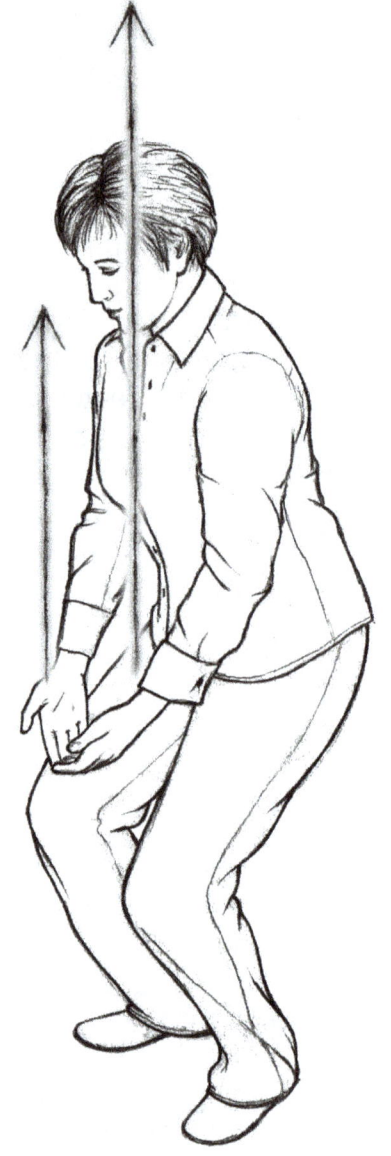

18 Our Fundamental Energy Balancing Exercise and its Variations: FEBE, QEBE and EEBE

The Full Energy Balancing Exercise (FEBE) - what it and why it is so powerful

The Full Energy Balancing Exercise (FEBE) combines all the primary movements of Energy Balancing in one complete and powerful exercise. This short two-minute sequence will quickly help you come into balance and center. It will clear your mind, center your emotions and balance your energy.

Not only will it be effective each time you do it, but its effects are cumulative. Each time you do it you are etching in more deeply these energetic pathways, taking you deeper and deeper into the richness of who you are.

To perform the physical movements alone is valuable. But to understand what each movement is doing and to give it the "right attention" through presence and the use of awareness to move energy, will bring you much greater benefit.

Once you understand what each movement is doing and how the "right attention" -through presence and awareness - moves energy, will it bring you much greater benefit.

We have several versions of this exercise. The FEBE covers the full spectrum of Energy Balancing in 2 minutes, though you can repeat it multiple times sequentially. The short version, the Quick Energy Balancing Exercise

(QEBE) can be done in 30 seconds. There is also an Extended Energy Balancing Exercise (EEBE) which can take anywhere between 10 to 30 minutes and can be personalized according to your needs.

Links to Online-Videos of FEBE and QUEBE

You can find video clips of these exercises on our website at www.energy-balancing.me that best illustrate the entire process.

An Overview of the Full Energy Balancing Exercise (FEBE)

There are several stages in FEBE that reflect the main materials covered in earlier chapters:

1. Centering to bring your energies in Grounding to bring your energies in the here and now

2. The upwards stream to create alignment and awaken the heart

3. Opening the energies out to expand

4. Bringing the energies in to come back to yourself

5. Lifting the energies to the crown and above to invoke the higher (invocation)

6. Opening yourself for the energies evoked (evocation)

7. Bringing down theses frequencies to embody and ground them

8. Ending by coming back to center, now with a clear and defined field

As a preparation for doing the FEBE, choose a space with as little distractions as possible. Things like ringing phones, electronics or other person can easily interrupt your practice.

Performing the FEBE

Exercise 18.1: **The Full Energy Balancing Exercise (FEBE)**

1. Centering (IN)

Stand with your feet shoulder width apart. Place your hands on your heart, close your eyes and come to center.

2. Grounding (DOWN)

Inhale. Now, on your exhale, with palms facing the ground, bend your knees slightly and move your hands slowly downwards to your base.

3. Lifting Energy up to the Heart (UP)

As you inhale, use your hands, palms facing to the ceiling, to lift the energy up the core channel to your heart.

4. Opening Yourself (OUT)

As you exhale, move your hands slowly from your heart forwards and to the sides to open yourself out. Palms are facing up.

5. Bringing Energy back to the Core (IN)

Inhaling, bring your hands back to the front in an arc and towards your heart to center.

6. Reaching up to the BEYOND (UP)

Exhale and with palms facing up lift the energy with your hands from your heart upwards over your head as high as you can reach to invoke the Higher (invocation).

7. Inviting the Higher (DOWN)

Inhale and evoke the energies of your crown down by slowly opening your arms to the sides, palms facing up (evocation).

8. Grounding the Higher (DOWN)

As soon as your arms reach the level of the heart, exhale, turn your palms to the ground and continue the movement down to the base.

9. Repeating the Cycle twice

Continue the cycle by lifting your energy UP to the heart, (no.3) and repeating the succession from no.3 to no.8 another two times.

10. Resting in CENTER

End your last cycle by lifting your energy up to the heart and then, exhaling, letting your hands rest on your heart. Come back to your center.

Quick Reference Points:

1. *Centering (IN)*
2. *Grounding (DOWN)*
3. *Lifting Energy up to the Heart (Up)*
4. *Opening (OUT)*
5. *Bringing Energy back to the Core (IN)*
6. *Reaching up to the BEYOND (UP)*
7. *Inviting the Higher (DOWN)*
8. *Grounding the Higher (DOWN)*
9. *Repeating the cycle twice (no.3-no.8)*
10. *Resting in CENTER*

1. Centering (IN)

The Quick Energy Balancing Exercise (QEBE)

The QEBE lifts you in 30 seconds out of the normal chaos with two simple movements, which we call "One Sweep – One Flow":

The Extended Energy Balancing Exercise (EEBE)

The EEBE is a free form version of the Full Energy Balancing Exercise. When working with your own energy you will sometimes feel that one direction or aspect of energy needs more attention than another. Perhaps you are too much out and feel you need to spend more time bringing yourself in to center. Or perhaps you are too much UP in your head and need to get grounded.

With the EEBE you spend as much time as you need in each section. When you feel complete in that section, move on to the next step. Tailor the exercise to your specific needs. You can change the order or do just those steps that you feel you need right now.

Exercise 18.2: The Quick Energy Balancing Exercise (QEBE)

1. DOWN

Stand with your feet shoulder width apart. Inhale and with your exhale bring your hands, palms facing down, to the base. Slightly bend your knees.

2. UP

Let yourself now 'collect' the energies of your base and imagine holding them in your hands. Inhaling, strongly "sweep" the energy with your arms, palms facing upwards, all the way up over your head as high as you can comfortable reach.

3. OUT

As you exhale, let your arms open out slowly to your sides and continue the movement slowly all the way down to your base.

4. Repeat

"Sweep" the energy with vigor up again and repeat **"One Sweep, One Flow"** at least another two times.

5. IN

Close your eyes to go in and take note of your center.

DOWN

UP

OUT

REPEAT

IN

Purpose of each of the 7 steps for the EEBE

1. Clear your Field	Gets the "stuff" out – whether it be your own disturbed emotional or mental energies or the energies from other people, from machines or the environment.
2. Go In and Center	Brings you back in when you feel yourself too much out of yourself, which can come from strong emotions, relating to others or being caught in doing,
3. Charge your Base	Brings vitality for when you feel: low energy, tired, frozen, fearful, blocked thinking, collapsed, needy, shame or guilt. Activates the Kundalini (life force).
4. Go Upwards	Helps you for when you want to step out of personality chaos; supports vertical alignment and connection to your essence or higher resources.
5. Connect to the Beyond	Connects you to your potential, to higher wisdom, intuition and inspiration.
6. Bring the Higher Down	Anchors your higher energies in your body; brings consciousness, new insights and perspectives into your system and life; helps to manifest your vision, come into potency and be proactive.
7. Build a Ring-Pass-Not	Contains your energy vibrantly; gives clear boundaries; builds a protective edge to your field.

Exercise 18.3: **The Extended Energy Balancing Exercise (EEBE)**

1. **Clear your Field and get the Stuff out**

- **Clearing the field.** *Use your imagination and visualize the stuff that's clogging your energy field. Move your hands, with palms facing outwards, through your entire field away from your body. "See" yourself sweeping out the dust and energetic debris.*

2. **Go IN and center in your Core Channel**

- **Gathering your energies:** *Start with arms extended to the front, palms facing your body. Now begin to gather in your energies from all around you, slowly bringing them into your body.*

- **Resting in your core channel:** *Put one hand on your breast bone and one on your pubic bone, parallel to your core. Take a moment to breathe into your core. Tune to the peace that comes with being centered and of resting in who you are.*

3. **Charge and awaken the Fire of your Base**

- **Pumping:** *With your knees slightly bent and your hands to your sides, bob up and down. With your palms facing down push the energy towards the ground. Let a deep-throated sound "HUH" come every time you pump downwards. Do this for at least 3 minutes.*

4. **Move the Charge UP in your Core**

- **Charging the core channel between base and heart:** *On your next inhalation breathe the charge you've built in the base up to your heart. Then exhale the energy back down to your base. Repeat several times, until you feel a stronger vibration in your core channel.*

- **Helping hands:** *As you inhale, let your hands, palms facing up, lift the energies up from the base to your heart. Turn your palms and push the energies with your exhale back down to your base. Repeat this sequence several times in a Tai Chi like movement. End the sequence with your hands on the height of your heart.*

5. Connect to the Beyond

- **From the Heart up to the Higher Self:** *Let the breath in your heart now become softer as you enter the more subtle energies in the upper part of your body. Exhale and lift your energies with your hands from your heart up through the top of your head and beyond.*

- *Inhale deeply and let your arms open to the sides, slowly coming back to your heart area.*

- *Again lift the energies from your heart up to the Higher Self, about one foot over your head. Repeat at least 3 times.*

- **Aligning yourself vertical:** *After the last repetition, hold your arms up as high as possible, palms facing each other over your head. Hold for a moment, breathe as relaxed as possible and feel the stretch.*

6. Bring the Higher down and anchor it

- **Fanning the Higher from Beyond to Base:** *Bring the energies slowly from above your crown down to your base, palms facing the body, Imagine gently fanning higher frequencies- light, consciousness and wisdom - into your energy field. Repeat several times.*

- **Grounding the Higher:** *Continue the down sweep to your feet. Take time to increase the flow of higher energies through your legs and joints into the earth.*

- **Growing Roots:** *Imagine yourself like a tree and see your "roots" expanded and anchored deeply within the ground. Feel the solidity this gives you - anchor and relax into it*

7. Build a Containing and Protective Ring-Pass-Not

- **Radiating from Center:** *Visualize your base grounded, the top of your head connected up, and your center radiating out about three feet in all directions.*

- **Defining your Boundaries:** *To help your system better contain this wonderful energy, move your hands from far out towards your body, palms facing in. See yourself condensing the boundary edge of the field up to about ten inches.*

- *Solidify your entire field – front, back, side, top and bottom.*

- When your energy field forms a clear and well-defined boundary, let your hands rest and relax.
- **Vibrating with the Higher and Holding your Center:** *Imagine your field now vibrating with higher energies of your core potential and at the same time holding a healthy Ring-Pass-Not.*

    Quick Reference Points:
    1. Clear your Field and get the Stuff out
    2. Go IN and center in your Core Channel
    3. Charge and awaken the Fire of your Base
    4. Move the Charge Upwards
    5. Connect to the Beyond
    6. Bring the Higher down and anchor it
    7. Build a Protective Ring-Pass-Not

19 Issue Quick Reference List

Look up issues - Diagnose problems - Find solutions!
A quick-reference resource to quickly guide you to the answers you need

Issues and Symptoms	Possible Energy Cause	Proposal for an Energetic Intervention	Refer to
Emotions			
Difficulties in relationship	Care, Love or Sucking Violation	Check if any kind of Care, Love or Sucking Violation is active. Take in "good" energies, block "harmful" energies; distinguish which is which.	**Chapter 12:** Love Violations (p.193) Care Violations (p.193) Sucking Violation (p.194) **Chapter 6:** Let the good Stuff IN 6.2 (p.114)
Turn on the 'Flame of your Heart'	Heart-flow blocked, limited or withheld	Open your heart. Awaken your heart. Ignite more love.	**Chapter 7:** Open Yourself 7.2 (p.129) **Chapter 14:** Awaken your Heart 14.1 (p.217) Ignite more Love 14.2 (p.218)
Aggravating emotional symptoms that throw you off balance, yet don't have an obvious cause	Transference - unconsciously resonating with another's emotions; picking up Energetic Goop	Identify the source of unwanted emotional energies. Clear "Goop" out of your energy system.	**Chapter 2:** Your Sensitivity to Energy **Chapter 3:** Dust your Energy Field 3.3 (p.51) Scoop the Goop 3.4 (p.59)

Feeling emotional numbness, frozenness or shock	Too much IN – unhealthy IN; field contractions	Open your contractions back up with Melting and with Energy Modelling.	**Chapter 9:** Melting an unhealthy IN state 9.1 (p.150) Using Energy Modelling to open unhealthy IN 9.2 (p.152)
Over-pleasing or overly care-taking others	Energy field is off center – too much OUT and in front	Come back to yourself. Experience your core channel.	**Chapter 4:** Bring your Field back to Center 4.1 (p.71) Core Channel Experience 4.2 (p.77)
Over-invested/ caught in other lives or them in yours	Overwhelm violations	Discover why love/ care can cause difficulties.	**Chapter 12:** Overwhelm Violations (p.191)
Overwhelming others with your emotions	Too much OUT and losing your energy	Check Energy Leakages.	**Chapter 8:** Seal your Energy Leak 8.2 (p.144)
Step out of emotional drama; becoming more of a "watcher"	Over-active lower chakras	Move the energy up. Shift to a higher level of consciousness. Discover the "Watcher" in you.	**Chapter 14:** Breathe to the Heart 14.2 (p.218) From Belly to Solar Plexus 14.3 (p.221) From Drama to Watcher 14.5 (p.225)

Domination and Control

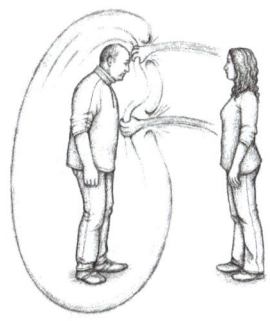

Overly dominating or controlling others - aggressive, bossy or pushy.	Too much OUT - spun up in Solar Plexus and charged in Base	Read about Aggression and Will Violations. Look into the 'Art of Impacting' and 'Offering versus Imposing'.	**Chapter 4:** Bring your Field back to Center 4.1 (p.69) **Chapter 12:** Aggression Violations Will Violations (p.186) **Chapter 11:** Offering versus Imposing 11.5 (p.178)

Ending up in confrontations	Unconsciously picking up or transmitting anger	Clear yourself. Read in chapter 10 about "Conscious and Unconscious Creatorship".	**Chapter 3:** Dust your Energy Field 3.3 (p.51) Scoop the Goop 3.4 (p.59)
			Chapter 10: Creatorship (p.160)
Manipulating others	Willing; Trespassing other's boundaries	Learn about Will Violation. Build a Ring-Pass-Not to contain your energy. Learn to give directions consciously.	**Chapter 12:** Will Violation (p.188)
			Chapter 8: Build a Ring Pass Not 8.1 (p.140)
			Chapter 11: How you give Directives 11.4 (p.178)

Self Confidence and Empowerment

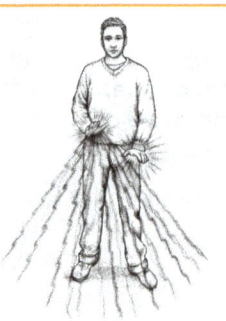

Being willed, dominated or manipulated by others	Energy violations; how others may be violating you; how you create this	Learn about Energy Violations. Take your personal space back. Saying "NO". Build a Ring-Pass-Not.	**Chapter 12:** Aggression Violations Will Violations Sucking Violations Taking over via Resonance and Leading (p.187-195)
			Chapter 7: Personal Space (p.125) Protect yourself 7.1 (p.127) Saying "NO" 7.4 (p.136)
			Chapter 8: Build a Ring Pass Not 8.1 (p.140)

Others dump their emotions or "stories" on you	Unhealthy IN; Not taking your personal space	Protect yourself by not taking in negative energies. Build healthy boundaries.	**Chapter 7:** Protect Yourself 7.1 (p.127)
			Chapter 8: Build a Ring Pass Not 8.1 (p.140)
Oversensitive, getting hurt, offended or knocked over easily	Too much IN - unhealthy boundaries; taking too much in	Come back out again with "Melting". Take next step with "Allowing Go".	**Chapter 4:** Back to Center 4.1 (p.71)
			Chapter 8: Build a Ring Pass Not 8.1 (p.140)
			Chapter 9: Melting unhealthy IN 9.1 (p.150)
			Chapter 13: Allowing GO! 13.1 (p.198)
Need for protection	Not protecting yourself	Build a protective wall.	**Chapter 7:** Protect yourself 7.1 (p.127)
Need for appreciation	Too much OUT – not connected to your core	Do the "Core Channel Experience". Shift you awareness from Belly to Solar Plexus. Connect with the Essence you already carry inside.	**Chapter 4:** Back to Center 4.1 (p.71) Core Channel Experience 4.2 (p.77)
			Chapter 14: From Dependency to Empowerment 14.3 (p.221)
			Chapter 13: Bring your Essence Qualities OUT 13.3 (p.203)

Disconnection

Feeling disconnected from your body or ungrounded	Too much UP - not grounded	Become more physical. Ground yourself as much as you can.	**Chapter 4:** Back to Center 4.1 (p.71)
			Chapter 16: Exercises to ground Yourself 16.1 – 16.9 (p.254-257)
Escaping mentally	Too much UP – and in the mind	Come fully back into the body, engage in the world and become more effective.	**Chapter 11:** Impacting Exercises 11.1 to 11.4 (p.173-178)
Spinning- or "Spaghetti"- Mind	Your Third Eye is clouded or overspun	Clear your head and your energy field. Do the "Tree Exercise".	**Chapter 3:** Dust your Energy Field 3.3 (p.51)
			Chapter 4: Tree Exercise 4.3 (p.80)
Daydreaming, being unrealistic or too "spiritual"	Higher disconnected from Lower - not effective	Ground yourself and bring your ideas and dreams down. Learn about sending energy with the right impact to the right location.	**Chapter 16:** Exercises to ground Yourself 16.1 – 16.9 (p.254-257)
			Chapter 11: The Art of Impacting (p.170)
Feeling cut off from the good stuff in life, lonely, emotionally starved	Walls closed your energy system	Learn to take the good stuff in again. Check out what your good energy sources are.	**Chapter 6:** Taking the Good Stuff IN 6.1 (p.107) Good Energy Sources List (p.116)
Disconnected from deeper self, inner feelings	Your vulnerability has become unavailable to you and others	Read more about "Conscious Vulnerability". Open yourself back up.	**Chapter 7:** Open yourself back up 7.2 (p.1299

Lack of Energy

Feeling clogged, sluggish, chaotic or cloudy	Energy field is clogged with "Energetic Stuff"	Check the quality of the energies of the people and places around you. Clear and dust your field from the energies you've identified.	**Chapter 2:** Your Sensitivity to Energy (p.29) **Chapter 3:** Dust your Energy Field 3.3 (p.51)
Lost your drive, feeling tired, flat or lazy like a "couch potato"	Too much DOWN – energy is flat	Center yourself to come back to your Self. Awaken your base physically and energetically to find new energy.	**Chapter 4:** Back to Center 4.1 (p.71) **Chapter 16:** Pump your Base 16.4 (p.255)
Feeling frustrated, hopeless, sad or depressed	Too much DOWN – energy is collapsed	Lift your energies UP.	**Chapter 14:** Moving from Lower to Heart 14.4 (p.223)
Suffering from addictions – food, drink, drugs, sex	Energy Leakages; disconnected from your higher energies	Learn more about Energy Leakages and seal them. Shift your awareness from lower to higher. Connect to your wisdom. Meet your higher self to find inspiration and purpose.	**Chapter 8:** Seal your Energy Leakage 8.2 **Chapter 14:** Moving from Lower to Higher 14.4 (p.223) From Personality to Wisdom 14.6 (p.228) **Chapter 15:** Meet the Magic 15.1 (p.239)

Manifestation

Juggling too many balls, spun-up or scattered in your actions	Too much OUT and hyped/spun up	Center yourself to come back to your Self. Ground and align yourself with the Tree Exercise.	**Chapter 4:** Back to Center 4.1 (p.71) Core Channel 4.2 (p.76) Tree Exercise 4.3 (p.80)
Longing to create the life you want - effective, empowered and joyful	Held back energies; not yet recognizing your potential or using your full energy	Become your own master. Read about Creatorship and "Conscious Ownership". Learn the art of sending energy from center and creating the impact you really want. Enhance and strengthen your Essence.	**Chapter 10:** Creatorship and Conscious Ownership (p.167) **Chapter 11:** The Art of Impacting (p.170) **Chapter 14:** Shift in Consciousness (p.209) **Chapter 13:** The Art of Bringing your Essence OUT (p.196)

Energies in Motion

The 4 directions of energy flow		FEBE and QEBE create alignment and balance in your energy system.	**Chapter 18:** **Orchestrate your Energies:** The Full and the Quick Energy Balancing Exercise 18.1 and 18.2 (p.269 and 272)
Got time for more		Learn more about the purpose of each of the 7 steps of the Extended Energy Balancing Exercise (EEBE) and try it out.	**Chapter 18:** The Extended Version of the Energy Balancing Exercise (EEBE) 18.3 (p.275)

Growth of Consciousness

Shift and grow your consciousness		Lift your energies up to higher centers of consciousness.	**Chapter 14:** The Shift in Your Consciousness (p.209)
Meet the Magic		Get more insights into the significance of your Higher Self and the Beyond.	**Chapter 15:** Meeting the Magic of the Higher (p.230)
Grow beyond personality into wisdom		Discover your crown as a center of wisdom, intuition and insight.	**Chapter 14:** Moving from Lower Six Centers to Crown 14.6 (p.228)

Support your own personal and/or spiritual growth		Read more about the tools and the purpose of Energy Balancing, Energy Psychology, Meditation and Inner Work.	**Chapter 17:** Energy and the Unfoldment of your Consciousness (p.259)

Knowledge

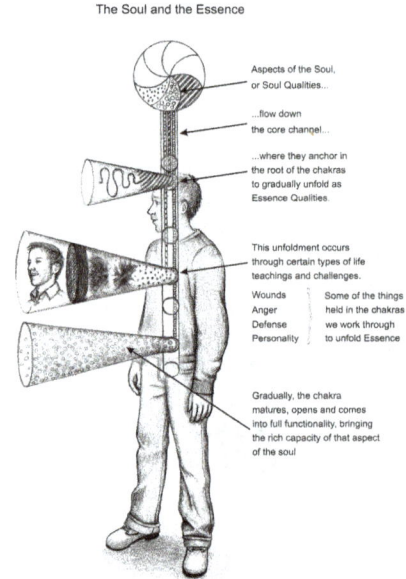

Plane of Action and Plane of Consciousness		Read about Vertical and Horizontal, the Circular Flow of Energy and IN-UP-DOWN-OUT.	**Chapter 4:** The Four Directions of Energy Flow (p.67)
Search for a term, an Energy Principle or a Definition		You'll find all 18 Energy Principles at one glance in Chapter 20. The glossary offers our definition of most of the Energy terms.	**Chapter 20:** 18 Energy Principles at one glance (p.287)
			Chapter 21: Glossary (p.290)
Continue Energy Balancing		Check our website for current programs in your area and for online-trainings.	**Chapter 22:** About the Energy Balancing Institute (p.297)

20 All 18 Energy Principles at one Glance

Number	Name	Energy Principle	Image	Chapter:
1	The human energy field is an antenna	The human energy field is like an antenna of the finest sensitivity.		2
2	Energy – the subtle fabric that underlies everything	The term Energy as we use it refers to a subtle world of forces that exist within ourselves, flows between us and other people, and is everywhere and in everything.		3
3	Energy is substance	Our thoughts, our feelings and our very life energy are a substance.		3
4	Everything is vibration	Not only physical matter, but life energy, thoughts and feelings are all composed of frequencies of vibration in the substance of energy.		3
5	Energy follows awareness	Energy flows where your attention goes		3

Number	Name	Energy Principle	Image	Chapter:
6	Energy Transference	Energy can be transferred between people, places and things.		3
7	The energy field has layers	A human being is like an onion, composed of many layers		3
8	Center – an energetic location	Center is an energetic location in the middle of your body. It is a vertical channel of energy running from the base of the spine to the top of the head		4
9	Center - an energetic state	Being centered is an energetic state where your energy is rooted within the core channel, creating alignment and integration throughout your entire energy system.		4
10	The four directions of energy flow	Energy flows in four primary directions relative to a human being		5
11	We are powerful transmitters of energy	Every moment we send out powerful energies from our energy field		10
12	Every layer of the human energy field creates.	Each layer creates and has its particular effect upon situations.		10

Number	Name	Energy Principle	Image	Chapter:
13	Energy lifts consciousness	The process of moving energy from a lower to a higher state lifts the level of consciousness		14
14	Higher consciousness opens at the top of the head	Directing energy to the top of the head stimulates higher states of consciousness		15
15	Invocation and Evocation	The relationship of invocation and evocation is one of cause and effect. When you reach up, the energy world will respond back.		15
16	The physicality of spirituality	Spirituality is an experience in the body		16
17	Manifesting the Higher	We are here to bring down the higher energies of our soul and give them form in our body, emotions, mind and actions		16
18	The higher calling of energy	Energy seeks to unfold higher vibration and higher consciousness		17

21 GLOSSARY of the most important Energy Terms

Term	Definition	Chapter
Alignment	*Alignment* refers to a state of the energy field when all energy centers are aligned, balanced and harmonious and functioning as an integrated whole.	4, 14
Beyond	*Beyond* represents a dimension of higher consciousness that is available to everyone – commonly referred to by names such as higher intelligence, soul, or spirit. It is accessed through a vertical channel of energy that rises above the head about 1 ft. where it connects to an 8th chakra or energy center.	5, 15
Boundaries (Conscious Boundaries)	*Boundaries* refer to the edge of the human energy field, like the eggshell surrounding the contents of an egg. A *conscious boundary* is the ability to put up a protective wall and not let things come in that shouldn't, or to contain your energies that they don't inappropriately flow out (also see *'Ring-Pass-Not'*).	7
Bridge	The *bridge* is the part of the core channel between the top of the head (the *Crown*) and the Eighth Center (or *Higher Self*), about one foot above the head. By directing energy up through this bridge we are stimulating and opening it and creating a more direct connection to higher consciousness and the magic of the Beyond (also see, *core channel'*, *'Crown'*, *'Higher Self'*, *'Beyond'*).	15
Center	The balanced position of your energy field. The field is centered, versus off center - too much in the front, back, sides, up or down (also see *'off-center'*). The location of the core channel in front of the spinal column in which energy runs vertically (also see *'core channel'*). The place and sense deep inside of you where you are in contact with your innermost and true Being. (also see *'Essence'*, *'Golden Being'*).	4, 11

Chakra Psychology	The emerging field of *chakra psychology* explores the seven energy centers (chakras) within the human energy system and the ways they affect our feelings, thoughts, body, behaviors and our energy.	17
Charge	*Charge* is a state of fullness in the energy field - like a charged battery. *Charge* brings vitality to everything you do.	6
Circular Flow of Energy	Energy Balancing is based on four directions of energy flow – IN, UP, DOWN and OUT. We speak of a *Circular Flow of Energy* when energy flows in a healthy way in these directions, nurturing, grounding and connecting you. The *Full Energy Balancing Exercise (FEBE)* gives a good example how you can integrate this *Circular Flow of Energy* into your daily life (see chapter 18).	5, 18
Clearing	*Clearing* is the process of removing unwanted energies from our energy field (also see 'stuff', 'dust', 'goop' and 'layers'.)	3
Consciousness	*Consciousness* is a "gestalt", a state of awareness and a way of looking at the world that includes feelings as well as thoughts.	14, 15, 17
Conscious creatorship	*Conscious creatorship* is when you are aware of the energies you radiate and are skillful in creating the effects you want (also see *'creatorship'* and *'unconscious creatorship'*).	10
Core Channel	The *core channel* is a vertical channel of energy located in the very center of your energy body that runs from the base of the spine to the top of the head. It parallels the spinal column but sits in front of it, in the middle of your torso.	4
Creatorship	*Creatorship* is our capacity to effect and shape the environment through the energy we send out (see also *Unconscious* and *Conscious Creatorship*).	10
Crown	The *crown* is an energy center at the top of our head. It is an important center in energy balancing as it's used for breathing energy *UP* to lift consciousness (see chapter 14). It is the *crown*, that enables us via the *Bridge* to experience the *Beyond* (see chapter 15, also see *'Bridge'* and *'Beyond'*). The *Crown* is also part of the Center exercise *'The Tree'* in which you bring energy up through the *core channel* up into the crown to open it like a tree's canopy (see chapter 4). (Also see *'Center'*, *'Core Channel'*, *'The Tree'*, *'UP'* and *'Beyond'*).	4, 14, 15,
Dynamic Center	*Dynamic center* is the experience of a flow of energy running through your core, from the bottom of your spine to the top of your head (also see *'The Tree'*).	4

DOWN	The direction of energy flowing *DOWN*wards into you. Also represents energy concretizing and grounding.	5
	An area of life: *DOWN* represents you being here in the body, this moment, in the here and now.	9
	The unhealthy position of your energy field when it's hanging in a position below center, too much down or 'blobby'.	4
	The action of moving your higher energies down into your body, and further down towards the earth *(grounding)*.	
Dusting	Through *Dusting* you remove what we could call the first layer of *stuff*, a layer that is constantly accumulating every day, every conversation, and that needs to be cleaned daily or even many times through out your day (see also '*stuff*' and '*goop*').	3
Energy	*Energy* is the subtle fabric that underlies everything. The term *Energy* as we use it refers to a subtle world of forces that exist within ourselves, flows between us and other people, and is everywhere and in everything. *Energy* is substance. Our thoughts, our feelings and our very life energy are a substance.	1
Energy Modelling	*Energy Modelling* is a tool to help you identify the flow, shape and structure of *energy* within the human energy field. You use your hands and/or posture to model the structure of *energy* in a specific location or in your entire energy field.	9
Essence	*Essence* is the most essential, fundamental YOU; the shining qualities that every one of us is born with. Though our *Essence* is One, it divides into many qualities, the way like light shining through a prism becomes many colors; for example vitality, joy, power, love, creativity, intelligence and intuition (also see '*Golden Being*').	Introduction, 9, 13, 17
Evoking	*Invoking* is your way of calling out to the beyond. Evoking is the response that comes back. You become receptive for a response from the Higher. It's the magic. What is evoked might be a feeling, an insight, a picture or a vision, it might be very subtle or powerful like a lightning bolt (see chapter 15 and '*invoking*').	15
FEBE	*Full Energy Balancing Exercise.* A simple 2-minute succession of movements that covers all directions of energy flow to create alignment, balance and uplifted consciousness (also see QEBE).	18
Golden Being	Synonymous with *Essence*. The *"Golden Being"* is your most essential and fundamental Being. (Also see '*Essence*')	9, 13, 15,

Goop	*'Goop'* is a type of energetic debris that enters your energy field and clogs it. *Goop* is a form of *"stuff"* and is related to *"dust"* (light weight energies that clog your field). *Goop* has more substance, is composed of thick emotions and thoughts, and affects particular areas of your field. *Goop* can have a powerful destructive impact upon you (also see *'stuff'*, *'dust'*, *'layers'*).	3
Grounding	Embodying something higher and giving expression in form to what was previously formless. Coming fully into your body, being dynamic and vital. Connecting yourself with the earth and nature. Responsibly dealing with practicals and tangibles.	16
Higher Self	The *Higher Self* or *Eighth Center* is a vortex of energy about one foot above your head, a higher part of your self carrying a high frequency vibration, containing higher aspects of consciousness (also see *'vortex'*, *'bridge'*, *'Beyond'*).	15
Horizontal Plane	The *Horizontal* is the plane of action and relating. Energy flows horizontally OUT from us to the world around and IN towards us from others and the environment; e.g. when you speak, when you connect to others, when you are in relationship to another - whether in love or anger, there is a horizontal flow of energy.	5
Impacting	The process of sending energies out to impact and change the environment (also see *'creatorship'*).	11
IN	The direction of energy flowing *IN* towards you from others and the environment. (also see chapter 6-7 on *"IN*wards energy flow", on taking or not taking energies in and on *"healthy boundaries"*). An area of life: *IN* is your inner life – the rich world of thoughts, feelings and sensations within. The unhealthy position of your energy field when your field is too far *IN* (contracted, shrunken or frozen). An action for when you've been too far out, away from center: taking your energies back *IN*.	4, 5, 6, 7, 8. 9
Inner Sense	The *inner sense* allows us to tune to our interiority – the rich world of our thoughts, feelings and energies.	9
Inner Work	*Inner Work* is the process of deliberately maturing yourself by directly 'working on' the various components of your psyche. The goal of inner work is clean yourself of limiting patterns, lift your consciousness, and live as fully as possible.	17

Invoking	*Invoking* is the process of reaching up to the *Beyond*. It's your way of calling out and saying hello, asking to feel the *Beyond's* presence or asking a particular question. You send words, intention, emotion and a stream of energy upwards to create an energetic pathway. With invoking you start a process that makes you available for the magic (see *'evoking'*).	15
Layers	Our energy field is like an onion, composed of many different layers. The outer layers hold more superficial and surface feelings and thoughts. The deeper layers hold more powerful and significant feelings and thoughts.	3
Leaks	*Leaks* are locations in the energy field where energy leaks out and is lost (also see *'ring-pass-not'*).	8
Level of Consciousness	*Consciousness* is a "gestalt", a way of looking at the world that includes feelings as well as thoughts. The levels of consciousness are connected to evolution and reflect earlier and later developments in our capacity of perception. The process of moving energy from a lower to a higher state lifts the level of *consciousness*	14, 15, 17
Lifting Consciousness	The process of moving *consciousness* from a lower center to a higher center is referred to as *lifting consciousness*.	14
Meditation	*Meditation* is the process of turning your awareness inwards and coming attuned to your inner life, particularly your higher aspects. *Meditation* is also a powerful methodology that guides energies through certain channels to open higher levels of energy, *consciousness* and perception.	17
Negative Energies	*Negative energies* are destructive and limit the flow of positive life energy (also see *'positive energies'*).	7
Off-center	Being *off-center* occurs when the energy field becomes positioned in front or behind you, up or down, or to the side. You are not rooted in your *center* (the *core channel*). Also see *'center'*, *'core channel'*.	4
OUT	The direction of energy flowing *OUT* from your field to the world around (also see chapter 10-13 on OUTwards energy flow: on creatorship, impacting the world around you and on bringing your essence *OUT*). An area of life: *OUT* represents the world outside of you – people, things and places. The unhealthy position of your energy field of being *OUT* of yourself; usually refers to the field being too much to the front, but can generally refer to any direction that takes you *OUT* of *center*	4, 5, 9, 10-13
Ownership	*Ownership* is an attitude of responsibility or "owning up" to the things that we create.	10

Personal Space	*'Personal space'* in regards to energy refers to the dimension of the human energy field that radiates approximately 3 feet in all directions around the body. (Also see *'boundaries'* and *'ring-pass-not'*.)	7, 8
Positive Energies	*Positive energies* are vitalizing, uplifting and healthy energies that do us good (also see *'negative energies'*).	6
QEBE	*Quick Energy Balancing Exercise*. A 30-second energy flow exercise, "One Sweep – One Flow", to lift you out of the "normal stuff" (also see *FEBE*).	18
Ring-Pass-Not	A *Ring-Pass-Not* is a soft boundary that keeps energies in; it keeps your energies from going out beyond a certain point (also see *'Energy Leaks'*).	8
Sensitivity (Sensitivity to Energy)	Everyone is *energy sensitive*; just most people don't know it. Due to various reasons people lose touch with their sensitivity. But everyone has a sense of the myriad of energies that are occurring. It might be just a subtle feeling in the body, or a shift in your emotions, but you are constantly picking up and reacting to energies.	1, 2
"Steh-auf-Männchen"	From German; the literal meaning is 'stand-up-person' and refers to a type of doll, which has a rounded bottom, filled with sand or water. When you knock them over they come back up. This is a metaphor for coming back to center quickly.	4
Stuff	"*Stuff*" refers to energetic debris that clogs your energy field. "*Stuff*" is the residue of your own and others emotions and thoughts, and discordant energies from machines, cell phones, computers and the like. There are two types of "*stuff*" - "*dust*" is lighter energies that go everywhere. "*Goop*" is thick emotions and thoughts that affect one area in particular (also see *'goop'* and *'dust'*).	3
Transformation	*Transformation* refers to the process of changing your energy from one state to another, usually from a lower to a higher state. Transforming your energy will change your perception of the world, your thinking, feelings and actions.	
The Tree	*The Tree* is a metaphor and exercise for becoming grounded (having roots into the ground), centered in your *core* (energy running up and down like in a tree trunk), and connected to the higher (like a tree's canopy *opening* to the sky above).	4
Unconscious Creatorship	*Unconscious creatorship* is where you are not aware of the energies you are sending out and the affects they are having (also see *'creatorship'* and *'conscious* creatorship').	10

UP	The direction of energy flowing Upwards in you. UP flowing energy raises the *level of consciousness* and vibration. Going *UP* connects you with the higher dimensions of life and gives you insight, wisdom and higher understanding (see chapter 14 and 15). An area of life: *UP* represents a dimension of higher consciousness that is available to everyone. *UP* represents the living in and through your higher energy centers that enable you to think and act from a higher perspective and *consciousness* – instead of living from lower centers and their instinctual patterns. The unhealthy position of your energy field when your energies are too much *UP*. The action for when your energies are too low: bringing your energies *UP* to higher places of *consciousness*.	4, 5, 14, 15
Vertical Plane	The *Vertical* is the plane of consciousness. It is an internal dimension, having to do with energy flowing within our core channel. The way the energy flows here changes the quality of our thoughts and feelings. Though we describe the *vertical* as internal it also has an external aspect to it as well, as the *vertical* connects and grounds us to the Earth below and opens us to the wonders of *consciousness* above.	5
Violation	Anything that enters your energy field without your willingness can be a *violation* to you. Inversely, you are violating someone whenever you step over their field *boundaries* without permission.	7, 12
Vortex (Energy Vortex)	A *vortex* is a focal point where many energies converge and change state and form. A human being is a large energy *vortex*, and within our energy field there are many smaller *vortexes*.	5
Vulnerability *(Conscious vulnerability)*	*Vulnerability* is our fundamental "touch-ability" and fragility; that capacity that makes us touchable and affected by a myriad of things. *Conscious vulnerability* is the ability to drop our walls and let our selves be touched.	6
Walls	*Walls* are protective layers of energy within our field that keep unwanted energies from coming in. *Walls* are necessary for our protection. However, they often become locked in place where they then restrict us and imprison our life energy.	7

22 Overview of all Energy Balancing Exercises

Section One
The World of Energy and You

2   **Your Sensitivity to Energy**
Key Principles of Energy Awareness
Exercise 2.1: Feel your Feelings p.34
Exercise 2.2: Feelings have Location p.34
Exercise 2.3: Watch your Hands and your Body p.35
Exercise 2.4: Think Energy p.36

3   **Clearing your Energy Field**
Exercise 3.1: Experience "Stuff" p.41
Exercise 3.2: Energy following Awareness p.49
Exercise 3.3: Dusting your Energy Field p.51
Exercise 3.4: Scoop the Goop p.59
Exercise 3.5: Clearing Energy in Public p.63
Exercise 3.6: Other Tools for Clearing in Daily Life p.64

4   **Centering Yourself**
Exercise 4.1: Bringing your Energy Field back to Center p.71
Exercise 4.2: Experience Your Core Channel p.77
Exercise 4.3: Ground and Expand like a Tree p.80
Exercise 4.4: A Ten-seconds Centering p.83
Exercise 4.5: A Two-seconds Centering p.83
Exercise 4.6: Center while Walking p.84
Exercise 4.7: Center while in Activity p.86
Exercise 4.8: Center while Relating p.86

5   The Four Directions of Energy Flow
    Link to Video of The Full Energy Balancing Exercise (FEBE) p.101
    Link to Video of The Quick Energy Balancing Exercise (QEBE) p.101

Section Two

The Horizontal - The Plane of Action: IN and OUT
Part I - IN

6   Taking Energies IN
    Exercise 6.1: An Experiment for Today p.112
    Exercise 6.2: Let the Good Stuff in p.114

7   Not taking Energies IN
    Exercise 7.1: Protect Yourself p.127
    Exercise 7.2: Open Yourself back up p.129
    Exercise for today 7.3: Open or Protected? p.130
    Exercise 7.4: Saying "No" p.136

8   Energy Leaks and the Ring-Pass-Not
    Exercise 8.1: Building a Ring-Pass-Not p.140
    Exercise 8.2: Seal Your Energy Leak p.144
    Exercise 8.3: Energy Leak Awareness Exercise for Today p.145

9   The Healthy and the Unhealthy IN
    Exercise 9.1: Melting an unhealthy IN state p.150
    Exercise 9.2: Extended version: Opening an unhealthy
            IN state p.152

Section Two

The Horizontal - The Plane of Action: IN and OUT
Part II - IN

10   Creatorship - Your Power to Create
    Exercise 10.1: Look into the Energy of Creatorship p.164
    Exercise 10.2 for today: Watch Creatorship in Action p.166
    Exercise 10.3 for the day: Take Ownership for your Creation p.167

11 The Art of Impacting
Exercise 11.1: Toss the Energy Ball – Find the Right Impact p.173
Exercise 11.2: Appropriate or Inappropriate Amount of Energy? p.175
Exercise 11.3: Sending Energy to the Right Location. p.175
Exercise 11.4 for today: How you give Directives p.178
Exercise 11.5: Sending Energy to the Edge of Another Person's Field p.180
Exercise 11.6: Release the Arrow – Come Back to Center p.184

13 The Art of Bringing Your Essence Out
Exercise 13.1: Allowing Go and Being Total p.198
Exercise 13.2 for today: Totality inventory of your activities p.200
Exercise 13.3: Bringing your Essence Out p.203

Section Three
The Vertical - The Plane of Consciousness: UP, BEYOND and DOWN
Part I - UP and BEYOND

14 UP - The Shift in Consciousness
Exercise 14.1: Turn on the Flame of Your Heart p.217
Exercise 14.2: Ignite more Love – Breathe Energy to the Heart p.218

Shift Up #1: From Dependence to Empowerment
Exercise 14.3: Moving from the Belly to the Solar Plexus p.221

Shift Up #2: From Animal Man to "Divinely Human"
Exercise 14.4: Moving from the Lower to the Heart p.223

Shift Up #3: From Drama to the Clarity of the Watcher
Exercise 14.5: Moving from Drama to the Awakened Third Eye p.225

Shift Up #4: From the Personality to Wisdom
Exercise 14.6: Moving from the Lower Six Centers to the Crown p.228

15 Beyond - Meeting the Magic of the Higher
Exercise 15.1: Accessing Beyond - Meeting the Magic p.239

Section Three

The Vertical - The Plane of Consciousness: UP, BEYOND and DOWN
Part II - DOWN

16   **Bring the Higher Down - Make it Real**
     Exercise 16.1: Breathing Down p.254
     Exercise 16.2: Bring your Energy Down p.254
     Exercise 16.3: Grow your Roots p.255
     Exercise 16.4: Pump your Base p.255
     Exercise 16.5: Drop your Arms: p.256
     Exercise 16.6: Stamp the Ground p.256
     Exercise 16.7: Simply Move p.257
     Exercise 16.8: Tune to the Physical p.257
     Exercise 16.9: Advanced Grounding Intervention p.257

Section Four

Orchestrating your Energy

18   **Our fundamental Energy Balancing Exercise and its Variations: FEBE, QEBE and EEBE**
     Exercise 18.1: The Full Energy Balancing Exercise (FEBE) p.269
     Exercise 18.2: The Quick Energy Balancing Exercise (QEBE) p.272
     Exercise 18.3: The Extended Energy Balancing Exercise (EEBE) p.275

23 The Energy Balancing Institute

Personal Trainings in Energy Balancing

- Would you like to learn more about energy?
- Would you like to gain a whole new ability to analyze and understand the energies in situations you are in?
- Would you like to learn to use your energy consciously to create your life more optimally?

Come take a course in Energy Balancing. Our programs take the materials in this book to a whole new level. They are experiential, dynamic and alive. It will be a profound step into the energy world and the skills you learn will be with you for a lifetime.

We offer various live and online trainings available for beginners to advanced practitioners.

Advanced Energy Balancing Trainings

Our advanced programs are for people who have already experience in Energy Balancing and want to take it to a deeper level. These include exploration of the energy centers (chakras), more advanced work on the energyfield, as well as relationship and action skills.

Professional Energy Balancing Trainings

The professional trainings in Energy Balancing teach you to work with others as an Energy Balancer. In addition to your training to give Energy Balancing sessions you learn advanced energy skills to enhance your quality of life. We also offer certification programs to lead Energy Balancing Groups and train others in Energy Balancing.

See our website for details
www.energybalancing.me

ENERGY BALANCING

24 Coming soon...

... the new book by Kabir Jaffe and Ritama Davidson:

What are the secrets that some couples discover that makes love flower? Why do even the most loving couples often end up in trouble?

The Energy of Love

by Kabir Jaffe and Ritama Davidson

"Energy of Love" looks at the energetic dimension of relating. It takes an x-ray view at what's really going on in a love relationship – the energies that flow between a couple. Through understanding energy you see exactly why so many authentically loving relationships still end up in struggle. And most importantly, you learn how love can really flower through working with energy.

Some of the subjects explored:

- The energetic basis of relationship
- The underlying forces at work in a love relationship
- The energy traps that sabotage love
- How energy can open the doors to intimacy, respect and friendship
- Conscious relationship and the higher possibilities of love
- The seven levels of love

"This is a break-through book in the field of relating, a must-read for every couple. It shows you the traps you are almost guaranteed to stumble into due to the ways energy works, and provides direct solutions that everyone can use to bring joy to relationship."

Go to www.essencetraining.com/energyoflove and add yourself to our notification list to receive an email when The Energy of Love is released.

25 Indigo Adults

Kabir Jaffe and Ritama Davidson

A new type of person is coming into incarnation right now, almost a 'next step' as humanity progresses. These people are visionary and creative, progressive and independent. They carry new ways of thinking and feeling that hold great promise for the future.

You may be familiar with the concept of 'Indigo children,' and never realized that there are also Indigo adults. Might you be one of them? Perhaps you have wondered why you've often felt different?

- Frustrations and dissatisfactions with the 'normal' world
- Not easily fitting in the system, and often feeling alone, separate, or not understood
- A pressing need to contribute to creating a better world
- Unusually sensitive
- A deep feeling, thinking, and introspective nature
- A powerful longing for 'something more'

Indigo Adults helps you identity if you or your children are Indigos, and can help you understand more clearly your nature and purpose here on Earth. The authors also put into perspective the bigger picture of the changing of an Age and its effect on our current world events.

www.indigoadults.com

I wanted to share with you how much your book is helping me. It is giving me a sense of belonging, understanding, forgiveness and acceptance. Thank you deeply.

—Karina Hadida

26 ESSENCE training

The Inner Work School

Do you aspire?
To a more fulfilled state of being
Where your heart is open
Your mind clear
And you're in your energy and power?
Imagine now our Earth filled with people this whole

We believe it's possible

The New Consciousness
The Essence Training Inner Work School is an environment for this new consciousness to flower.

Exploration - Energy - Awakening
The School is an environment for self-exploration, entering the energy world, and awakening to the higher consciousness of the Soul.

Science - Psychology - Spirituality
Based upon the Science of Human Potential, the pioneering work of Kabir Jaffe and Ritama Davidson, the School offers an intensive process of discovery and transformation through training in the chakras and the human energy system. This powerful synthesis of science, psychology and spirituality embraces the totality of a human being, from our earliest evolutionary origins to the greatness of our soul.

Dynamic process
The School combines dynamic group processes, personal work, energy training, meditation and teaching to create a rich environment for personal transformation and professional development.

To the point

The School programs are direct, intense and to the point. Each focuses upon one particular chakra and it's themes. This in-depth exploration includes identifying and clearing the blocks which inhibit us in that area, opening the Essence Qualities of that center, and learning to bring these energies into dynamic daily living.

Are you ready?

    Do the deep work

        Discover your Essence

            Become the person you know you can be

www.ingramcontent.com/pod-product-compliance
Lightning Source LLC
Chambersburg PA
CBHW080239170426
43192CB00014BA/2495